Matthew A Roman

MOSAICS WEST8

MOSAICS
WEST8

BIRKHÄUSER
BASEL · BOSTON · BERLIN

This publication was made possible through the support of the Municipality of Rotterdam, Art and Culture Department, and the Stichting Harten Fonds, The Hague.

Editing and translation
Fanny Smelik, Chidi Onwuka, Daphne Schuit, Victor J. Joseph and D'Laine Camp, Rotterdam

Concept
West 8, Rotterdam

Design and typesetting
Tony Waddingham, Klerken

Printed and bound in Belgium by
Die Keure, Bruges

Bibliographic information published by the German National Library
The Deutsche Nationalbibliothek lists this publication in the Deutsche Nationalbibliografie; detailed bibliographic data are available in the Internet at http://dnb.ddb.de

Library of Congress Control Number: 2007936983

Basel · Boston · Berlin
P.O.Box 133, CH-4010 Basel, Switzerland
Part of Springer Science+Business Media

Printed on acid-free paper produced from chlorine-free pulp. TCF ∞

ISBN 978-3-7643-7404-4

www.birkhauser.ch

9 8 7 6 5 4 3 2 1

CONTENTS

FLATNESS

ADRIAAN GEUZE

The landscape fashioned from the bottom of the sea is the soul of Dutch culture. In this landscape of polders and waterfront towns, a unique metropolis has emerged: the Randstad, the urban conglomeration of towns and cities in the west of the Netherlands. In the absence of an efficient planning strategy, this metropolis is losing its vitality and, through an inexplicable self-loathing, its magical empty centre with horizons and skies lined with low-hanging banks of clouds. Without this vast polder land, its inhabitants are mentally orphaned, as impotent as the Swiss without their mountains and as lonely as Italians without their food.

In less than two centuries, the immense swamps and the precarious *vloedvlaktes* (floodplains) of the rivers and coastal areas of the Delta were reclaimed. An achievement that was unprecedented at the time and is still scarcely comprehensible today.

What drove the medieval inhabitants of this non-land to construct a brand-new existence on the misty, impenetrable peat forests? While Europe was building its cathedrals, engaging in a contest for the highest possible spire with the most delicate structure, here the horizon was being built. Was it because man wanted to show what he was capable of and to compete against others? Or was it a religious motivation that spurred on this dynamism? After all, man had not been able to abide by the injunction not to eat the forbidden fruit, and God had thrown Adam and Eve out of Paradise. There was nothing left for man to do but toil away in drudgery, in the hope of creating his own paradise – if need be in perilous places not made for the purpose.

The fen streams and deep gullies that left the new land vulnerable to the sea and the rivers were *afgedamd* (dammed). Monks and farmers cut their way through the thick forests and dug thousands of kilometres of ditches so that the swamps could *afwateren* (drain off) and then be ploughed as arable fields. This new landscape, which we now know as the *veenweide gebied* (peat pasture region), with its infinite rhythm of narrow, parallel land parcels, existed nowhere else in the world. Sometimes the ditches were oriented to the church spires and spread out in a gorgeous *waaierverkaveling* (fan parcel allotment). This land, fashioned without the use of blueprints, combed into fantastic lines by a steady hand, nourished a rapidly growing population and provided resources for more than 200 new waterfront towns, built on dams and at the hubs of the waterways. Around 1300, the land reclaimed by these impassioned colonists covered 15.000 km^2. A mosaic of more than 3.500 *polders* with regulated drainage stretched from the terp-mound region in the north to the Schelde. The birth of a *Nieuwe Land* (New Land) seemed at hand.

However, the efficient drainage turned on its creators. Through a spectacular process of *inklinking* (subsidence) of the mostly organic soil layers, vast polder areas reclaimed at great cost dropped to as much as four metres below their original elevations. Areas that had once been comfortably above sea level sank to the level of the sea or below it. Around 1400, an unrelenting series of storm tides and catastrophic floods seemed to seal their fate. Huge tracts of land in West-Friesland were washed away. Polders around the mouth of the IJssel and along the Rhine were under constant assault from the water. The old Mastenbroek Polder, in the IJssel Delta, became the tragic champion of floods and dike breaches. The Groote Polder behind Dordrecht, at the time the most prosperous of the polders, vanished during the St Elizabeth Flood in 1421. The sea did not simply flood this land, it literally devoured it! The farms, the villages, the cattle, the people, but also the soil, were all swallowed up. What remained was an immense inland sea, where the moon held dominion over the tides, a true Atlantis, a fate that was seared into the collective memory of the inhabitants. They perceived God's hand in the permanent menace of the water, as the inevitable punishment for failings and sins. In their vernacular, the angry waves of the sea were henceforth dubbed *zondvloed* (tides of sin) – a neologism that would occur in no other language.

The succession of disasters forced the inhabitants to move on to the next stage in the creation of the New Land: *de bedijking* (the building of dikes). To protect it from the sea, the

Potato fields near Lelystad, Province of Flevoland, Ger Dekkers

subsiding land had to be diked. *Molens* (windmills) and *sluizen* (locks) were invented to drain the sinking land, which no longer *afwaterde* (drained naturally) into the sea. *Waterschappen* (water districts) proved to be an efficient organisational form, far more advanced than the usual feudal structure. Even before words for it existed, the New Land had an early form of representative democracy. Control of the water could only take place through communal management of the hundreds of kilometres of linked dikes, windmills and waterways, with proportional suffrage and equitable tax levies.

Meanwhile, rapid innovations in timber construction technology for ships, windmills and locks and for the building of wharfs, jetties and abutments provided the second condition for a unique concept, a stunt without precedent: draining the sea!

In the sixteenth and the early seventeenth centuries, areas outside the dikes and treacherous inland seas were *ingepolderd* (impoldered) and transformed into fertile land. The advent of engineering made it possible to *aandijken* (dike up) new land in the northern headland of Holland, in Zeeland and in the new tidal areas left behind by the St Elizabeth Flood. The shallows outside the dikes were made to rapidly *aanslibben* (silt up) by building long protruding jetties. In short order, enough sediment had collected to reclaim a new, oblong polder from the sea, thanks to a *ringdijk* (ring dike). The sea floor blossomed on these crusts of newly diked land. This made possible the creation of West-Brabant within a short interval.

For the first time, this technique was grounded in a scientific approach. Andries Vierlingh achieved great fame as an engineer. Using ingenious locks and culverts, the water was *gespuid* (sluiced out) at low tide. The new polders were works of art designed by the surveyors, who worked from predetermined planning charts. Their well-conceived Cartesian creations, in which the meandering patterns of the now *ingedijkte* (diked-in) brooks provided contrast, were cartographic masterpieces. The razor-sharp orthogonal landscape, in which the ditches marked out beautiful rectangular parcels, surpassed the previously created New Land in every respect. Skilful impolderers moved on to the north and established colonies on the New Land of the Frisian Middelzee, which was reclaimed from the sea in record time.

A breakthrough in windmill technology was the windmill with a revolving top, which could be oriented to the direction of the wind. These efficient machines made it possible to *droogmalen* (drain using windmills) deep inland seas. Every lake north of Amsterdam could be vanquished by placing windmills in a line and removing water of great depth to transfer it into a ring canal. These *molengangen* (windmill corridors) were marvels of ingenuity. The history of the New Land reached a new climax with the *droogmakerijen* (impoldering works) of North Holland, which underwent a true metamorphosis. Within 20 years the impoldering was completed and the former sea clay in these polders was being cultivated. The notion of the ideal world, with its energetic horizons of hundreds of windmills, was more than farmland: it was the proud possession of a people, the identity of a new nation. Unlike previous efforts, this had not been the result of mere reclamation – it had been literally created. Making land had a cultural dimension. It had become a form of art.

The new windmills were able to permanently drain the previously reclaimed peat soil to far below sea level. Other large peat moors were excavated for *turf* (peat) that served as fuel for the towns. New lakes were created. To visitors, the New Land was a revelation. The system of waterways and *trekvaarten* (barge canals) linked all the towns with unprecedented efficiency according to a reliable schedule. From the noiseless tow barge or from an open sailboat with its sails half-unfurled, one could see the New Land glide by from a low perspective.

The empty land in which silhouettes moved against the horizon was enchantingly beautiful, even stunning! Towns had fortifications, canals, quays, water gates, churches with graceful spires and bulwarks with windmills. Their waterfronts, lined with fish, merchandise and wharfs, bustled with activity. At the anchoring roadsteads, boats big and small waited for the right tide or for the wind. The towns seemed singled out for glory, in their flat, vast surrounding setting of villages and pretty countryside. The livestock of the polder land had a reputation. For milk, cream, cheese and hams, there was no place like this one. The sea clay and loam of the new polders produced fresh vegetables and grain. Nor was there any lack of fowl, fish or shellfish. The Delta had come into full bloom. The New Land between the Rhine, the Maas and the Schelde became Europe's Mesopotamia. All the toiling in the wet soil and the obsession with making land were rewarded in the Gouden Eeuw, the Dutch Golden Age that more or less spanned the seventeenth century.

The pioneer spirit of the polders, coupled with a talent for commerce, now proved to be the foundation for the emergence of a new nation. A birthing process that was triggered by the violent secession from Catholic Spain. War, voyages of exploration, commerce, religious strife, science and art went hand in hand. The spiritual and cultural enlightenment of the Golden Age would demonstrate how much the New Land had been the foundation for the mindset and the identity of the Dutch.

The soul of the people who had succeeded in creating the polder land had yearned for a religion that would provide salvation from the difficult existence below the waves. In their flat world, every position was equivalent. The unavoidable process of coordination elicited preoccupations that led to thoughts about equality. The flat plain denied superiority. The horizon cut every ambition down to size, and storm tides did not discriminate either. Potentates or popes had no place here.

Surrounded by a hostile nature, the polders could bear no nuances or half-truths. There were but two conceivable positions: *binnendijks* (inside the dike) or *buitendijks* (outside the dike). The New Land of the polders compelled a straightforward and principled worldview in which 'participating' or 'being excluded', 'right' or 'wrong' and 'pure' or 'sinful' were the only alternatives. The iconoclastic campaign of the Beeldenstorm, which first raged in the southern Netherlands in 1562, swept like a hurricane over the polders. The ideal attitude to life was felt to be encapsulated in the viewpoints for which Luther and Calvin had provided ideological principles.

The inhabitants of the Delta had chosen their version of the Protestant faith, which offered a value system in which sacrifice, consistency and a bent for purity were virtues. You were born a sinner and had to earn heaven by doing battle with the sea. Dogma had become the mental equivalent of toiling in the heavy clay, and theological quibbling was the supreme stage of land surveying.

The polders not only entailed a strong faith, they also stimulated the senses. The atmosphere above the flat plain held a unique heavenly light with a wide spectrum. Its fast-changing moods provided the ideal decor for painters. They were overwhelmed by the beauty of the New Land, with its horizon, the religious dimensions of its light, the clouds, the waves, the livestock, the windmills and the ships. They glorified its moods and its changeable nature. While their Italian and Flemish contemporaries shut themselves away in their studios, Holland's artists took their paints and brushes outside, to paint the New Land in the light. They were drawn into the polders and made innumerable sketches during their strolls. For the first time in history, the landscape itself became the subject of painting. It was recorded and catalogued outside the studio. Landscape painting, now such a completely self-evident part of the character of the age, was born, a genre that would develop into a vast array of schools and movements. The euphoria about the flat plain produced the Dutch Masters, who together immortalised every aspect of the New Land.

The young Paulus Potter was a specialist who concentrated on the genre of livestock painting. As a West Frisian, he had witnessed the enormous transformation of his native region and the birth of the Beemster. Was it coincidence that in his famed painting *The Bull*, the nation seems to be symbolised by a vain bullock in a landscape whose horizon he drew through the animal's legs?

The Bull, Paulus Potter, ca. 1647, Mauritshuis Royal Picture Gallery, The Hague

View of Haarlem with Bleaching Grounds, Jacob van Ruisdael, ca. 1670–1675, Mauritshuis Royal Picture Gallery, The Hague

Jacob van Ruisdael and Philips Koninck climbed up the flanks of the inner dunes and the Heuvelrug moraine in order to experience the breathtaking emptiness of the New Land even better. Beneath their banks of low clouds, the insignificance and transience of toiling man in his self-made creation were inescapable. They exalted the banks of clouds over the Atlantic and the abundant light. In Koninck's *Panoramic View of Dunes and a River*, the wildly meandering river has trouble leaving the beautiful polder land. In Ruisdael's *View of Haarlem with Bleaching Grounds* a mighty sky covers the town of Haarlem, the elect, among the lowlands. Like Haarlem, Rhenen on the forelands of the Rhine was also painted, where the St Cunera Tower reigned over the Betuwe. In one of Ruisdael's melodramatic works, *A Stormy Sea*, an approaching storm lashes wooden jetties. The painting, with its sky of inky clouds, places considerable emphasis on the two wooden jetties and the beacon, probably the harbour entrance used by engineers to protect the accesses to the waterfront towns. Ruisdael, who also produced an oeuvre of fanciful romantic landscapes, was fascinated by the soul of the New Land, as expressed by the sky, the water, the windmills and the engineering works. One of his most famous pieces is *The Windmill at Wijk bij Duurstede*, a grain mill on the town rampart. He devoted numerous studies and sketches to the windmills of the polders, even climbing the Westertoren to sketch the windmill corridors of the Stadspolder west of Amsterdam. Rembrandt van Rijn would sketch the same horizon of windmill corridors.

Meindert Hobbema painted the polders created by the recent diking operations. *The Avenue at Middelharnis* was an ode to land surveyors, a glorification of the orthogonal world.

Albert Cuyp was the master of the forelands, the muddy land outside the dike in which cows served as foreground for his panoramas of Dordrecht. He cherished the becalmed wind, the impotent peace of the handing sails as an exorcism of the ever-looming fate of storm and flood.

Both Johannes Vermeer and Rembrandt used the magic of the polder light. Rembrandt borrowed the effect of backlighting in a dark approaching front pierced by sunlight in only a few places in order to light a single fragment of the landscape each time. This divine light, taken directly from the landscape, would form the foundation of his entire oeuvre. The clear light of the flat plain was never so well captured as by Vermeer, who did not even need to paint the landscape to suggest it none the less. A window through which the polder light spattered an interior sufficed. His marzipan women bathed in that light. With his milkmaid who seems a woman made of cream, fresh bread on the table and peat in the stove, Vermeer is crowing with delight about the lusty abundance of the New Land. The carefully dripping trickle from her milk jug is nothing less than an allusion to the foreplay to an actual orgasm: the eternal love for the maiden from the fertile polders that would later form the Westland. The way in which he has his own town of Delft rising out of the empty polder is unequivocal. Delft is the pearl of the polder land. The city glows in the morning light, mirrored in the Schie. The red roofs bask in the early sunshine.

Rembrandt took long walks through the countryside around Amsterdam. He was besotted by the daily life in the polders and sketched the hamlets, the barns and windmills tucked away near Diemen, the Gein and the Amstel. He did not

Panoramic View of Dunes and a River, Philips Koninck, 1664, Museum Boijmans Van Beuningen, Rotterdam

The Avenue at Middelharnis, Meindert Hobbema, 1689, National Gallery, London

fail to spot the spectacular view of the city from the west, from which he painted the city ramparts of Amsterdam pulverised by the sails of dozens of windmills, which had to spin continuously to keep the Stadspolder, menaced by the raging Haarlemmermeer, dry. He also drew the brand-new polders of Het Bildt in Friesland, home of his wife Saskia.

The livestock, the windmills and the ditches of the New Land figured on an endless number of paintings that now adorn the walls of museums all over the world. These also house the paintings in which the water looms and waves crash against the dikes, or others in which the polder land is shown wrapped in a lovely winter blanket. In Ruisdael's work, the snowy plain is cold and frozen stiff; in Hendrick Avercamp's, the people of the polder are enjoying themselves on the ice of the ditches and canals. How they loved their self-made land.

THE MYTH

Despite all these blessings, a people whose existence is so easy is doomed to sleep. Just as the gold of the Americas had given Spain an embolism, the excessive self-importance of the polders and the unquestioned trade from the colonies carried with them a distressing complacency. The drive to create was over. For more than a hundred years, no further expansion of the New Land was attempted. The economic centre of gravity had shifted to England, where the miracle of the Industrial Revolution was unfolding. At the end of the eighteenth century, the polders were annexed by France and the Dutch fleet was blown to smithereens by the English. Napoleon, who had contemptuously dubbed the country the alluvial backwash of the French Empire, left it bankrupt and robbed the polders of 23.000 farmers' sons who died with *La Grande Armée* in Russia. Like the French, the water would ultimately shake the polders out of their slumber.

At the beginning of the nineteenth century, catastrophic floods took place throughout the river region. Because of ice jams in the rivers that had frozen solid, the river dikes were breached three times in 15 years, and all of the polders from Nijmegen to Dordrecht were flooded. In response, still under French occupation, the *Civiele Waterstaat* (Civil Water Authority) was founded. It would take another half a century before adequate solutions for the river region were found. For a long time, abandoning the polders was even considered.

With the Water Authority, engineers re-entered the scene, and how! North of Rotterdam, one lake after the other was drained using English steam-driven pumping stations, something that had been impossible using only windmills a century and a half earlier. Polders of staggering depth would be added to the mosaic of the New Land. In part assisted by the works of King William I, the nation rediscovered the spirit that had been characteristic of the generations that had created the New Land. Under his leadership, new sea canals were dug to the Marsdiep and the Haringvliet. Maastricht and 's Hertogenbosch were linked by the Zuid-Willemsvaart. The secession of the much more enterprising Belgian section of the country in 1830 was an omen of how much the polders had fallen behind.

Midway through the nineteenth century, after Johan Thorbecke had introduced the Constitution, the country set out on a spectacular catch-up operation. Development companies

Windmill on a Polder Waterway ('In the Month of July'), Paul Joseph Constantin Gabriël, ca. 1880–1889, Rijksmuseum, Amsterdam

Polder Landscape with Windmill at Abcoude, Willem Roelofs, ca. 1870, Collection Gemeentemuseum, The Hague

were set up to drain the Haarlemmermeer and develop the northern peat districts. As in the seventeenth century, the certificates the companies issued could be used to speculate on the stock market.

The Haarlemmermeer Polder had once been dreamed up by the brave mill builders of the Golden Age. However, they had been unable to achieve what the three gigantic steam-driven pumping stations were now doing: pumping out five metres of water despite the tremendous and permanent seepage of brackish water. It took years to build the pumps, which had pistons that were lubricated with sheep fat and could displace a formidable quantity – 27 square metres – with each stroke. The three giant machines, with parts manufactured in Liège and Leeds, were so ingenious and ground-breaking that they literally thumped the barely awakened Netherlands back to life. The impulse of the Industrial Revolution had finally reached the country. The Haarlemmermeer became the biggest of all the polders.

Once more the New Land reached completion. Never before had so much land been made according to a plan. Although the total surface area set a new record and the parcel allotment was efficient, the actual development was a disaster, because the new polder had been primarily conceived as a speculative venture. It would take three generations before the farmers were able to make a profit. But the *Waterwolf* had been tamed, and history had been made.

In short order, a web of railway lines was laid down. Even the polders with soft ground were crisscrossed by railway embankments, which often followed the lines of the old barge canals. The towns were outfitted with stations with large covered concourses, like those that been built earlier in neighbouring countries. In Amsterdam, the railway line and the station were built right in the middle of the IJ. The rivers inspired the engineers to come up with athletic structures. Permanent crossings with swing bridges were built over the Waal, the IJssel and the Maas, as well as over the innumerable canals. The Hollands Diep and the Nieuwe Maas at Rotterdam were spanned by spectacular railway bridges. A new waterway was dug through the dunes for sea-going ships, for the Port of Amsterdam as well as the Port of Rotterdam. New ports with quays, cranes and warehouses brought steamships into the cities. The North Sea Canal was part of a grand plan that included a sea lock and the impoldering of the entire IJ. It seemed Holland's answer to the Suez Canal built by the British. Entirely against its historic orientation to the Zuiderzee, Amsterdam's centre of gravity rotated towards the west, and Rotterdam expanded across the Nieuwe Maas.

The big rivers were canalised and safeguarded against the formation of dangerous ice jams. New fortifications and the New Holland Water Defence Line made the old city ramparts obsolete. Romantic parks were designed atop the bulwarks, where the citizenry could stroll. The towns were finally able to expand, and the fast-growing population found accommodation in new quarters in the polder land. The mad plans for the impoldering of the Zuiderzee and the Waddenzee were a testament to the decisiveness of the late nineteenth century and demonstrated the eagerness of the engineers of the New Land. On the other hand the impoldering of the Haarlemmermeer and the peat industry of the north and the Peel were linked to miserable social situations that showed a different, less heroic side of the story. The New Land was on its way to the modern era.

The great works of the late nineteenth century and the steady expansion of the New Land took place at the end of the Romantic period. Life in the world of steam and steel elicited a profound longing for nature, for the harmonious existence of the past. Inspiration was found not in the town or the new landscape of railway lines, but in the idealised, archetypal landscape of the moors and the familiar polder land. This longing found a predictable expression. Dutch landscape artists once more established a great new genre that added a dimension to the polder land. The pre-Romantic tradition of the Golden Age had its sequel in the Impressionism of the late nineteenth century. For the Dutch, the polder land was a magnet. Like Don Quixote, the artists were hypnotised by the windmills, which became indispensable motifs in their landscapes.

Vincent van Gogh, who eventually produced an oeuvre out of madness and joyful colour-blindness in the south of France, was gripped in his youth, before he was able to escape the polders, by their willow-grey desolation – the unmistakable quality of the lowlands. In his *Polders at Dordrecht*, with its gloomy windmills and black earth, the polder land is doomed. Dordrecht would never recover. Johan Hendrik Weissenbruch, who as a young artist had dared to paint Haarlem from the same perspective as Ruisdael, soon became the master of the light and the mood of the weather. He always chose a position with the water in the foreground. It is as if the anatomy of the polder, with the barge canal or the outlet into which the mills sluice out their water, had to be made explicit. He was lyrical about nature in the polder land, which displayed its beauty mainly in stormier weather conditions. His polders might be new-born out of the mist or golden in the evening sun. Spring, summer or autumn, morning or evening, he conjured it onto the canvas. The melancholy of his watercolour landscapes was unprecedented.

J.B. Jongkind, like Weissenbruch and Van Gogh much admired in France, had to go and live with his sister in the Hoekse Waard when his fortunes were at an ebb. He did not shun the autumn in the surly polders either. He painted the islands of South Holland and the polders of the Schie in the rain and in sunshine. When he encountered the sun in the polders, Jongkind, the best colourist of his time, could paint the New Land in hues soft as butter. He made Maassluis and Overschie, for instance, shine like pharaohs in their crypt. They surpass the Delft consecrated by Vermeer and Ruisdael. The light dances on the orange roof tiles. The towns are nestled, inviolable, behind the dikes.

Paul Gabriël turned his attentions to any polder with windmills and cows. The IJssel Delta, central Holland and the rivers region were his domain. Although the lowlands were known for the drizzle and the raging storms that plague and threaten them, his polders are a manifesto for lethargy and peace. The wind refuses to ripple the water, and the windmills are on strike.

Anton Mauve painted the barge canal where the horse-drawn barge glided peacefully over the water, as though there were no trains cleaving the polders with steam, black plumes of smoke and noise.

Willem Maris and Willem Roelofs painted the peat pasture region of Holland and Utrecht as a land of creamy butter, as plains brushed by the wind. Their canvases were all windmills and cows. Roelofs's ditches were pregnant with plants, fish, birds and insects. There is more grass than the livestock can stand. The sky is blue and the clouds are reflected in the water. Maris and Roelofs painted the cows as though they were women. Always soft, preferably young and white, lying in the grass with their legs tucked under them or wading in the river or a ditch. These are the first pretty bathers in painting. Roelofs even went so far as to adorn the polder shamelessly with a magisterial rainbow. The New Land was Paradise Lost.

The nineteenth-century masters saw the polders as the perfect creation. The polder mosaic produced by man was given a religious dimension. There was no sign in their paintings, therefore, of sturdy bridges or mightily pounding steam-driven pumping stations belching out smoke from their chimneys as they forced water out of the newest polders. The subject was the Arcadia of the 'old' polder land. In Rembrandt's work this landscape had weeds, muddy pools and barns in need of paint. This version was definitively revised by Roelofs and his contemporaries. At the world fair in Vienna in 1873, a legendary selection of nearly 200 Dutch paintings was exhibited. The world was presented with a magical polder land, a landscape with a flat horizon and light of the sea, painted in an enchanting combination of realism and mood. Over the entrance of the Dutch pavilion hung a poetic canvas by Jozef Israëls, in which a woman ploughs the flat soil of the polder behind two horses.

The windmills on the Gein at Abcoude, the meadows north of the Nieuwkoopse Plassen, the polders along the Vliet and the Gouwe and the banks of the Schie have remained in international collections ever since. The nineteenth-century landscapes of the New Land, which now hold pride of place in the Louvre, the Tate and in Washington, relate the myth of the polder land.

THE FINE ART OF LAND MAKING

The tradition of reclamation and impoldering would reach its apotheosis in the twentieth century. Following the First World War, the decision was made to implement the Zuiderzee Works, which had been outlined nearly 50 years before. The approach to these works was entirely new. Having learned the lesson of the imperfection of the Haarlemmermeer Polder, the aim was for a different methodology, with sophisticated engineering, social/economic planning and democratic decision making. One noteworthy aspect is that research claimed an important position. Work was no longer based on an all-encompassing plan. The Zuiderzee Works were based on three pillars: perspective, research and implementation. Only after a period of conception and re-evaluation was the first sub-plan produced. Each subsequent phase and intervention was different from or better than the last. A progressive system of insight, as it were, was organised, in both an engineering and a social sense. The idea that not only new land but a new society was being made was continually kept in mind by explicitly addressing what this social structure should look like.

The Lely Plan, in which the ambition of the work was outlined, served as the driving perspective. A chain of scientific research institutions and laboratories was then recruited, as well as the business world, to organise an innovative, self-learning process. Risk analyses, variants, evaluations and trial-and-error were thus made an integral part of decision making. The renowned, Nobel Prize-winning Professor Hendrik Lorentz was appointed as chairman of the first state commission that was to set up the research effort. The third pillar was the installation of a statutory body, the Zuiderzee Commission (later the IJsselmeer Polders Department), which would be responsible for construction management, social accountability and democratic decision making.

The master plan-research-public accountability trinity became the foundation of this unprecedented success. It represents the climax of a long history, the fine art of land making. Never would the sea bed be celebrated on such a scale as in the New Land of the twentieth century.

Both the Zuiderzee Works and the subsequent Delta Works became a cultural act in which new technology, attitudes on the planning of society, architectural and hydraulic engineering principles were linked. The sublime phasing of trial projects and alternative solutions led to a rapid evolution in increasingly better polders and dams. The Flevo polders were a confirmation of a passion for making land bordering on obsession, which can only be placed in the context of the Dutch tradition.

The Zuiderzee project was inspired by the need for farmland, but as ever, the pretext was found in a flood, this time the Waterland Flood. The village of Andijk, where the sea dike was rescued during this storm disaster, was rewarded with a designation as the first *proefpolder* (trial polder). In the Andijk Polder, research would show how the process of soil preparation and the selection of crops for brackish soil would work out. Then began the genuine work, with the construction of the Wieringermeer Polder, the largest ever created. For the first time, a serious selection was implemented of the farmers who would cultivate the polder. During the construction of the dikes of this polder, scientific research into the optimal trajectory of the Afsluitdijk, or closure dike, also known as the IJsselmeer Dam, began.

The completion of the Afsluitdijk was turned into a national celebration captured on film, in photographs and in paintings. The filmmaker Joris Ivens and the artist J.H. van Mastenbroek would become famous with the film, and the paintings in which the *keileem* (boulder clay), dredged at Urk, was poured into the final *stroomgat* (closure gap) played the leading role. The Afsluitdijk became the first work in this long history to be commemorated with a monument immediately upon completion, a white look-out tower designed by the architect W.H. Dudok. In the anxious period of the Depression, the people were able to forget their worries for a moment and dream of the panorama over the waters of the Waddenzee and the IJsselmeer, which this dam, which could definitely be called the eighth wonder of the world, now separated.

Just before the Second World War, the construction of the Noordoost Polder began, with drainage completed during the war. This polder, for which much research was conducted at the newly established Hydrodynamic Laboratory in Delft, became the improved version of the Wieringermeer Polder. Rolling-stock manufacturer Werkspoor developed new, extremely powerful diesel engines for the main pumping stations in Urk, at Lemmer and at Ketelsluis. Despite the many variations in elevation, the accurate engineering made it possible to regulate the water table of each individual parcel independently, using intakes and floodgates. The polder design went beyond the grid of farming parcels with a surface area of 23 hectares. Serious work was implemented to achieve an ideal landscape, the image of which was strongly influenced by the myth of the nineteenth-century masters. Inspired by the school of Grandpré Molière, the young J.T.P. Bijhouwer was the first to develop landscape architecture. The new polder was given a landscape of avenues with bends, which gave the space scale and guided the observer's gaze. The future society was circumscribed in a hierarchical framework of farmsteads, villages and the central town of Emmeloord. Farmhouses, farm workers' houses, schools, shops and churches were positioned according to this predetermined model. Ultimately, it was even decided to establish a model village, an architectural experiment for a community based on International Style that would be designed by Dutch modernists. The present cohesion and equilibrium of society in the Noordoost Polder is no coincidence, it seems – this social engineering proved particularly effective. The polder, which was a showpiece of planning and in which engineering, design and society were integrated to a far-reaching extent, would later be designated by UNESCO as a World Heritage Site.

The devastation of the Second World War, the loss of the East Indies, the Cold War and the North Sea Flood of 1953 would spur the Dutch to acts of heroism. An unchained nation sought its salvation in reconstruction and development. The only tradition was embraced, that of planning, building and making land. The entire agricultural area was subjected to land consolidation, all the streams and rivers were canalised, new universities were founded, infrastructure, industry, merchant shipping, Schiphol Airport and the Port of Rotterdam were expanded and the cities allocated extensive expansion districts. But above all, the traditional enemy, the sea, was subjugated by the Delta Plan, which provided for the damming of the tidal basins of Zeeland and the rebuilding of all sea dikes according to the most comprehensive safety standards in the world. There was no hesitation in linking the huge works, predicated on the newest engineering techniques, to other improvements to the physical landscape that were deemed imperative. Necessity was turned into a virtue. For the duration of the works, special legislation was enacted, the *Deltawet* (Delta Act), and the *Deltadienst* (Delta Department) took charge of day-to-day management and implementation. The Delta Works ultimately produced marvels of civil engineering. The tidal dam in Oosterschelde, despite the numerous cost overruns, became the nation's pet dam. Like the Afsluitdijk earlier, it became a requisite feature of school excursions for Dutch children as well as a destination for international delegations. The reconstruction projects were opened to enthusiastic applause by successive queens and recorded in innumerable Polygoon news bulletins.

The Zuiderzee Works were carried out with great energy. East and South Flevoland would become the next two IJsselmeer polders to be constructed, with a *Randmeer* (fringe lake) that shielded the deep polders from the seepage of the Old Land. Like the Delta Department, the *Rijksdienst voor de IJsselmeerpolders* (IJsselmeer Polders Department), which built its offices in the future capital of the polders that were to form a new province, was a beehive of innovative powers and go-getters. As a generous tribute, the capital built for growth was named after Cornelis Lely, the engineer and statesman responsible for the Zuiderzee Works, and the last pumping station to be built was named after the chairman of the first state commission, V.J.P. de Blocq van Kuffeler. Unlike in the quasi-romantic Noordoost Polder, the Flevo Polders were once again based on the shameless principle of the most efficient farmland parcel allotment. All seepage-prone or excessively low-level areas were zoned as nature areas and forests. The entire southern corner was reserved for the building of Almere, which it was presumed would grow into the country's fourth-largest city. The remaining acreage of these polders of 45.000 hectares was allocated to farmers and partitioned into very large parcels. The layout was such that crop dusting could now be done with airplanes! The monumental farmland that was born here has no equal among the 4.000 polders of the New Land. The scale of the landscape and its unique horizon are overwhelming. Motorists, who can literally whiz along the sea bed, fancy themselves not in Europe but in the New World.

The perspective and the excess inspired a large number of artists and photographers. And like the polders of the Golden Age and the nineteenth century, the land of Lely, beaming with self-confidence, was recorded in all its moods and glory.

The advent of De Stijl, a movement of which Piet Mondriaan became the most famous artist, cannot be dissociated from centuries of polder parcel allotment and the graphic qualities of the horizon and the livestock. The order instilled by the land surveyors finds its crowning glory in Mondriaan's abstract compositions. Within the Stijl group, a schismatic debate had taken place about the diagonal line, which had pitted artist Theo van Doesburg against Mondriaan. To Van Doesburg, the diagonal line brought greater dynamism to compositions, whereas Mondriaan stayed true to the static order of horizontals and verticals. In effect it was a battle between the windmills and the horizon: which is the most characteristic of the image?

Photographers like Cas Oorthuys, Frits Rotgans, Aart Klein, Ger Dekkers, Harry Cock and Peter van Bolhuis became the new masters of the landscape, whose work fit in with the tradition of the great masters.

Oorthuys conjured up a modern milkmaid, roaring with laughter as she empties a big bucket of milk in one fell swoop into a milk churn. Vermeer's creation poured a measly trickle compared to Oorthuys's woman of prosperity who thinks in hectolitres. His muscled farm workers were barely able to harvest the over-abundant crops. He was not content with the horizon and photographed the new polders from the air. The New Land, with its silver ditches, sparkled amidst a black sea.

Dekkers rhapsodised about the perspective in which the trees, ditch embankments, dikes and furrows displayed themselves to the observer. He made square serial portraits of the Flevo Polders that tested the Renaissance rules of perspective geometrically. The horizon, in each of his photographs, is sharper and more flawless than in Potter's work.

Haymaking with Horse and Cart, Cas Oorthuys

Apart from its unsurpassed expansion in Zeeland and in the Zuiderzee, the most startling manifestation of the New Land was that of the Holland polders. This highly layered and original polder land suddenly acquired an aura, a fringe of towns and cities. In the 1930s it was Albert Plesman (founder of KLM) who had first recognised this phenomenon and dubbed it the *Randstad* (the fringe city). From the air, he had observed that the towns of Holland formed a ribbon structure around the polder land. The rapid growth of the towns and cities had created a unique metropolis, anchored in the historic waterfront towns and lacking a centre. That is to say, its centre was the rich agricultural landscape of the New Land. The peat pasture region of Holland and Utrecht had literally been framed. A green heart of polders, peat extraction fields, lakes and drainage works. A landscape that everyone was familiar with, with its graphic qualities of a square natural environment of cows and windmills, which could transform into grey clammy desolation or a startling snow-covered skating realm. A grateful land that in the spring and autumn was born anew each day out of mist and fog. An area that was best appreciated from a car or a train, from which one could experience the rhythm of the ditches like music, like jazz. An emptiness that constantly reminded the city dweller of the seasons and the changeable Holland weather. The green heart of this metropolis was the succinct 'non-city' that withdrew from neurotic modern society. This empty expanse was not simply a vacuum: it was a monument to the tradition of Holland. The layered history of seven centuries of New Land, which mirrored the soul of a people and was immortalised in a thousand poems and paintings.

Just as the Bosphorus was a gift to Constantinople, Table Mountain to Cape Town and the heavenly Guanabara Bay to Rio de Janeiro, the New Land was a gift to the Randstad. Its cities naturally claimed their individual positions on the sea, in the inner dunes, on the IJ, the Heuvelrug moraine or the rivers, but they shared the primeval polder land in between, the unique, open central area. The metropolis that encircled these lowlands was blessed. This land was a precious possession, a sweet love and a myth: an empty expanse in which Randstad dwellers, in their daily journeys through it, were reborn.

The framework that had grown out of a topographic accident of history, the fringe city with a green heart, was soon embraced as a planning ideal. Even internationally, the Randstad with its *Groene Hart* was hailed as the ideal urban design model for a modern metropolis that would compensate for all the drawbacks of the nineteenth-century metropolis.

When new motorways were added between the four largest cities of the Randstad in the 1960s, literally hundreds of thousands of people were able to enjoy the horizon in the morning mist or the setting sun to their heart's content. The car added an extra dimension to the myth: the association with *freedom*. While getting around in other metropolises was viewed as unpleasant but necessary, traffic in the Randstad was a triumphal march through the landscapes of Rembrandt and Jongkind. Just imagine how the underground metro commuters of London or Paris, hanging onto straps and handles, would pine for such a piebald panorama of clouds and cheering light.

THE LOST HORIZON

Starting in the 1970s, a diabolical development took place, an unforeseen catastrophe. The generation that was born after the war and for whom the great works had been carried out resolutely turned against tradition. The dynamic drive of their parents was placed in a negative light by plans such as the construction of a new town in the Bijlmermeer Polder, the demolition of the old city centre of Utrecht to make way for the Hoog Catharijne complex and numerous other projects they considered fearsome. The flipside of unrestrained development also became painfully obvious: environmental damage, contamination scandals and a loss of the human scale. Around the world, the realisation grew that trees could not grow into the heavens, and that the earth, as a natural system, was fragile. The new generation shifted the focus from physical and spatial development to social and cultural development. Society would have to be drastically rearranged. Education and culture, especially, would have to be revamped. The emphasis on social and human proportions was coupled with an aversion to entrepreneurs and scientists.

An impressive planning doctrine was established, geared toward a 'harmonious' development of the land based on what was now called Spatial Planning. This quickly evolved from a modest sector into an immense planning industry that provided work for tens of thousands of lawyers and planners and was supposed to vouchsafe the country from lurching developments by fits and starts and overly ambitious interventions. This doctrine was based not on perspectives or works but on policy and procedures. The policy served as an exorcism of the recalcitrant reality and provided mantras with which ministers and municipal aldermen could substitute a politically correct mental framework for this complex reality. The lawyers and later the system managers were placed above the engineers. Engineering sketches became taboo. Cratefuls of thick policy papers were published, written in a secret jargon and illustrated with bombastic charts of arcs and arrows. All of this was enshrined in a legislative framework: the *Wet Op De Ruimtelijke Ordening* (Spatial Planning Act).

This legislation outlined a staged process with an infinite number of feedback loops. Spatial Planning had deliberately been inserted into the Thorbeckian power vacuum among the three layers of government. Spatial development in the hands of lawyers, with significant input from provincial authorities and lower-level authorities... a greater break with the tradition of land making would be hard to imagine.

Every infrastructure intervention necessary to society, including obvious works, new train connections, dike reinforcements or improvements to the Port of Rotterdam was taken completely out of its context. They went into the planning machine as a clear plan and came out as spaghetti. Delays spanning several years, continual financial overruns and adjustments to every element of the programme of requirements became the norm. No project was owned by a single administrator or agency any more. They became anonymous and procedural phantom processes, without accountability and devoid of pragmatism. This monstrous planning labyrinth eventually proved impenetrable even to the lawyers.

The consequences were telling. However much the politically correct sham planning system exuded circumspection and stagnation, the world outside was the opposite of peace and quiet. Through simple exegesis of policy papers and regional plans and planning-speak, every municipal alderman had the opportunity to implement any random plan on any site within city limits. Out of precaution, pension funds and developers bought up the entire polder acreage of the Randstad and offered their services. In so doing, they literally drove the farmers, who were subsisting on their farms thanks to government-mandated milk quotas, from their pasture land. The real estate prices made a mockery of the farmers' labours. The landscape became the ultimate speculative venture. Within a span of 15 years, this cynical process would culminate in the systematic rape and perversion of the Groene Hart.

CRUMBLING

How precisely could this unique landscape of 1000-year-old peat polders, with their unparalleled horizon and ode to low skies, be devastated? Just as the Taliban in Afghanistan had not been able to stomach the ancient Buddha statues and had blown them up with brute force, a succession of municipal aldermen trampled the mighty polder land underfoot. A single decadent generation contrived to carve out and fritter away the mystical heart of the metropolis. Without the Randstad gaining any new sense of urbanity, quality or recruitment power, the polders were crushed under endless suburban guilelessness, a twilight world between life and death.

The roads across the plain became corridors of banal commercial estates with hangars and sheds. Developers used every exit to put up banal retail and showy office buildings. Even the fewer than 100 remaining windmills of the painters' land were not spared. One after the other, they were boxed in or moved. The naïvety of these acts and the lack of respect for their tireless spinning were shocking. It genuinely seemed as though the collective memory of the culture had to be erased. The fast-growing horticultural sector did not need to look for a new core area in the urban periphery. On the contrary, in the absence of planning or strategy, the very last open polders near the towns of the southern section of the Randstad were covered over with greenhouses.

The typical Holland dialogue between the city and its authentic surrounding countryside was abolished, by means of added buffers of soulless park land of copses, tree screens, hills, beaches and circuits that were supposed to please city dwellers. Had not the old painters in fact revelled in flattering their towns in the flat lowlands? And had not city dwellers always enjoyed strolling, skating and cycling along the canals and pastures? Outside the city of Amsterdam, this bicycle-addicted people were allowed no bike paths to the windmills of the Groene Hart. Nature-preservation organisations like the Provinciale Landschappen, Staatsbosbeheer and Natuurmonumenten in fact did not like the polders as farmland and focused their acquisition policy on other genres: woods, country estates, dunes and wetlands. Their stewardship was primarily geared toward creating archetypes of nature, through all manner of *natuurdoeltypes* (nature target types). Friesland, which for years had shown how keenly city dwellers could enjoy boating, did not open any eyes to linking the polder outlets of the Groene Hart.

Many critics and artists demonstrated their aversion to the new Holland horizon and the political indifference.

The Rotterdam photographer Jannes Linders made the dismantling of the urbanised landscape of the southern section of the Randstad visible. Pastures, ditches and dikes are still featured in his pictures – but as fragments of a new, impenetrable context. The landscape was orphaned, the people lost. On one of his walks through the area of the mouth of the Rhine, he found a farmer and his son dragging along two cows. As ever, the farmer toils with an unhappy expression. If one looks closely, one can see that the rest of the photo shows indifferent urban fringes and the billboard of a furniture outlet village. In the pasture are some hobby sheep and ponies. It is unclear whether this is a cynical critique or in fact a comforting understanding of the fragility of existence in the modern world.

Ellen Kooi still searched for the unadulterated polder landscapes of potatoes, poplars or heather. Her panoramas always featured girls. They hang in the trees, bend their little bodies backward like bridges over the ditch or stand adorably on their little legs in the fog. These unmistakable city types vainly try to make the polder land their own but ultimately get lost. Are these the milkmaids of today? Full of life and innocent yet not of this land? Her imposing pictures scream out how much humans want to possess this land, but also how wide the gap is between their imagination and reality.

Photographer Bert Verhoef looked into the countryside around Amsterdam in his album *De Boomgaard der Gelukzaligen* (The Orchard of the Blessed), the land that Rembrandt, Roelofs, Mondriaan and the poet Nescio had combed. Dikes crowded with people in tight Lycra, skaters, cyclists and joggers pushing prams, sweating and gasping for breath. An old but now suburban dike house, freshly thatched, on the Gein. The modern mass culture exploring, in hordes, the scarce passages in the cleaved landscape.

NO PRIDE, NO SHAME

The process of renouncing of the polders was able to thrive in a culture of 'No pride, no shame'. This self-loathing did not merely lead to the destruction of the historic New Land. The southern portion of the Randstad also declined as a magnet environment. Rotterdam, The Hague, Leiden, Delft, Zoetermeer, Gouda and Dordrecht had become all one city the rest of the Netherlands abhorred ever having to live in. The part of the country that, of all the polders, had most often been immortalised in paintings and had been the draught-horse of the economy for almost a century, was now experiencing a relocation imbalance. No business would establish a new operation there. The inner cities fell into decay as a result of the organised exodus of the middle class to the new-build ghettos in the wet polders.

The charm of the celebrated Holland landscape had vanished. The five million inhabitants of the Randstad were becoming increasingly orphaned from their own native soil. This once-privileged Randstad, the unique metropolis encircling a vast emptiness, had degenerated into a Los Angeles-like ghost town. Without a word about it ever having been written into official policy, or the people ever having been consulted, the planning elite had robbed city dwellers of their Sunday family bicycle outing to the cows and the cow parsley. The myth had died. The commuters stuck in traffic jams made their obligatory daily journey without windmills, without a horizon, without seasons, like zombies. Abroad, there was laughter.

The scale of the act was covered up in legal terms by proclaiming active support for the *Groene Hart beleid* (Green Heart policy) and at the same time constantly shifting its boundaries. Any thought of a tradition of creation and a New Land were long gone. In 1986, the baby-boom generation, by law, had jettisoned the last element of Lely's plans. There would be no Markerwaard. This decision was the symbolic death-blow for the land-making philosophy. The Rijksdienst was dismantled and its archives barely rescued in the nick of time by the Nieuwe Land heritage centre.

An even greater evil was perpetrated by the unfathomable decision, in 2006, to clean up the inert spatial planning process by devolving the management of planning to municipalities, developers and institutions. Local and regional consultative planning under the watchful eye of provincial authorities. The lame leading the blind.

A land without tradition has no future. Only the arch-enemy, water, could change all this. We must wait for a catastrophic storm to flush the orphaned polder land clean, so that future generations might embrace it again.

Velsen – Mist, Ellen Kooi, 2003

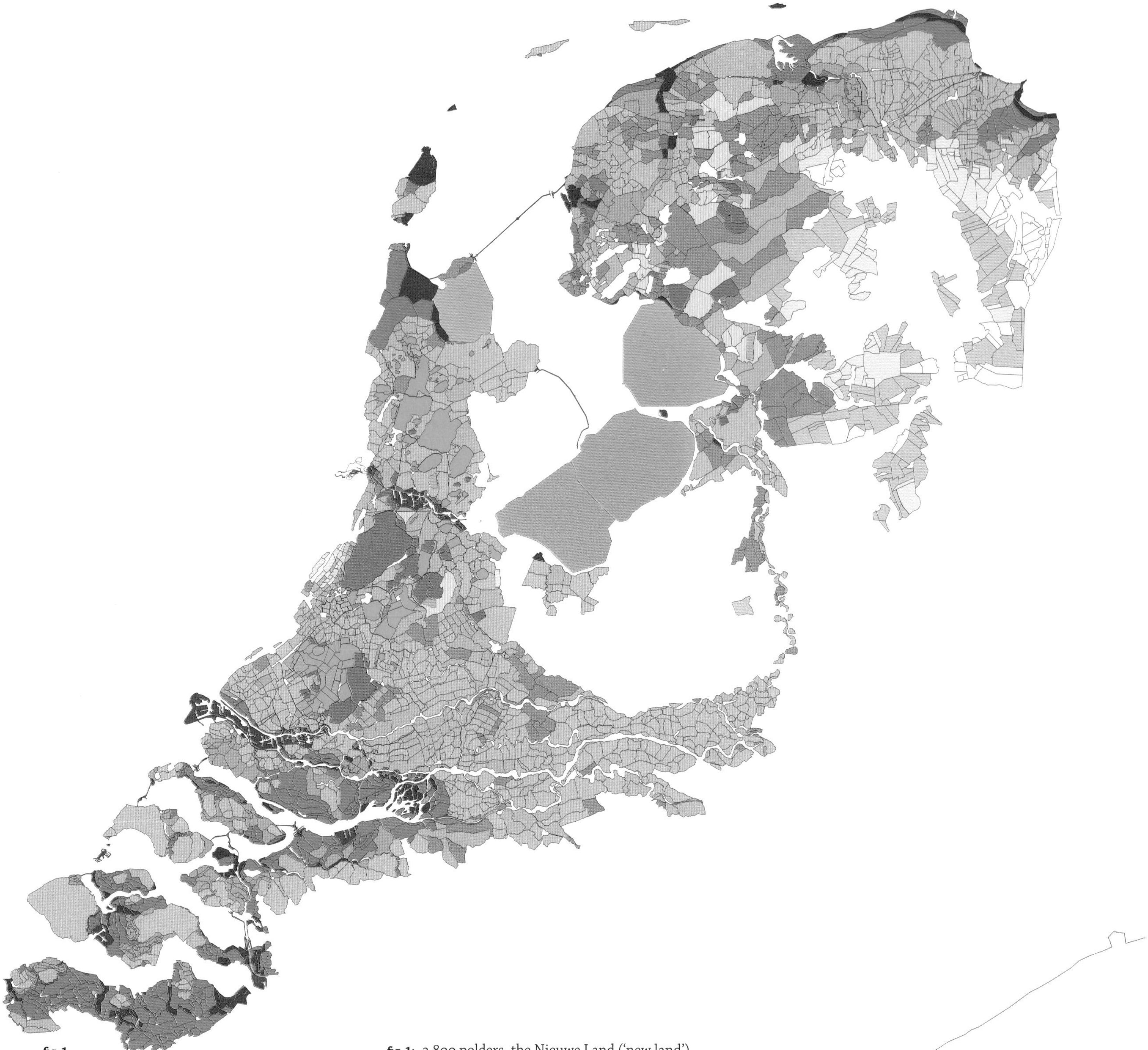

fig. 1

fig. 1: 3.800 polders, the Nieuwe Land ('new land')

fig. 2: Groene Hart ('green heart'), regeneration: 1958, 1991, 2006

fig. 3: Gebroken Groene Hart ('broken green heart'), 2008

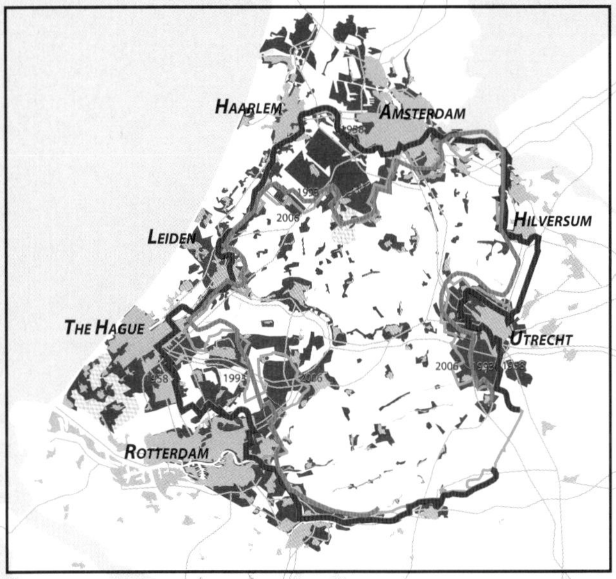
HAARLEM
AMSTERDAM
HILVERSUM
LEIDEN
THE HAGUE
UTRECHT
ROTTERDAM

fig. 2

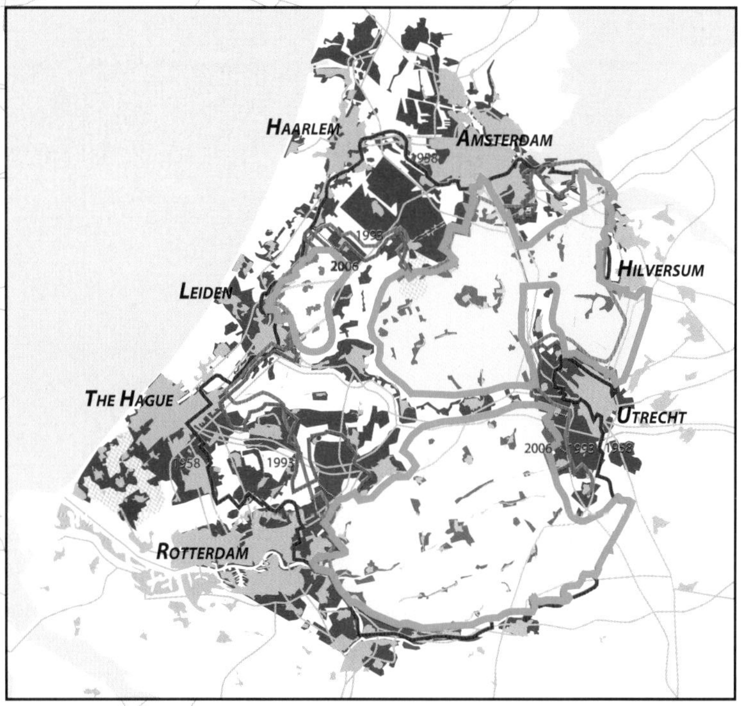
HAARLEM
AMSTERDAM
HILVERSUM
LEIDEN
THE HAGUE
UTRECHT
ROTTERDAM

fig. 3

1

1: Cow on location, along the A2
2: Cow inflation
3: Cow on location, along the A13

2

HORIZON PROJECT
THE NETHERLANDS

Three eight-metre-high cows are placed along the main highways in the Randstad as reminders of the unique Dutch horizon. They draw attention to the fact that the Dutch *veenweidelandschap* is not only of cultural importance but also essential as a place for self-reflection.

They are happy cows, posing like Potter's bull, framing the glorious horizon between their legs and, as is the case with Potter, fixing the onlooker with their bright eyes suggesting they know what's going on.

Interestingly enough, when setting up this project, the farmers we asked to provide us with suitable meadows did so without hesitation. They too knew what we were talking about!

3

4

5

6

4–5: Cow on location, along the A4
6: Cow deflation

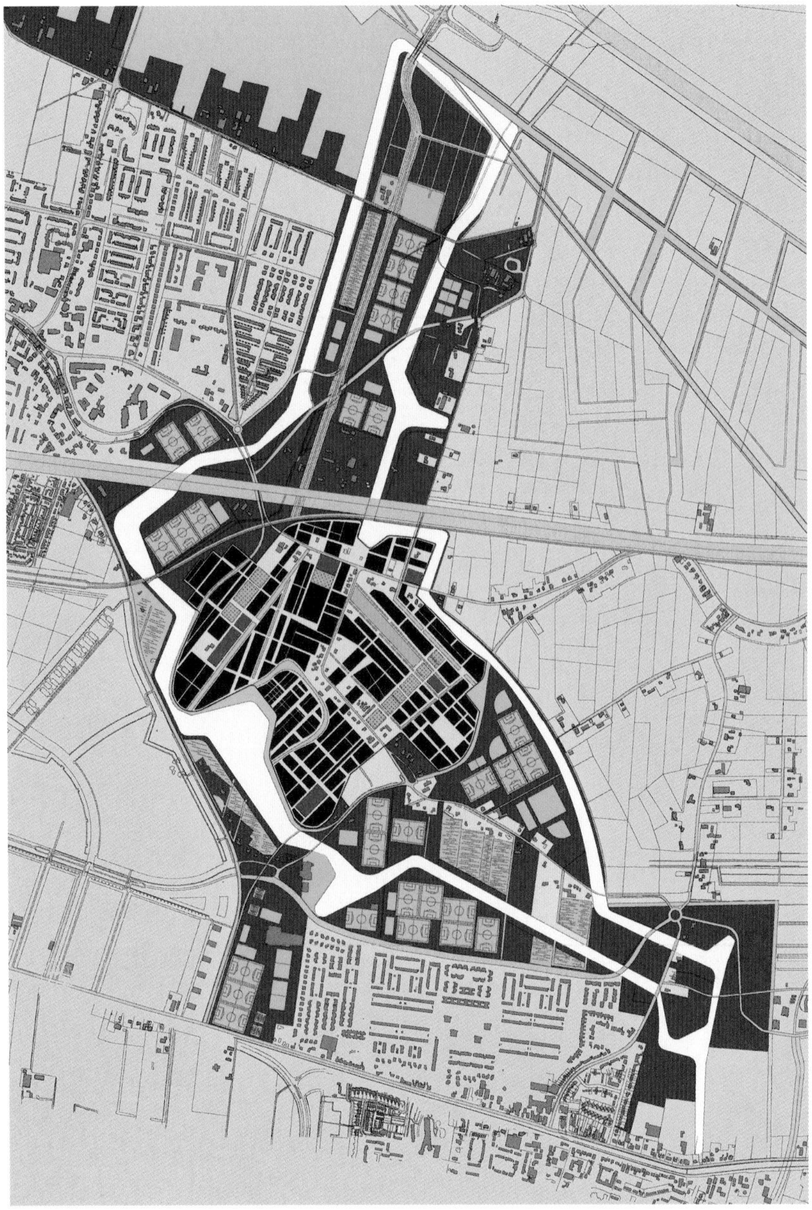

1

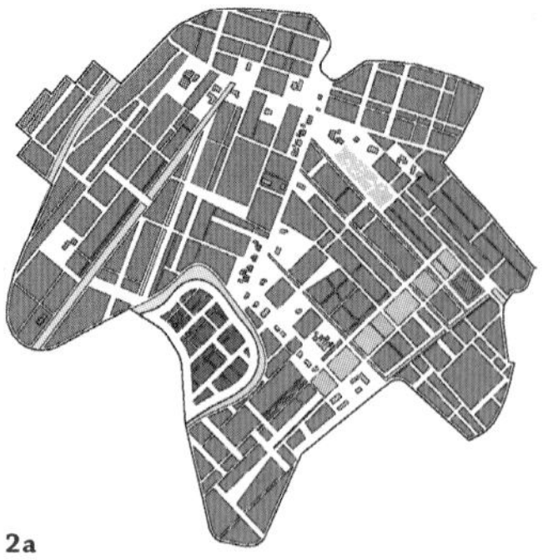

2a

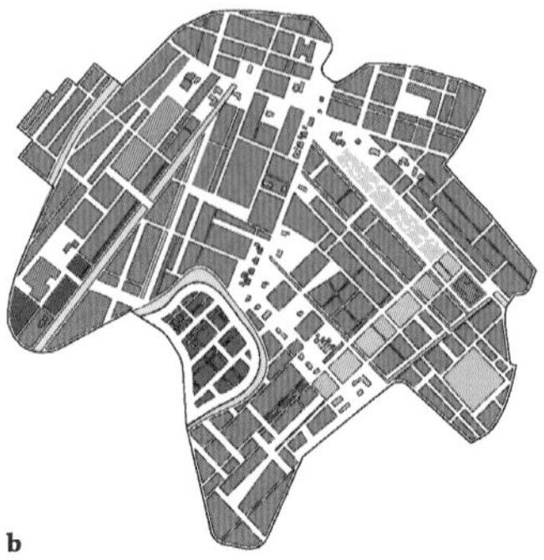

b

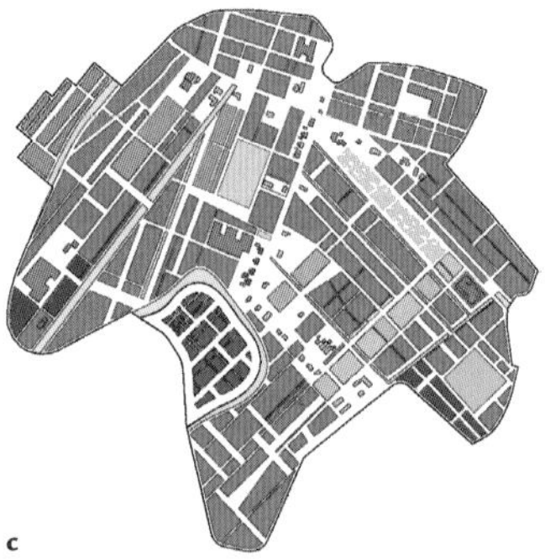

c

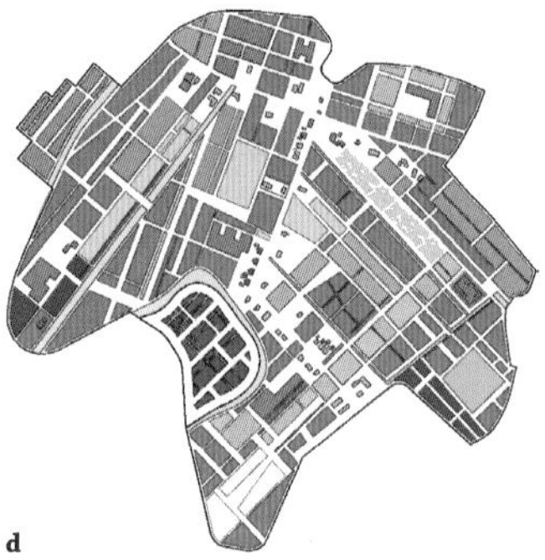

d

1: Competition design
2a: Phase 1: 10 years
b: Phase 2: 15 years
c: Phase 3: 25 years
d: Phase 4: 50 years

LEIDSCHE RIJN PARK

UTRECHT, THE NETHERLANDS

The design for Leidsche Rijn Park was the outcome of a design competition held in 1997. The concept for the park, to be constructed in a new residential district of 35.000 homes to the west of Utrecht, is based on creating three 'edges' – borders that shield the park from its suburban surroundings. The edges consist of a re-excavated meander of the River Rhine, a twelve-kilometre-long ecological ribbon with a track, and a five-kilometre-long park wall around the central section. Within the park, which measures 300 hectares in area, the 50-hectare walled *Binnenhof* ('courtyard') forms a climax. It contains woods, stream banks and avenues which create a secretive inner world that can be entered only through gateways. The waterways, woods and avenues are under construction. Sports grounds, a manege and allotments have already been completed.

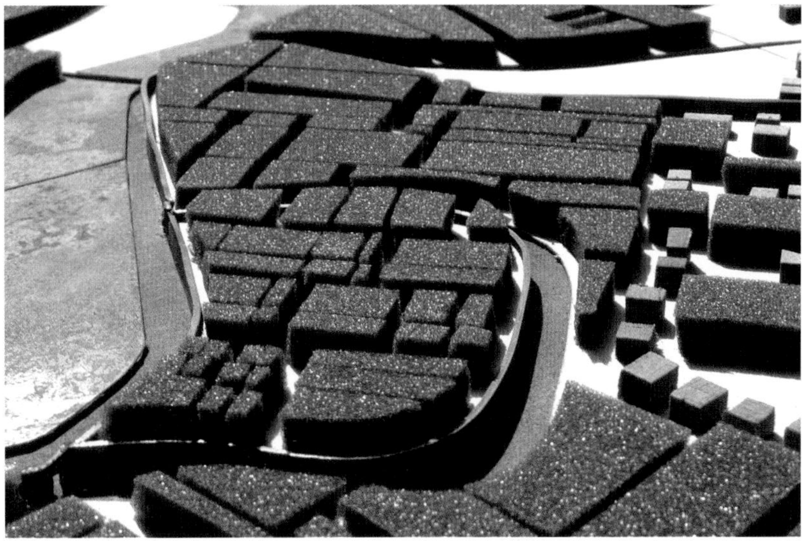

3

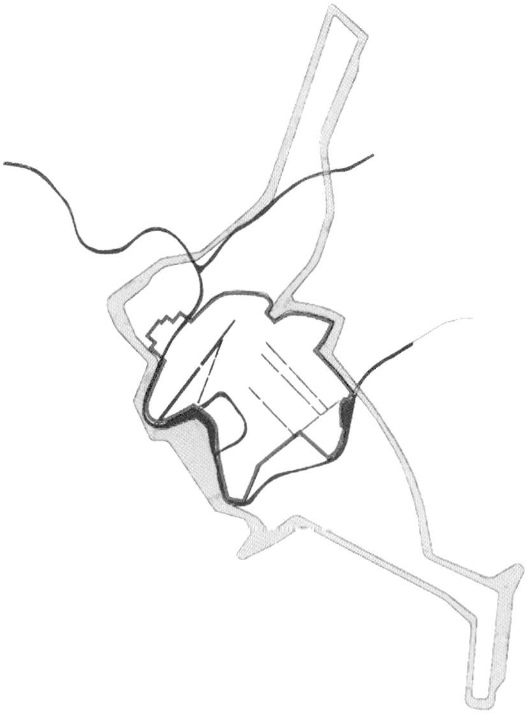

4

5

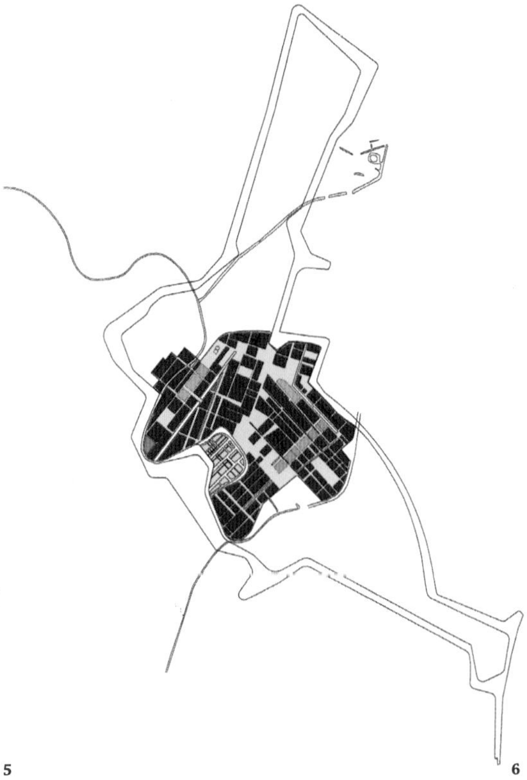

6

3: Scale model
4: 3 boundaries
5: Sports fields, vegetable gardens
6: Public park, Kremlin

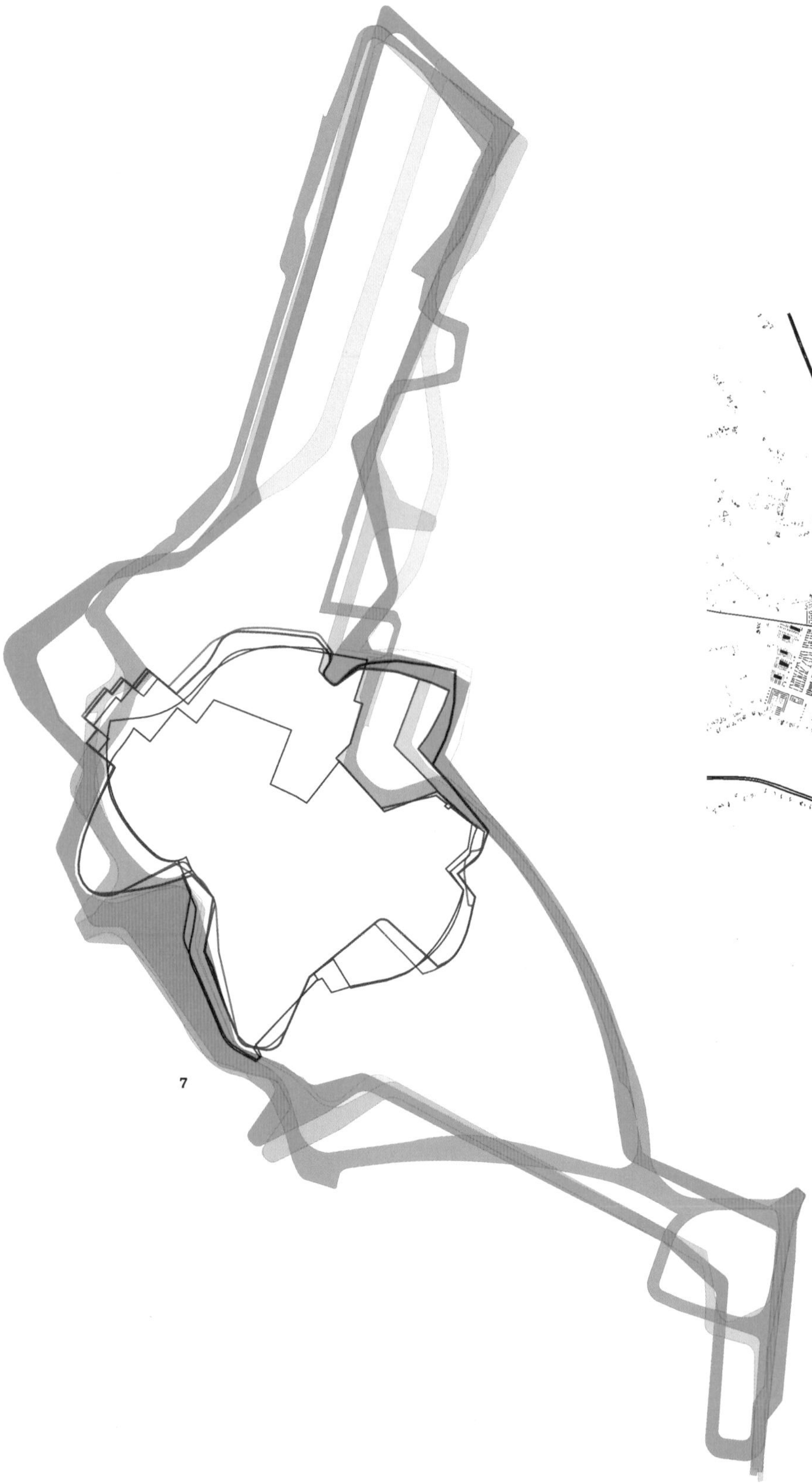

7

8

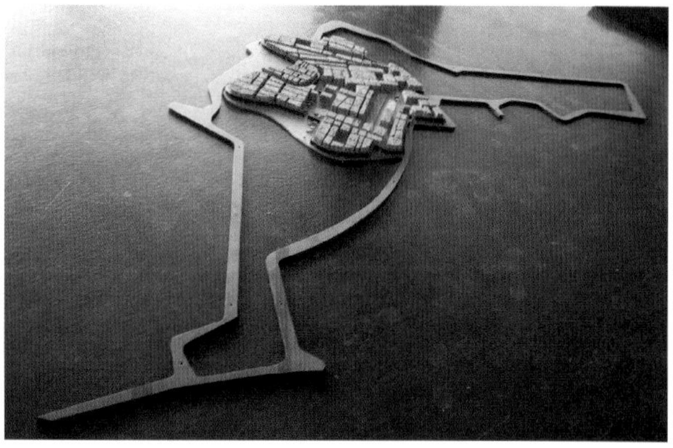

9

JACQ. P. THIJSSE LINT

7: Jacq. P. Thijsse Lint, wall, transformations
8: Situation in periphery Utrecht
9: Model
10: Aerial view, projection

11

12

13

CONCRETE KERB STONE FOR JACQ. P. THIJSSE LINT

11–14: Detail with daisy flower pattern

15

16

17

15–16: Soil samples
17: Geological location Viking Rijn
18: Vegetation plan
19–20: Young plants

18

BEPLANTINGSPLAN
Projectnummer 403.036
Behorende bij tekeningnr. 3036.CMT-1 (Concept 3), d.d. 09-01-2004
Status: concept 2
Datum 09-01-2004
Door S.X.M. Buiten

vaknummer	tot. opp. (m^2)	Latijnse naam	Nederlandse naam	kwaliteit	totaal aantal (st)
VAK B1					
mengsel b	8995				
		Quercus robur	Zomereik	veren / sel. / ned. herkomst	3399
		Fraxinus excelsior	Es	veren / sel. / ned. herkomst	850
		Fagus sylvatica	Gewone beuk	veren / sel. / ned. herkomst	567
		Alnus glutinosa	Grauwe els	zaailing	283
		Populus euram. 'Robusta'	Euramerikaanse populier		63
		Carpinus betulus	Gewone haagbeuk	autochtoon	100
		Corylus avellana	Gewone hazelaar	drietak / autochtoon	50
		Prunus padus	Vogelkers	autochtoon	200
		Cornus sanguinea	Rode kornoelje	drietak / autochtoon	60
mengsel 1a	1812				
		Quercus robur	Zomereik	autochtoon / selectie	3
		Tilia cordata	Winterlinde	autochtoon / selectie	1
		Fraxinus excelsior	Es	autochtoon / selectie	2
		Prunus avium	Zoete kers	autochtoon / selectie	2
		Carpinus betulus	Gewone haagbeuk	autochtoon / selectie	20
		Acer campestre	Spaanse aak	autochtoon / selectie	20
		Corylus avellana	Gewone hazelaar	drietak / autochtoon	25
		Rhamnus catharticus	Wegedoorn	autochtoon	20
		Crataegus monogyna	Eenstijlige meidoorn	autochtoon	25
		Viburnus opulus	Gelderse roos	autochtoon	125
		Euonymus europaeus	Kardinaalsmuts	autochtoon	175
		Cornus sanguinea	Rode kornoelje	autochtoon	120
mantel	1495				
		Mespilus germanica	Mispel	autochtoon	30
		Cornus mas	Gele kornoelje	autochtoon	35
		Ligustrum vulgare	Gewone liguster	drietak / autochtoon	120
		Prunus spinosa	Sleedoorn	autochtoon	50
		Rosa rubiginosa	Egelantier	autochtoon	95
		Sambucus nigra	Gewone vlier	autochtoon	25
populiercirkels	692				
		Populus euram. 'Robusta'	Euramerikaanse populier		54
VAK A4					
mengsel a	3785				
		Quercus robur	Zomereik	autochtoon / selectie	1430
		Fraxinus excelsior	Es	autochtoon / selectie	477
		Prunus avium	Zoete kers	autochtoon / selectie	119
		Tilia cordata	Winterlinde	autochtoon / selectie	119
		Populus eura. 'Robusta'	Euramerikaanse populier		13
		Alnus glutinosa	Grauwe els	zaailing	119
		Corylus avellana	Gewone hazelaar	autochtoon	75
		Cornus sanguinea	Rode kornoelje	autochtoon	75
		Prunus padus	Vogelkers	autochtoon	100
mengsel 1a	711				
		Quercus robur	Zomereik	autochtoon / selectie	3
		Crataegus monogyna	Eenstijlige meidoorn	autochtoon	10
		Acer campestre	Spaanse aak	autochtoon	8
		Cornus mas	Gele kornoelje	autochtoon	8
		Rosa rubiginosa	Egelantier	autochtoon	40
		Prunus spinosa	Sleedoorn	autochtoon	25
		Euonymus europaeus	Kardinaalsmuts	autochtoon	30
		Ligustrum vulgare	Gewone liguster	autochtoon	33
VAK A1					
mengsel a	2413				
		Quercus robur	Zomereik	autochtoon / selectie	912
		Fraxinus excelsior	Es	autochtoon / selectie	304
		Prunus avium	Zoete kers	autochtoon / selectie	76
		Tilia cordata	Winterlinde	autochtoon / selectie	76
		Populus euram. 'Robusta'	Euramerikaanse populier		8
		Alnus glutinosa	Grauwe els	zaailing	76
		Corylus avellana	Gewone hazelaar	autochtoon	75
		Cornus sanguinea	Rode kornoelje	autochtoon	75
		Prunus padus	Vogelkers	autochtoon	100
VAK C3					
mengsel c	4956				
		Quercus robur	Zomereik	autochtoon	2497
		Fagus sylvatica	Gewone beuk	autochtoon	624

19

20

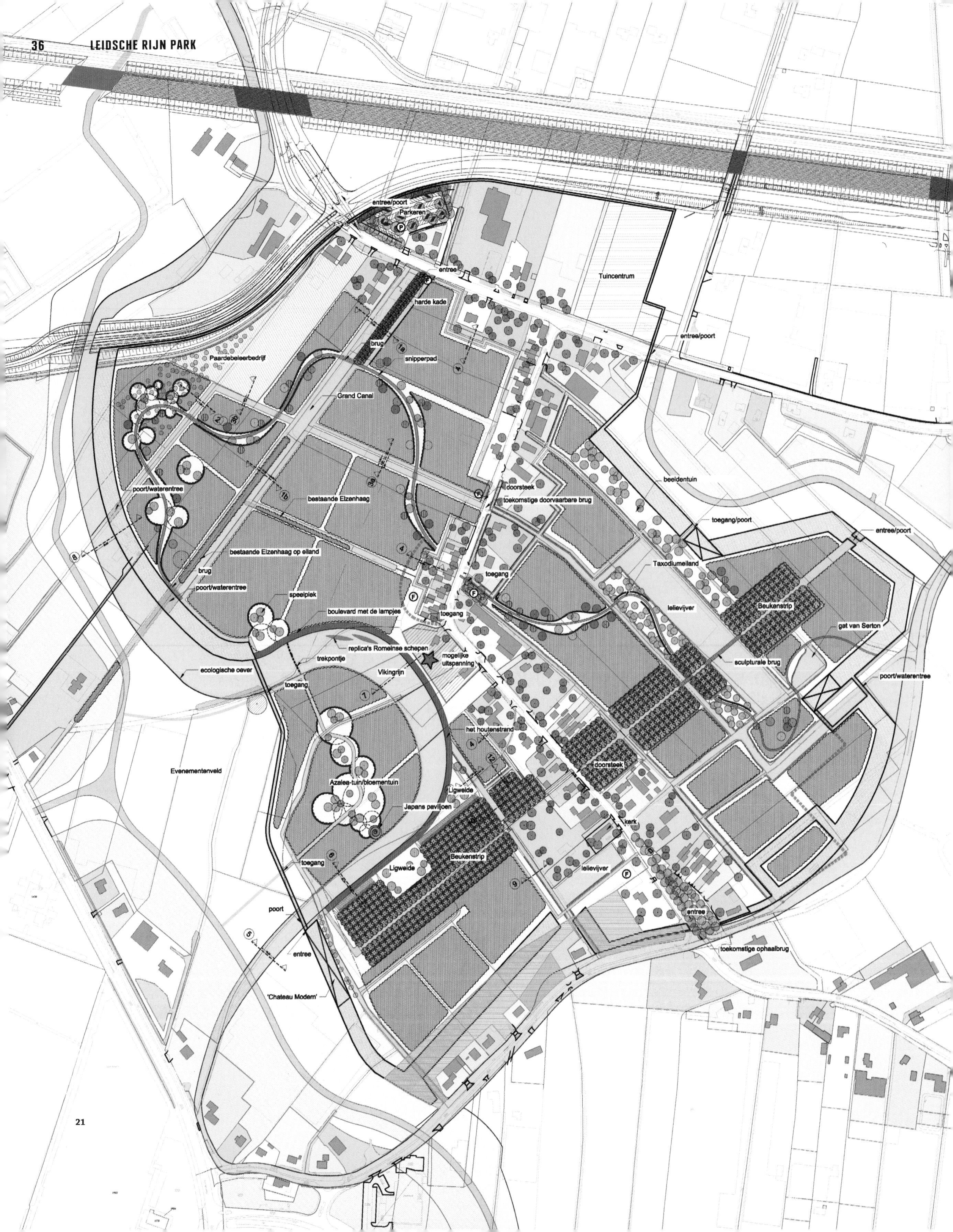
entree/poort
Parkeren
entree
harde kade
Tuincentrum
entree/poort
brug
snipperpad
Paardebeleerbedrijf
Grand Canal
poort/waterentree
bestaande Elzenhaag
doorsteek
toekomstige doorvaarbare brug
beeldentuin
toegang/poort
entree/poort
bestaande Elzenhaag op eiland
Taxodiumeiland
brug
poort/waterentree
toegang
speelplek
boulevard met de lampjes
toegang
lelievijver
Beukenstrip
gat van Serton
replica's Romeinse schepen
mogelijke uitspanning
trekpontje
sculpturale brug
ecologische oever
Vikingrijn
poort/waterentree
toegang
het houtenstrand
Evenementenveld
doorsteek
Azalea-tuin/bloementuin
Ligweide
Japans paviljoen
kerk
toegang
Beukenstrip
Ligweide
lelievijver
poort
entree
entree
toekomstige ophaalbrug
'Chateau Modern'

22

23

24

VEGETATION

21: Master plan
22: Lime trees
23: Mayor
24: Minister
25: School children
26–27: Avenue of beeches

25

26

27

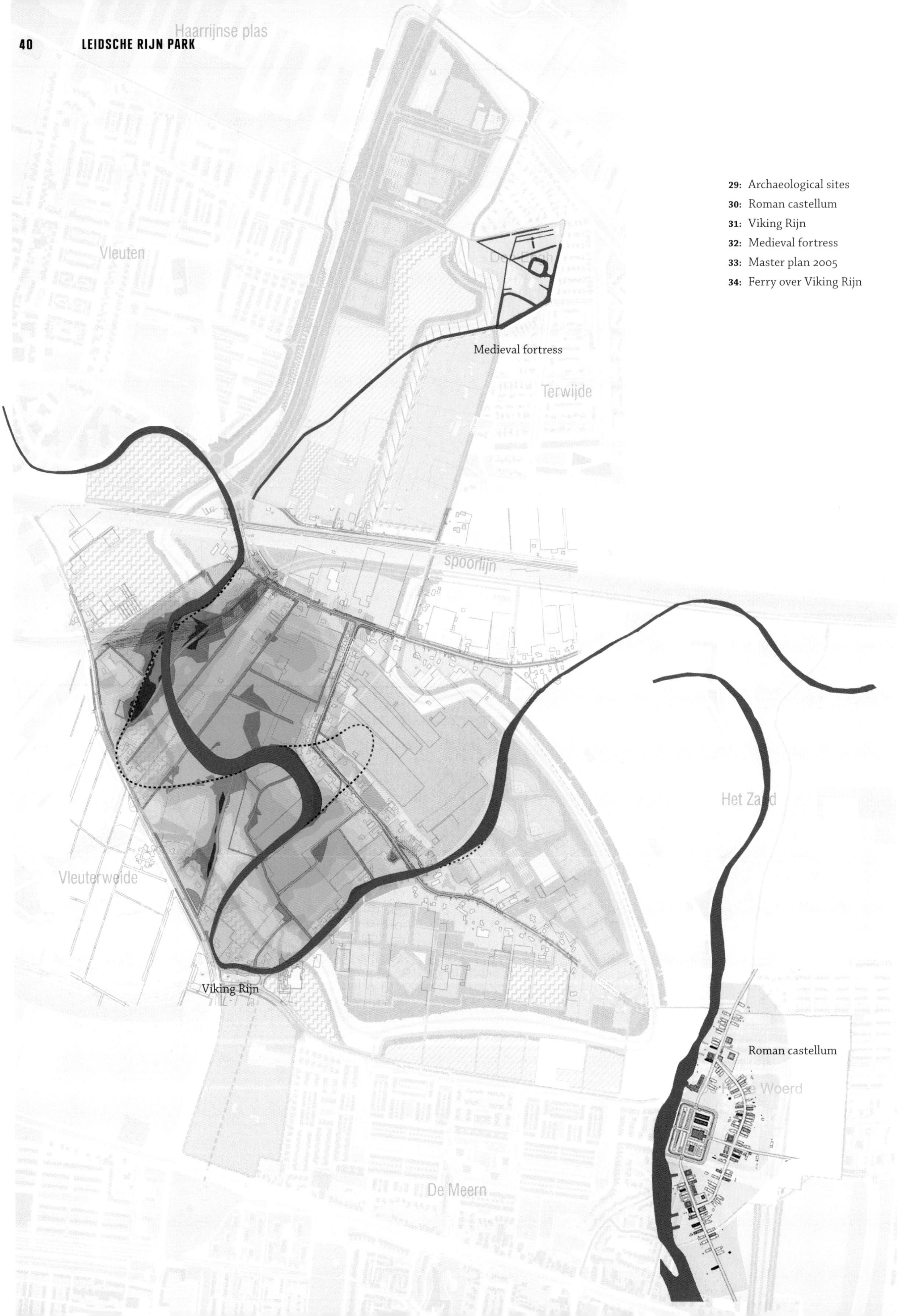

29: Archaeological sites
30: Roman castellum
31: Viking Rijn
32: Medieval fortress
33: Master plan 2005
34: Ferry over Viking Rijn

29

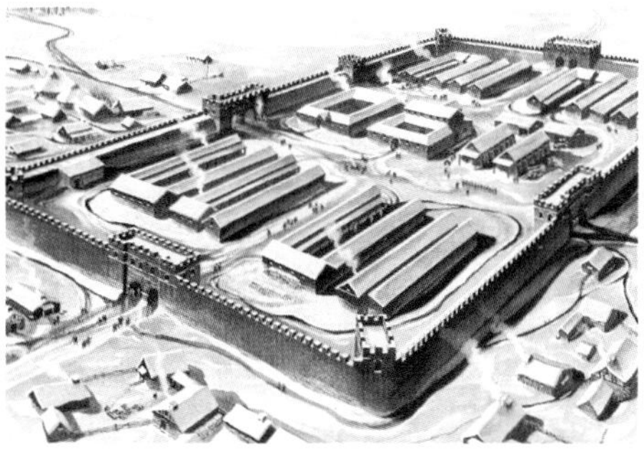
30

31

32

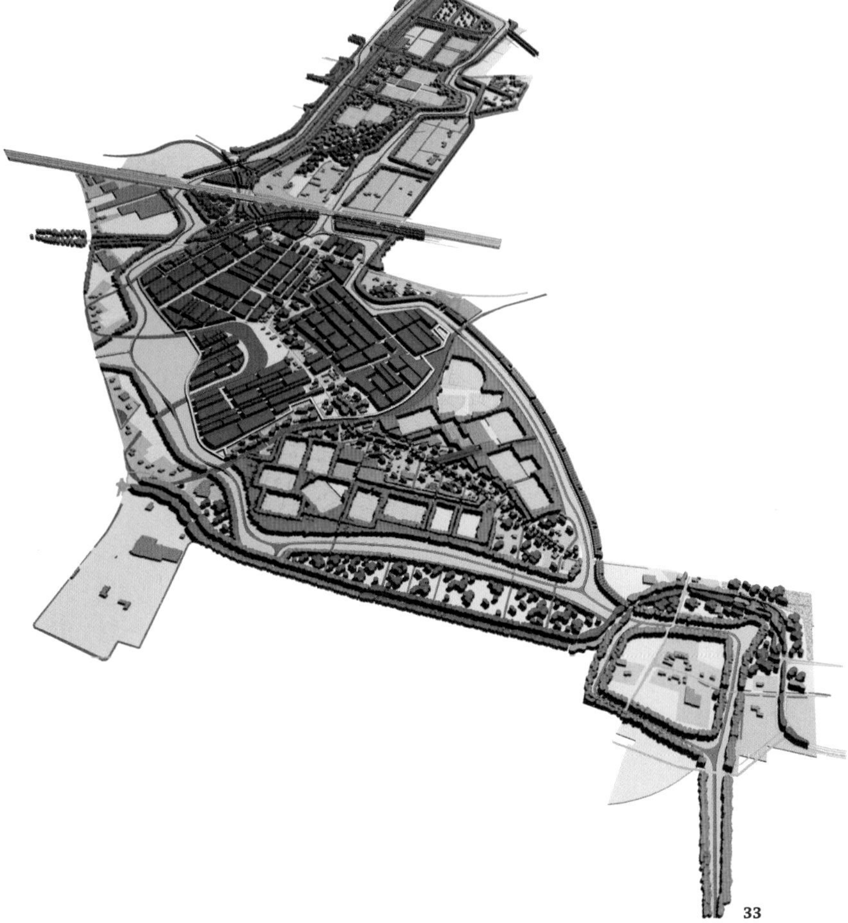
33

34

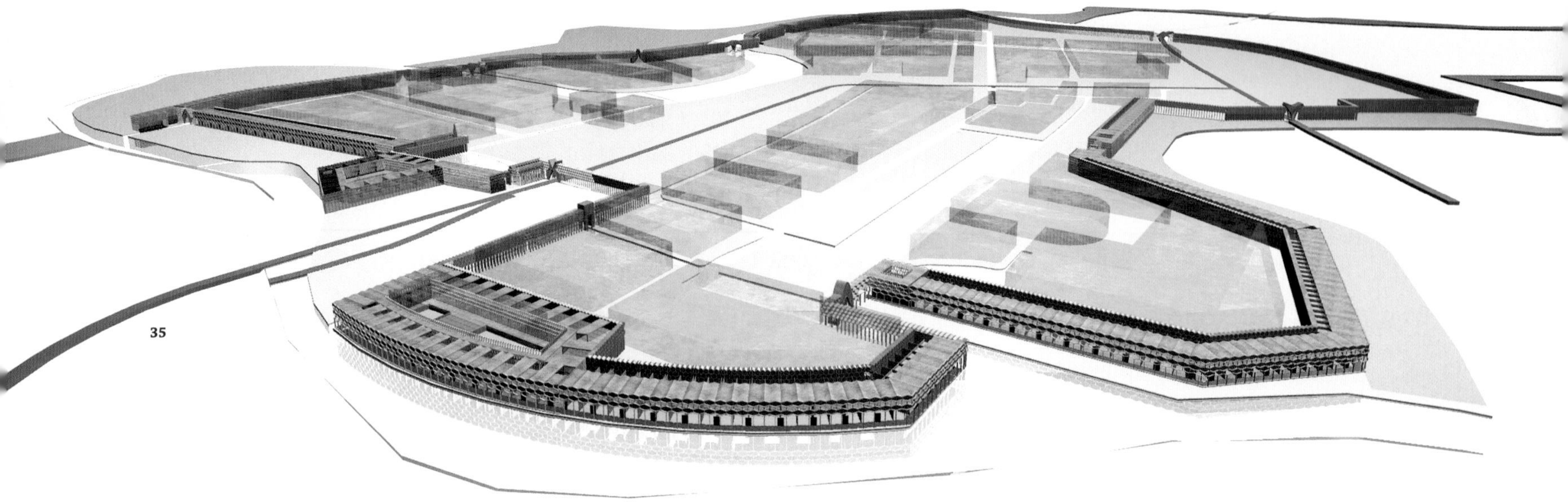

35

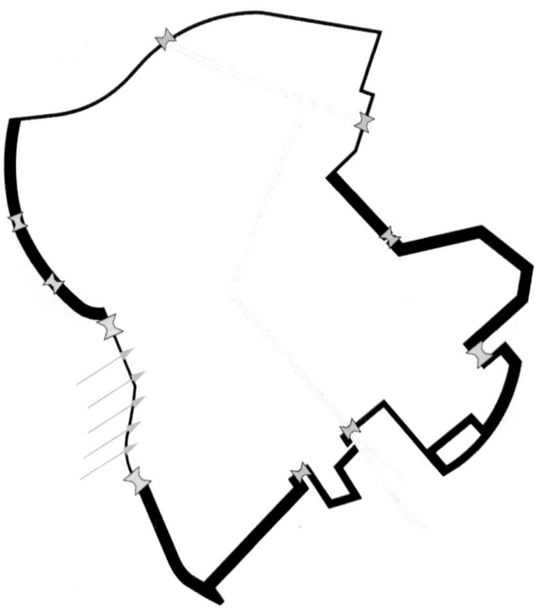

37

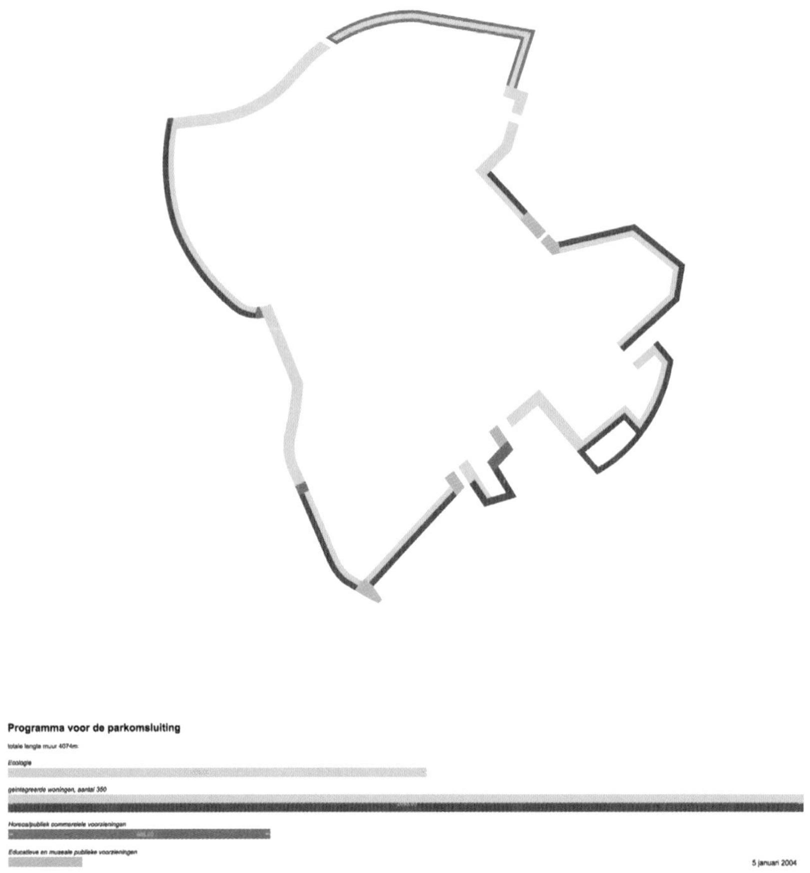
Programma voor de parkomsluiting
totale lengte muur 4074m
Ecologie
geïntegreerde woningen, aantal 350
Horeca/publiek commerciele voorzieningen
Educatieve en museale publieke voorzieningen
5 januari 2004

36

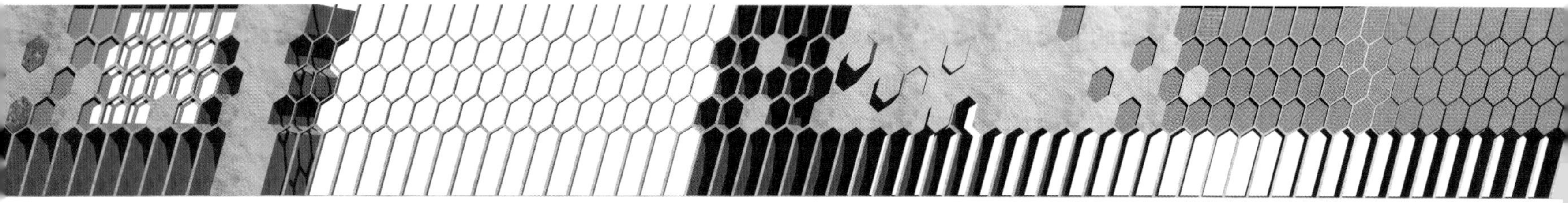

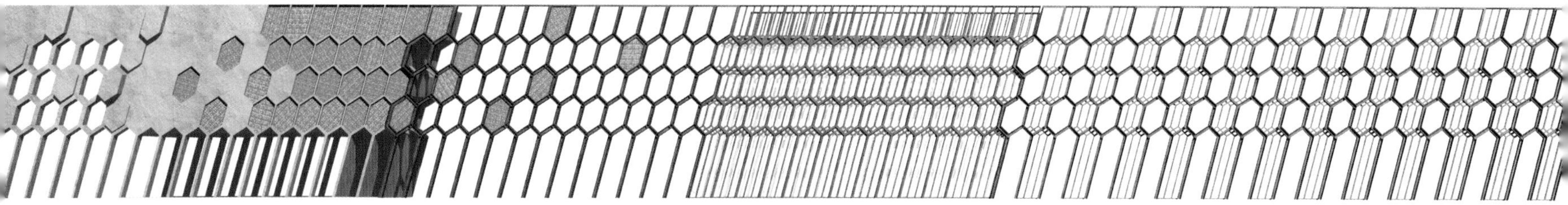

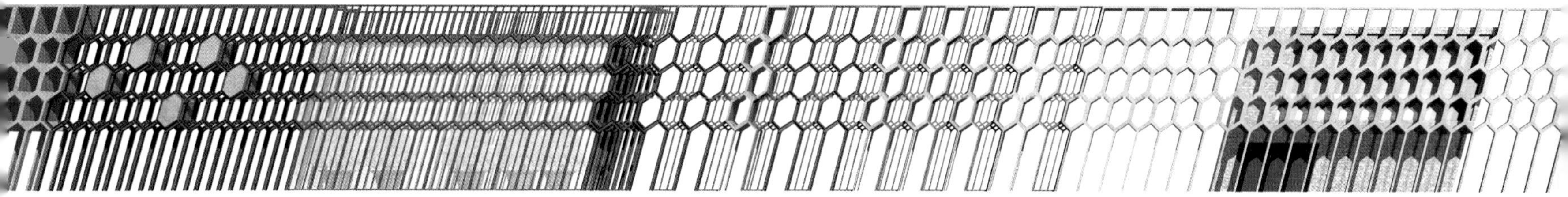

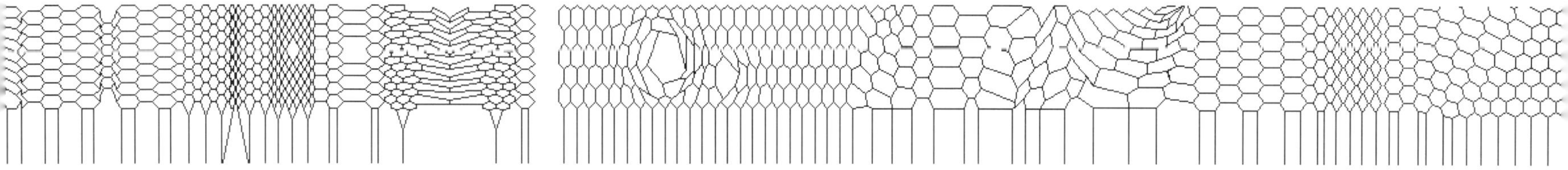

38

WALL

35: Design

36: Programme

37: Gates

38: Sketches

39

39–43: Artist's impressions

40

41

42

43

44

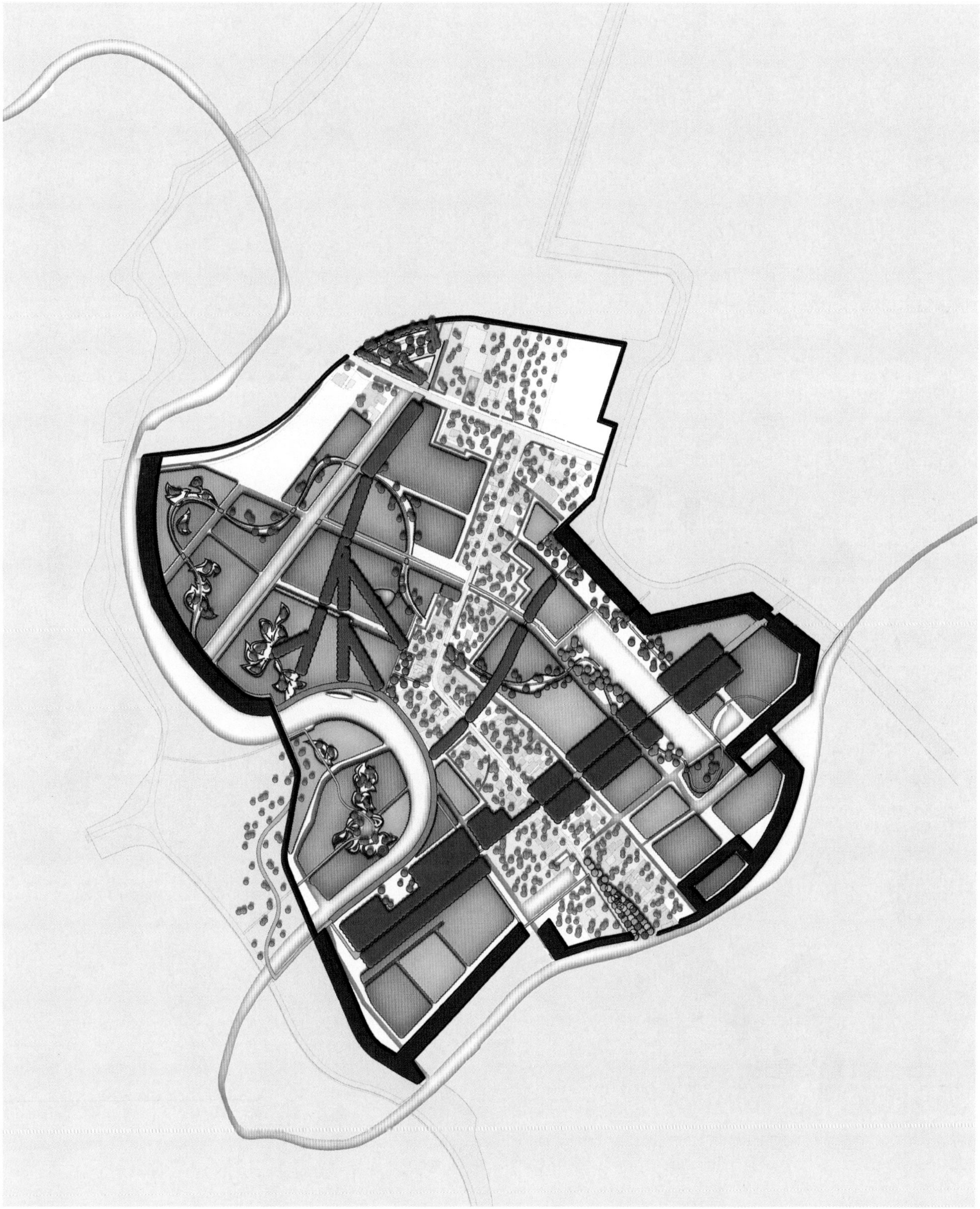

45

44: Swamp vegetation

45: Design sketch 2006

1

2

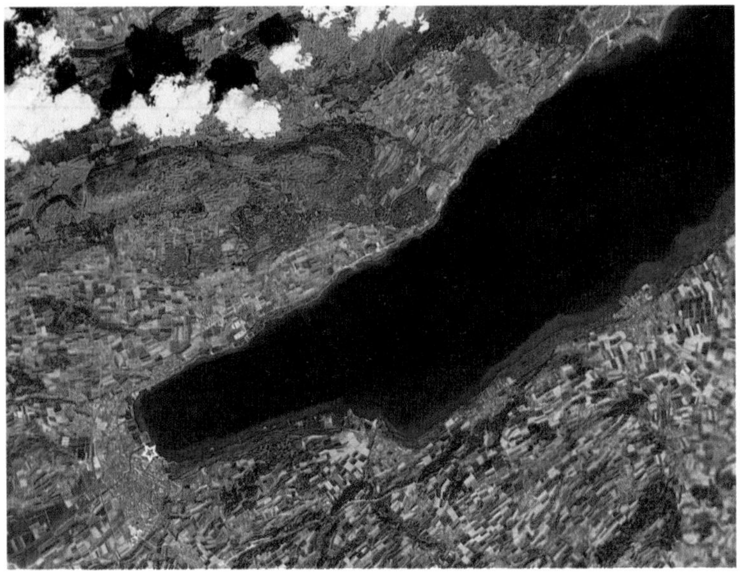

3

EXPO '02

YVERDON-LES-BAINS, SWITZERLAND

A design for an exhibition park on the banks of Lake Neuchatel. The Expo was a year-long festival celebrating Switzerland as a product. The challenge was to create an exhibition area without built architecture. In collaboration with the Zurich-based architects Vehovar Jauslin, West 8 created a master plan purely out of landscape and media elements. The design alluded ironically to a 'Dutch landscape lost in the mountains'. Surreal flower fields and an artificial cloud were placed in the context of the snow-capped peaks of the Jura Mountains. The team invited Diller Scofidio to design the cloud. The temporary Expo park, with hills covered in seasonal flowers and overlooking the restaurants and pavilions, became a popular summer attraction in 2002, with daytime and night-time events.

1: Cloud and tulips
2: Mountains
3: Site located at Lake Neuchatel
4: Man-made cloud
5: Tulips in the mountains

4

5

6

6: Master plan
7: First model
8: Early computer model

7

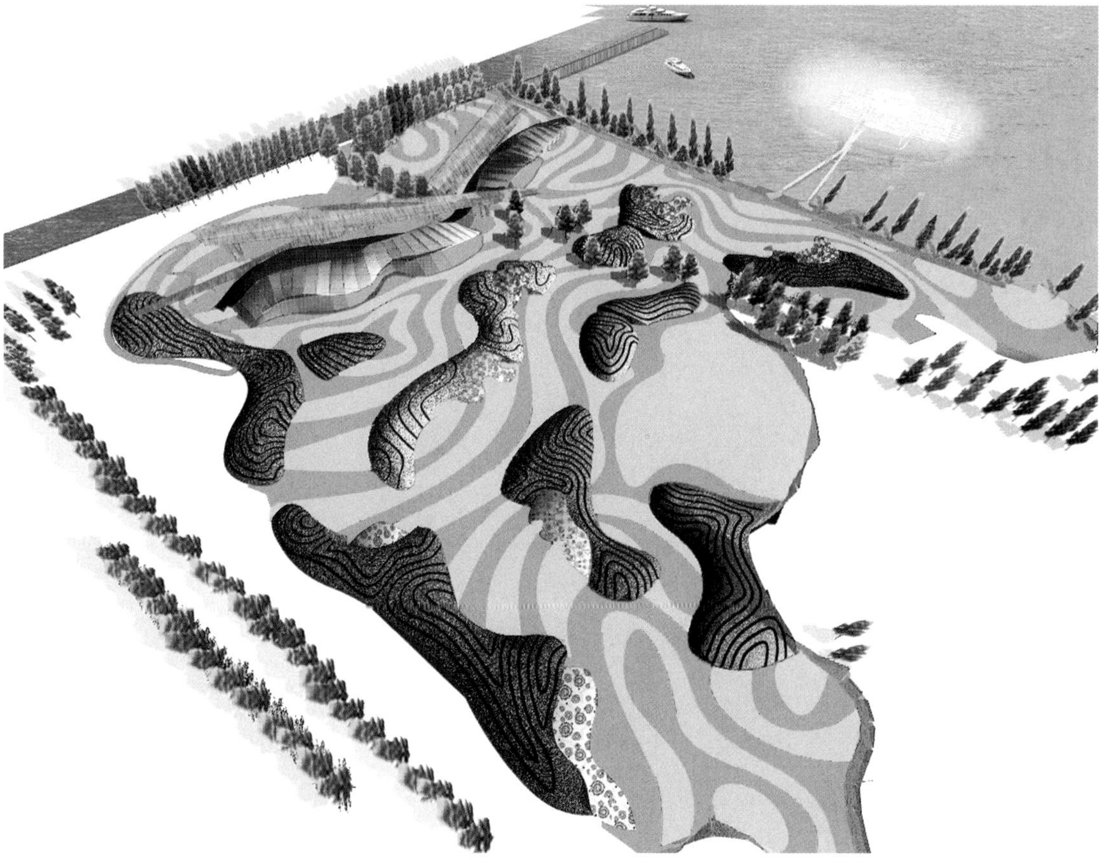

8

9

10

11

12

13

ARTIFICIAL HILLS

9: Timber for artificial hills

10–13: Construction of Hill #4 using traditional Swiss techniques

14: Planting begins

14

15

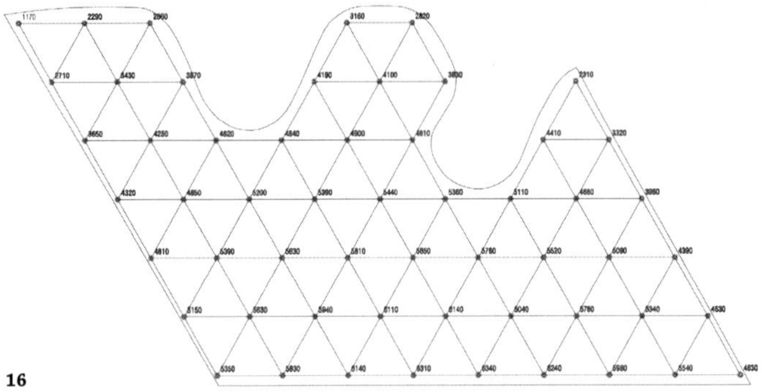

16

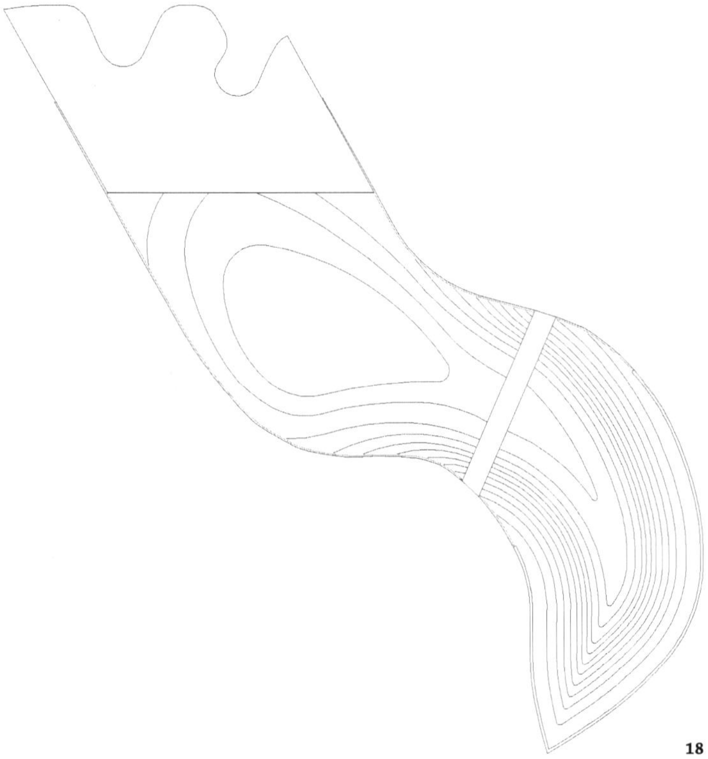

18

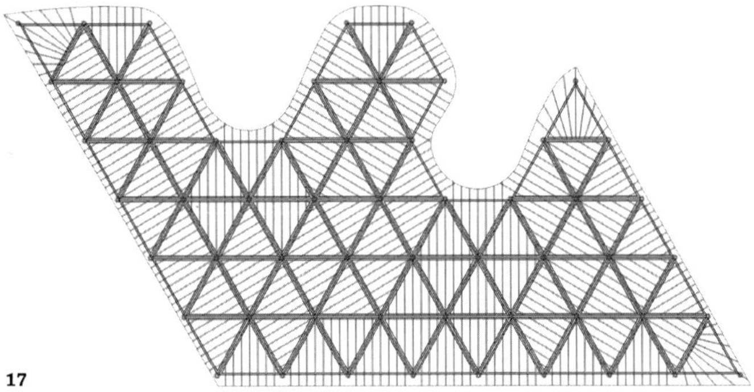

17

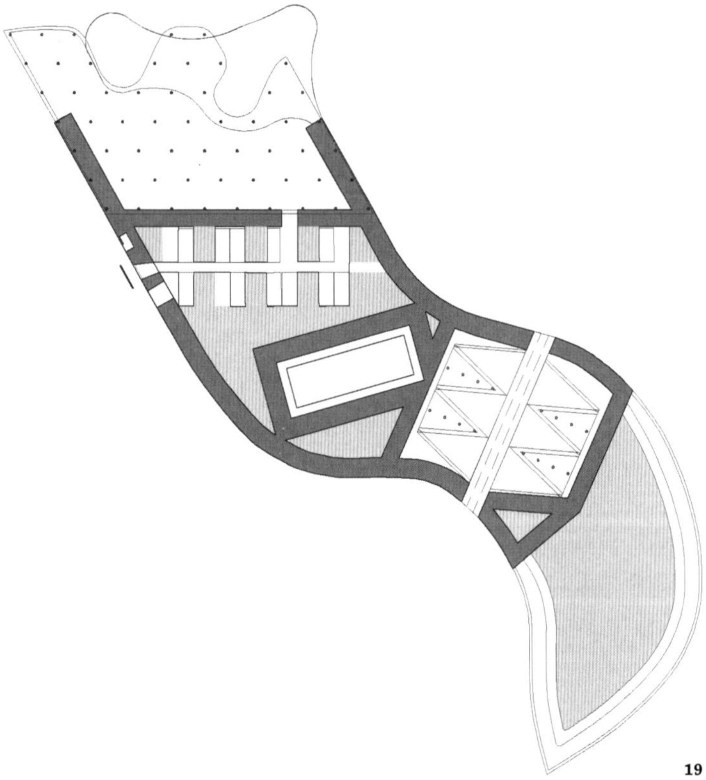

19

HILL #4

15: Site plan indicating Hill #4
16-17: Structural roofplan
18: Contour plan of Hill #4
19: Plan of Hill #4
20: Weights and timber roofing joint

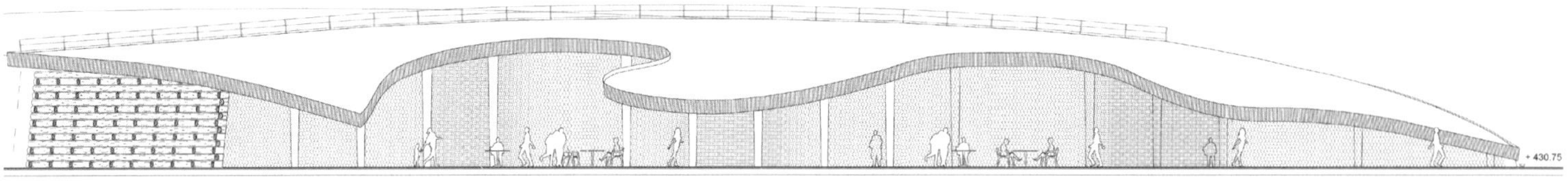

21

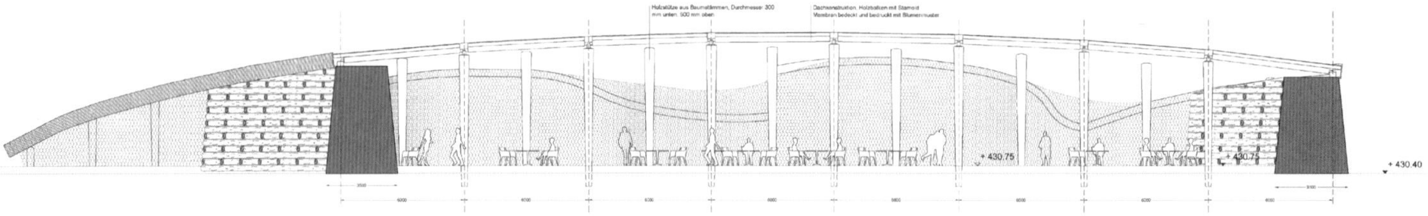

22

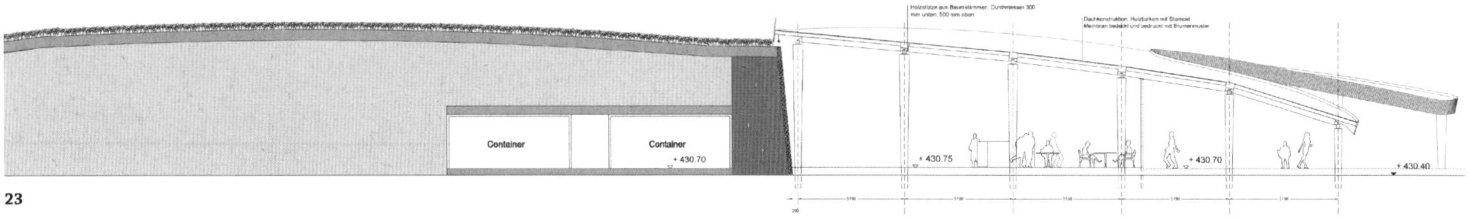

23

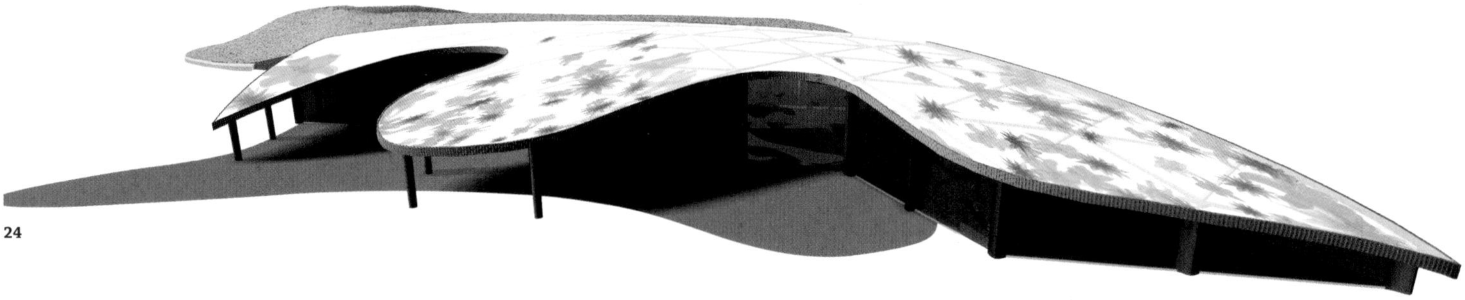

24

HILL #1

21: North elevation

22: South elevation

23: Section

24: Computer model

25: Tent roofing detail
26: Pavilion at night

25

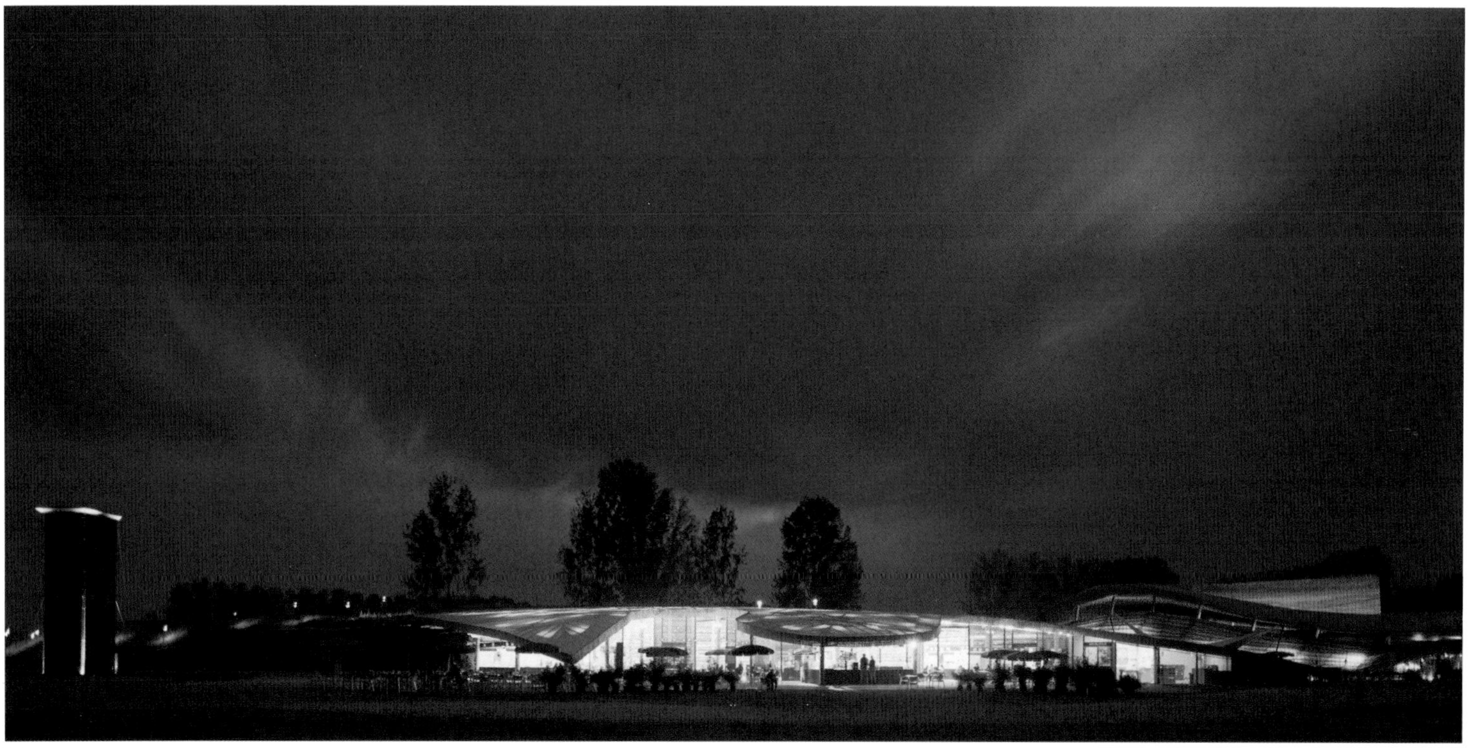

26

27

28

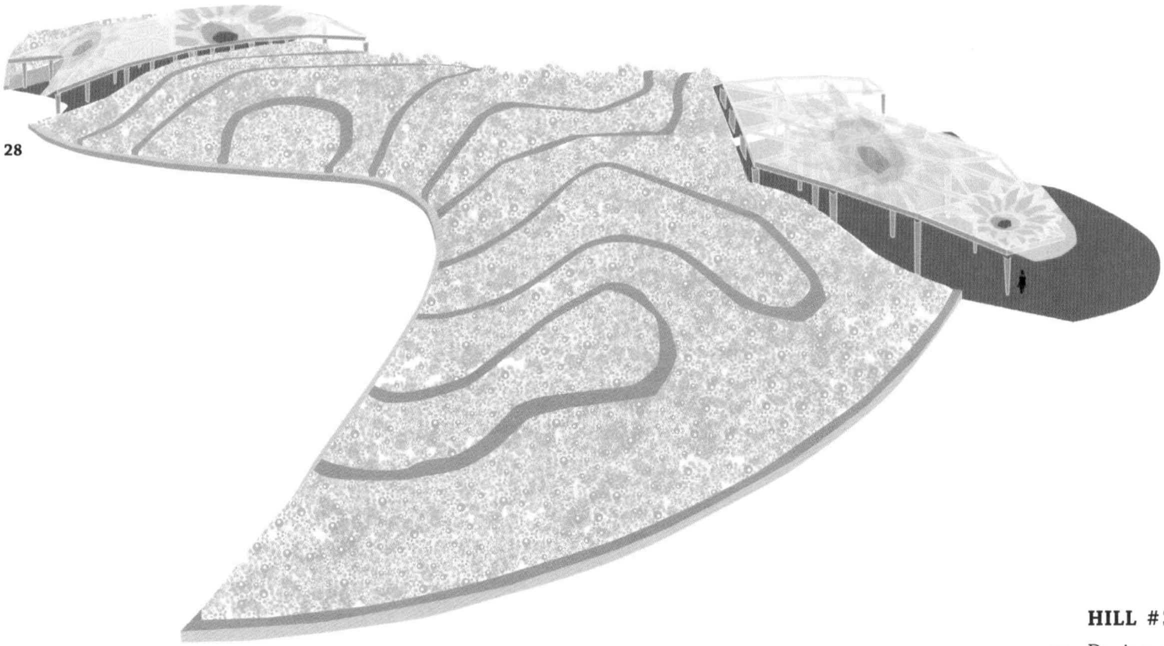

HILL #3

27: During construction
28: Computer model
29: Aerial view of Hill
30: Hill during Expo '02

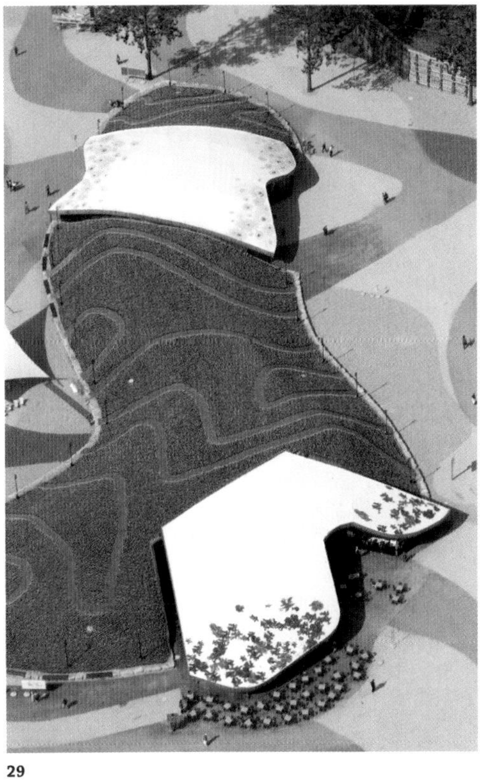

29

30

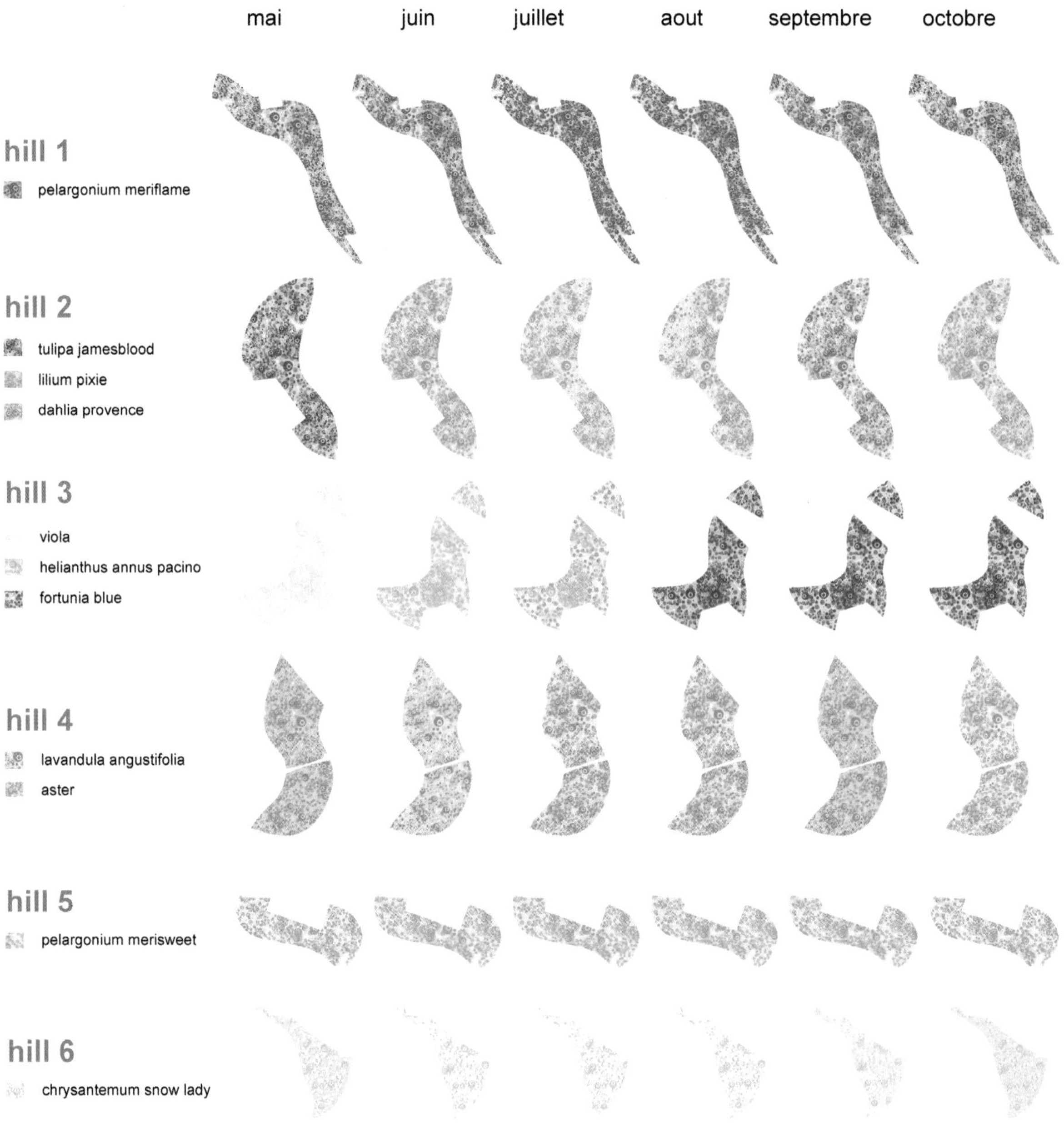

31

33

35

SEASONS

31: Seasonal plan for all 6 hills

32-33: Hill #2

34: Hill #4

35: Hill #3

32

34

36

37

38

36: Hill #1
37-38: Hill #4

39-40: Hill #3

39

40

41

42

41–42: Canopy at trainstation

43–47: Flower line, guiding pedestrians from station to Expo '02

43

44

45

46

47

THE CLOUD

48: Cloud (D.S.)

49: Aerial view Expo Park

50: In the cloud

48

49

50

51

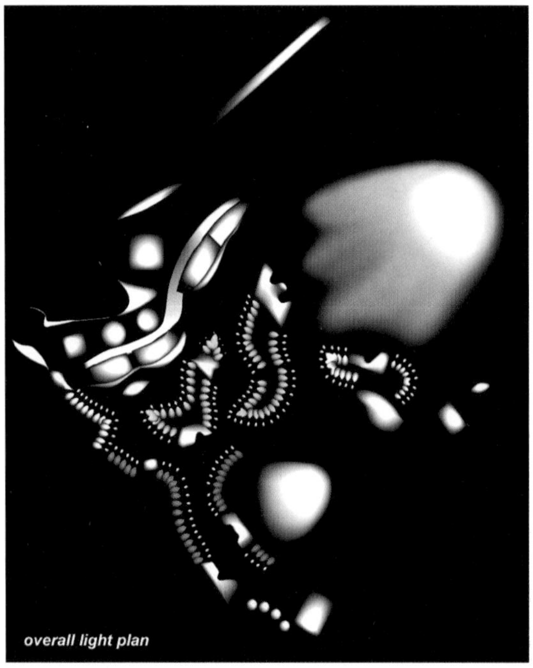

52

51: Night view
52: Overall lighting plan
53: Pavilions and hills at night

53

1

CHISWICK PARK

LONDON, ENGLAND

1: Enjoywork, lower pond
2: Site

Stanhope plc created the concept for a new business park in the West London Borough of Chiswick, based on service, lifestyle and efficiency: enjoywork.com! Following the integrated master plan, created together with Richard Rogers, West 8 designed a Chinese-inspired interior park with two pools and a waterfall, a sharp and coherent park edge which is the service and entrance space for the buildings, a small plaza for public events and the surrounding circulation and parking areas. The business park opened in 2001.

2

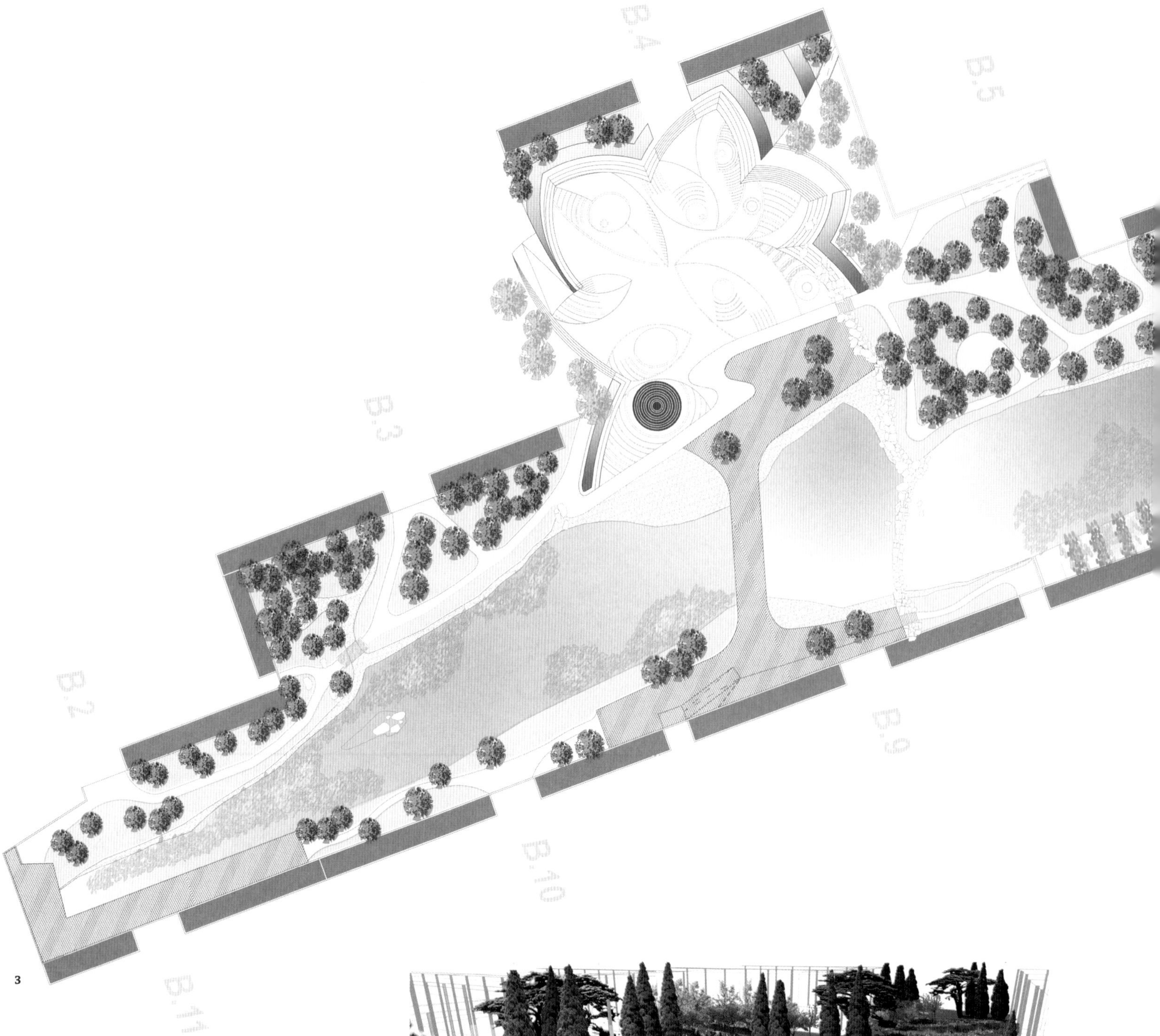

3

4

3: Plan

4: Inside lake, artist's impression

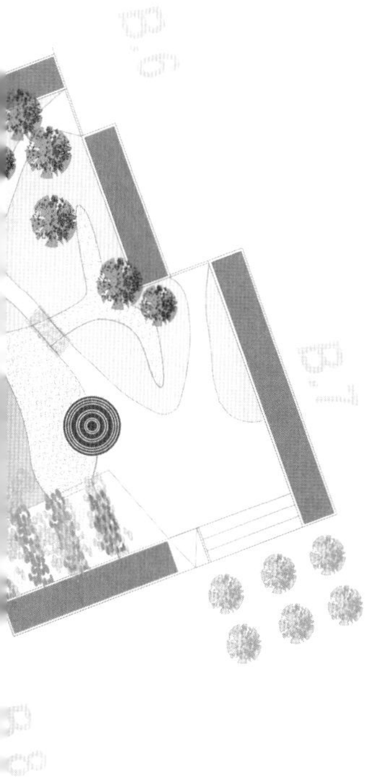

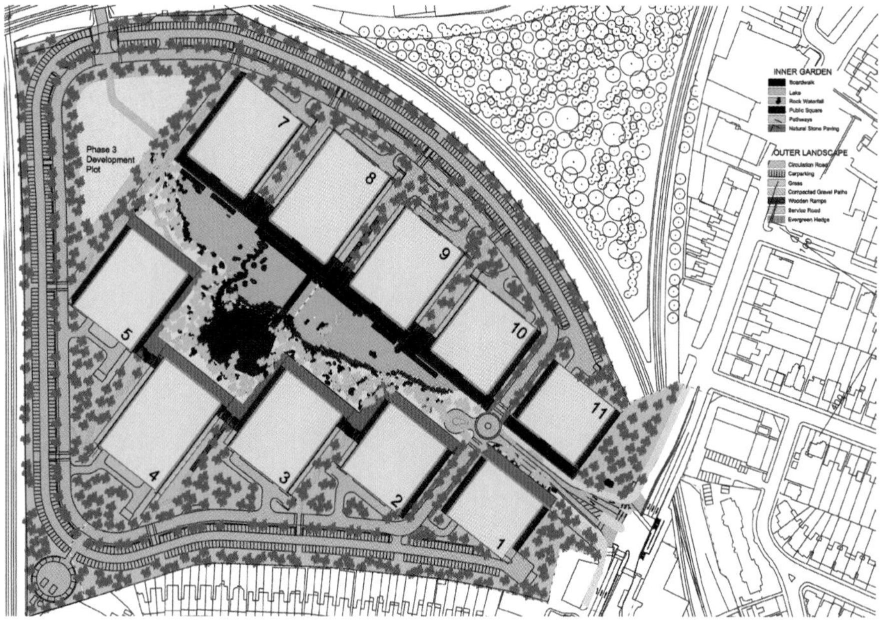

5

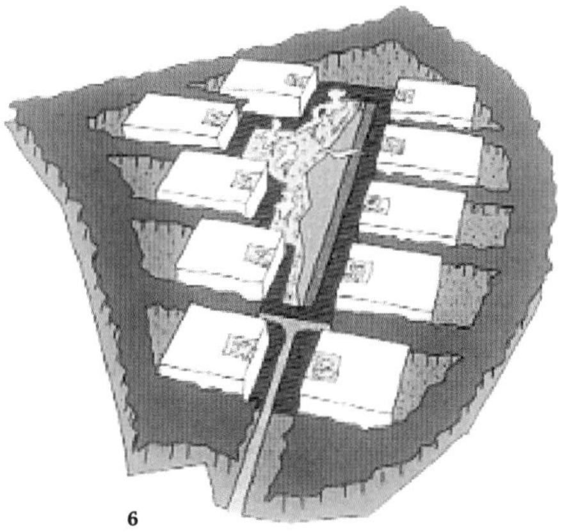

6

5: Master plan
6: Isometric overview
7: Interior, artist's impression
8: Model

7

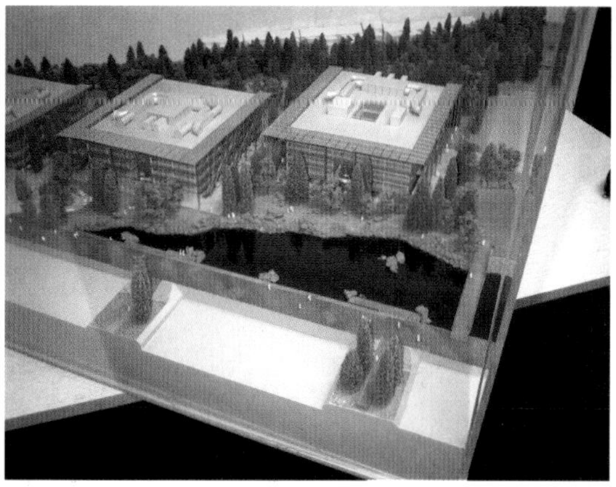

8

Chiswick Park
566
Chiswick High Road
LETTING ENQUIRIES CONTACT

9: Signage, entrance area
10: Trees with façade
11: View from the restaurant
12–14: Routeing for pedestrians

10

11

12

13

14

15

THE TIGHT FRAME

15: Pylon in the grass

16: Line in the grass

16

THE ROMANTIC INTERIOR

17–19: Dry stone river

20: Pebble beach

17

18

19

20

21

21, 23: Lower pond
22: Upper pond
24: Bridge over lower pond
25: Master plan

22

23

24

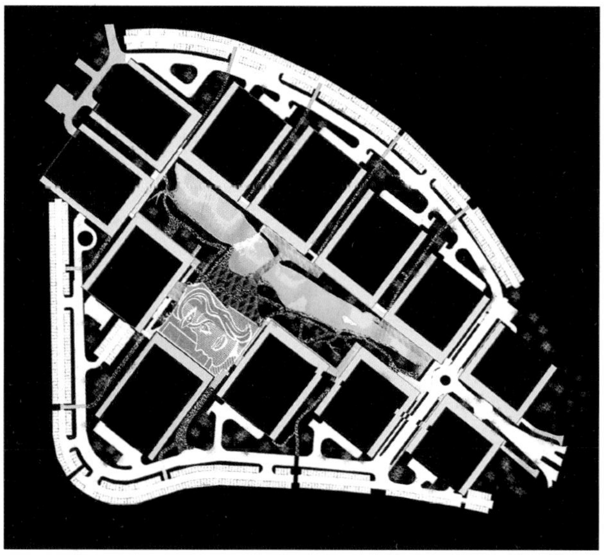

25

26

26: Water lilies
27–28: Rock formations

27

28

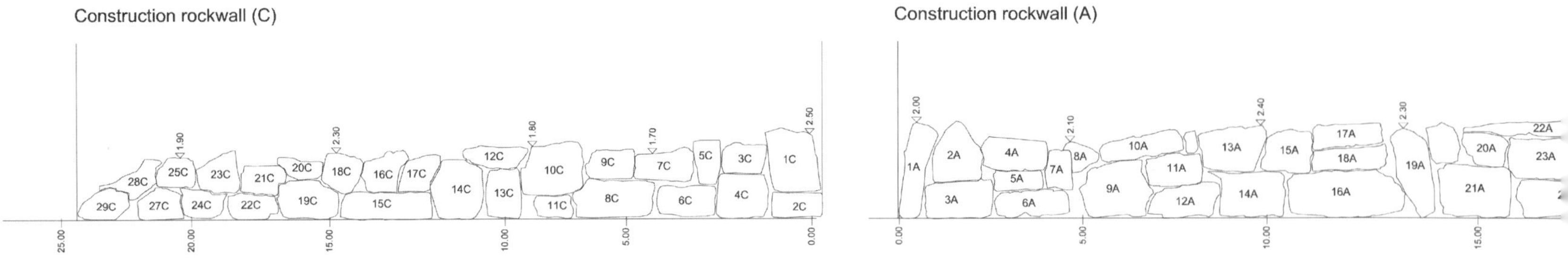

29

30

31

32

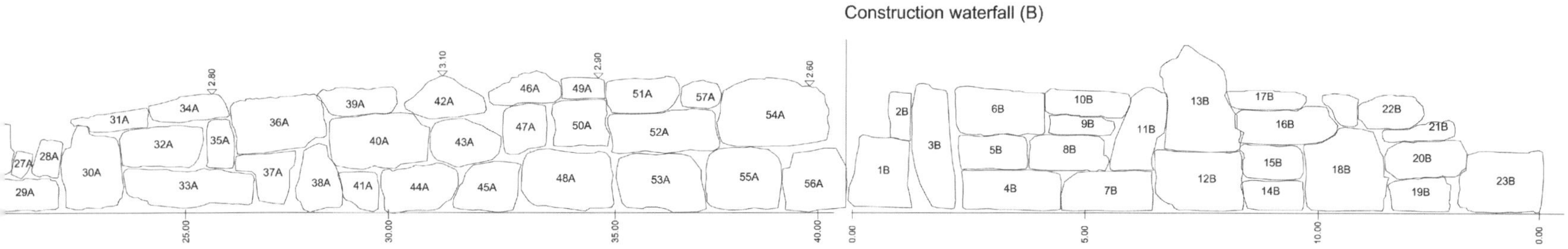

WATERFALL, ROCKS

29: Working drawing, position rocks in wall
30: Rockwall mock-up for the cascade (Wales)
31: Rolling rocks
32: Rock formation

33

Waterfall

34

35

36

DECKING

34: Bridge

35–36: Border, details

37

38

SQUARE

37: Transition to park

38: Steps

39: Overview

39

1 in 4
1 in 4
1 in 4
1 in 4
1 in 4

40: Square, plan
41–43: Painting pattern
44: Sketch drawing
45: Night view
46: Artist's impression

41

42

43

44

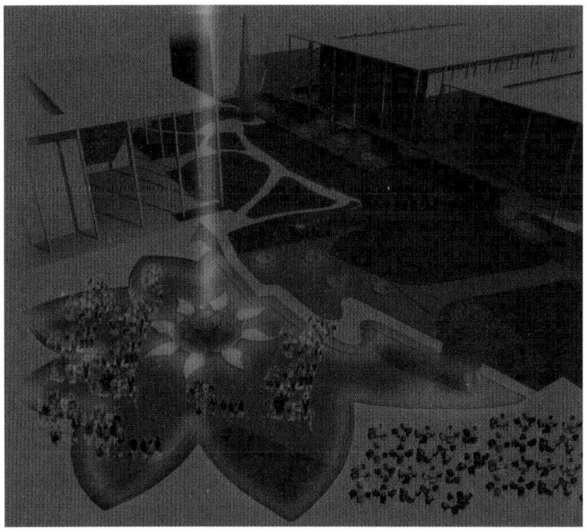
45

46

BURGEMEESTER E. RYCKAERTSPLEIN

BERCHEM, BELGIUM

Pending completion of the Antwerp Central Station for the high-speed TGV railway service, the station at Antwerpen-Berchem was designated for this purpose. This made it necessary to build a large underground car park, a bicycle park and a new bus and tram station. West 8 designed the master plan for the City of Antwerp, De Lijn and the NMBS and later the outdoor space above the underground car park. For the tram stops and the entrances to the underground car park, canopies were designed in perforated copper sheeting decorated with a floral pattern. The cheerful floral motifs present a contemporary note at the end of the monumental Cogels-Osylei, Antwerp's famous eclectic boulevard.

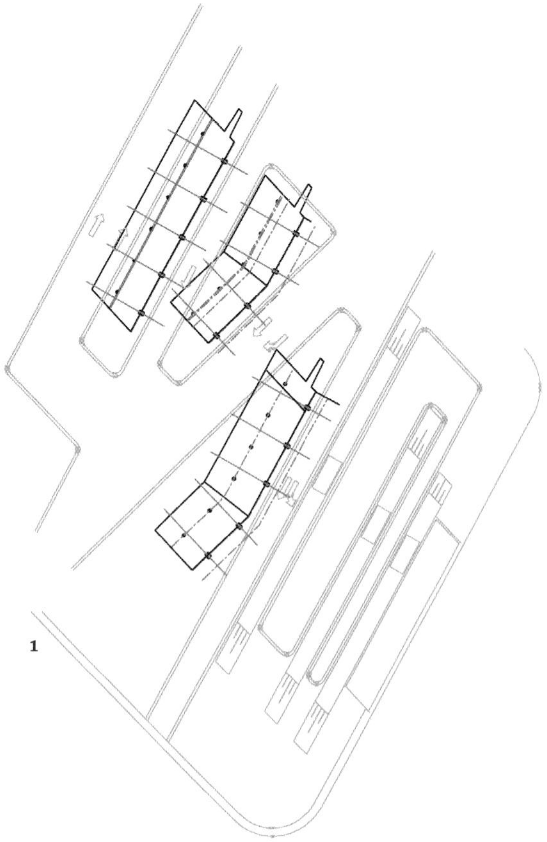

1

2

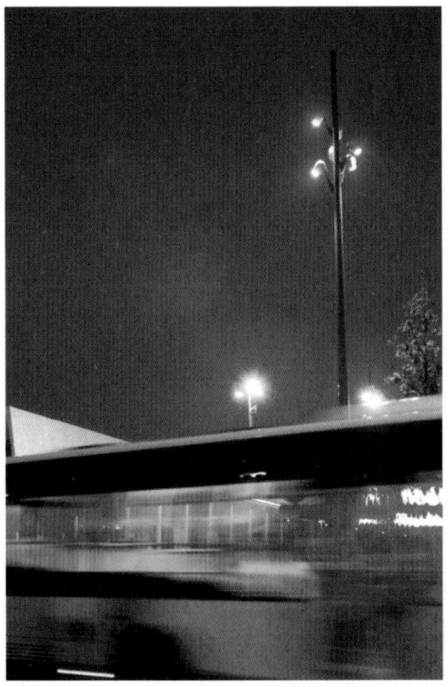

3

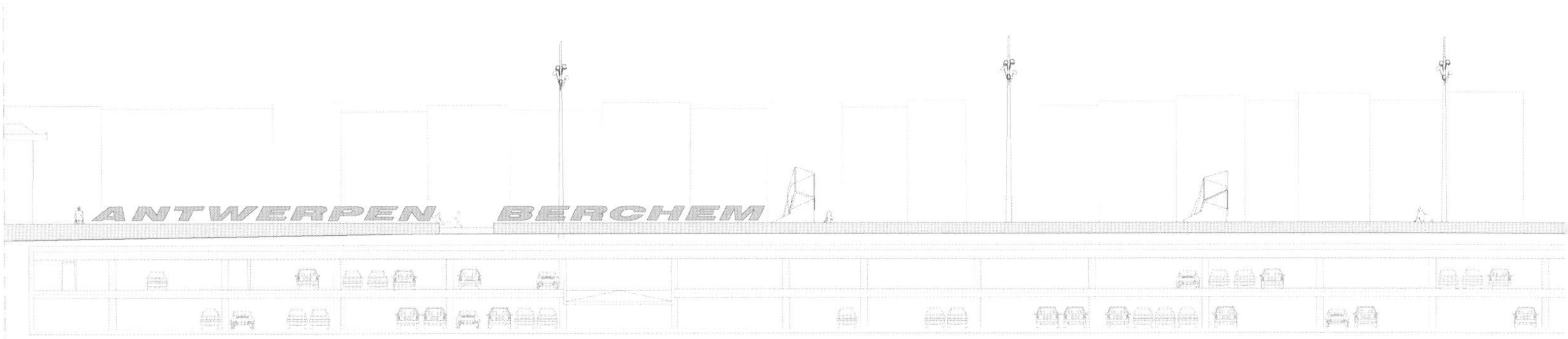

4

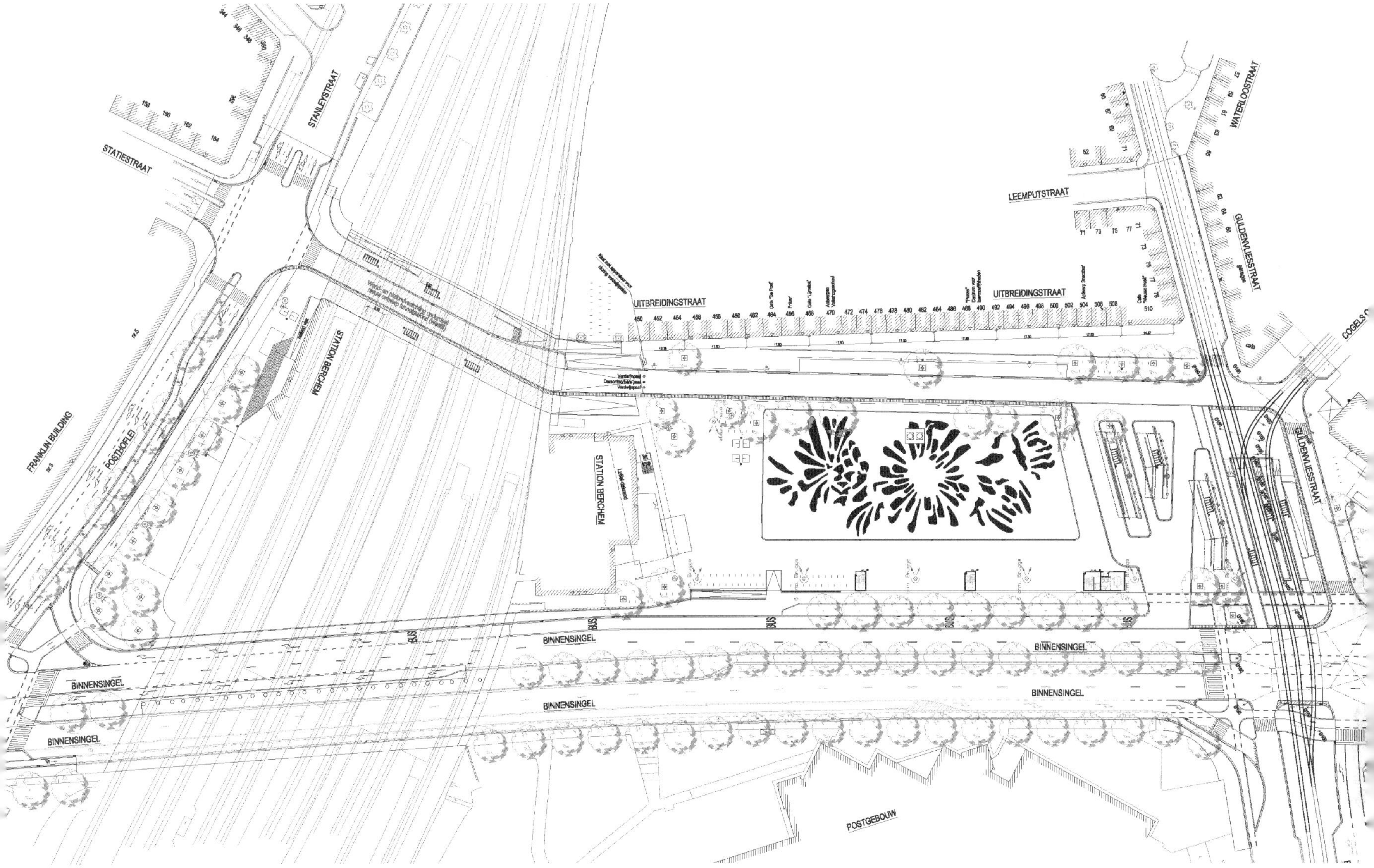

5

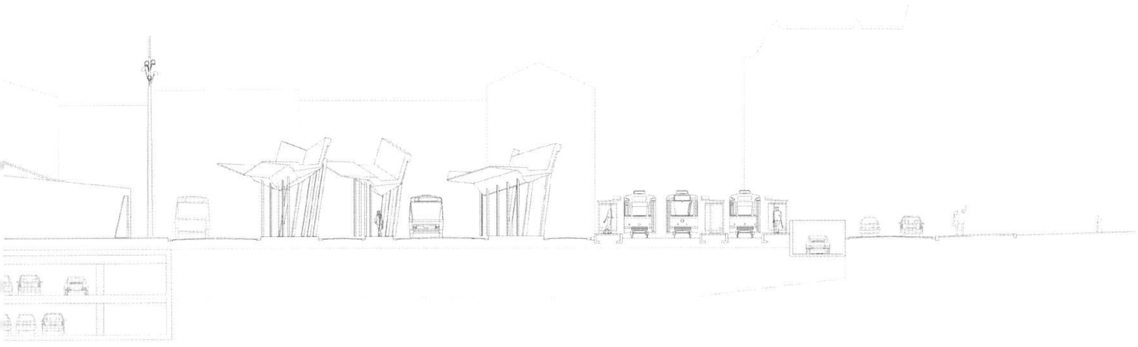

1: Bus and tram stop
2: Square, night view
3: Tram
4: Section
5: Master plan

6: Early design, computer sketch
7: Train, tram and bus station, diagram
8–9: Tram station, artist's impressions
10: Design drawing
11: Model study
12: Construction of underground car park

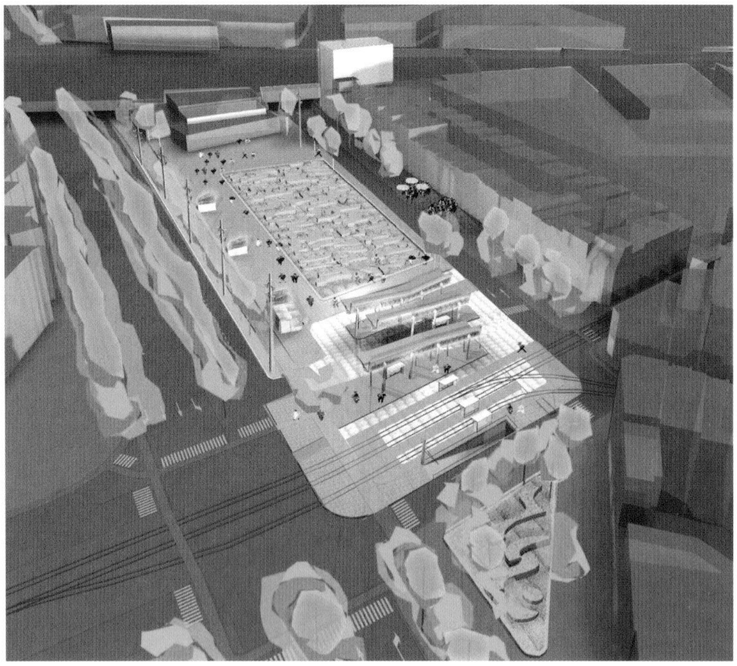

6

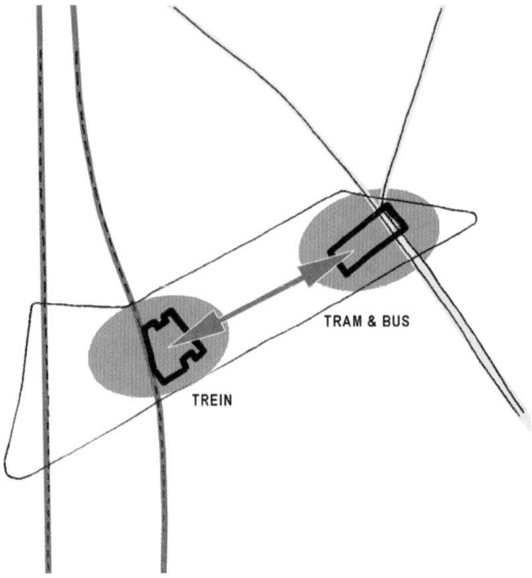

7

8

9

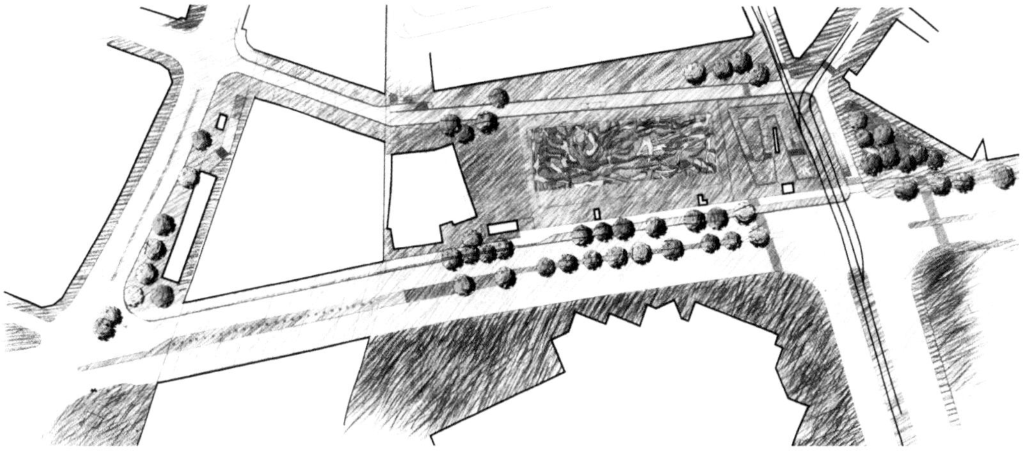

10

11

12

13

HEDGES

13: Night view

14: Situation

15: Technical drawing

14

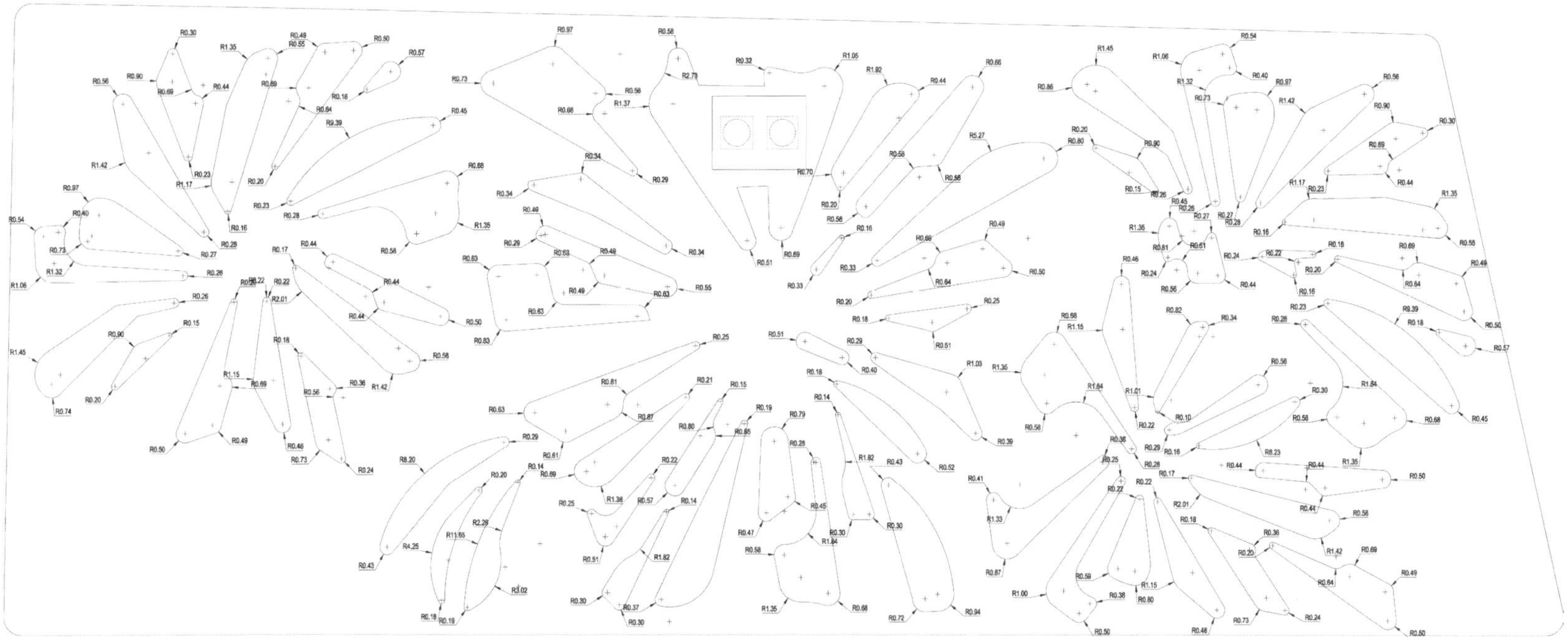

16

17

18

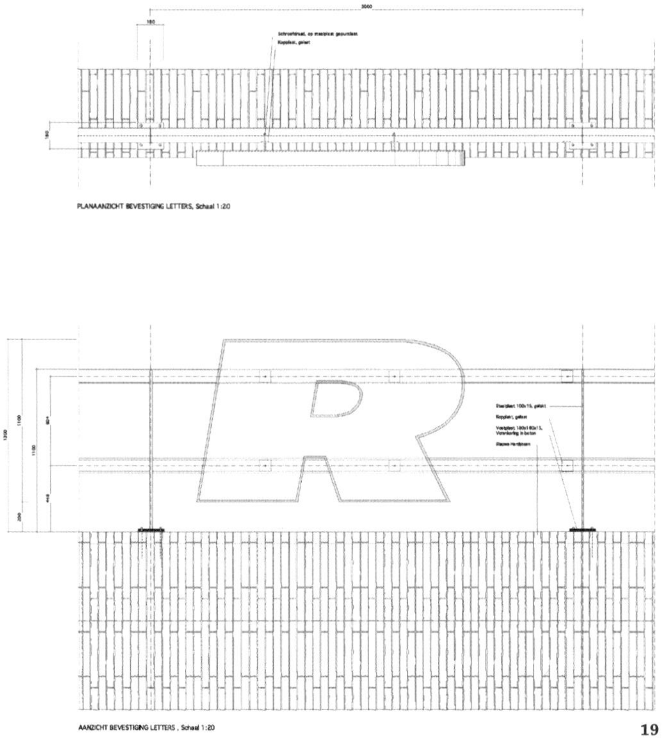
3000
PLANAANZICHT BEVESTIGING LETTERS, Schaal 1:20
AANZICHT BEVESTIGING LETTERS, Schaal 1:20

19

20

21

22

23

PAVEMENT

16–18: Blue stone
19: Wall with logo
20: Wall
21–23: Pavement

24

25

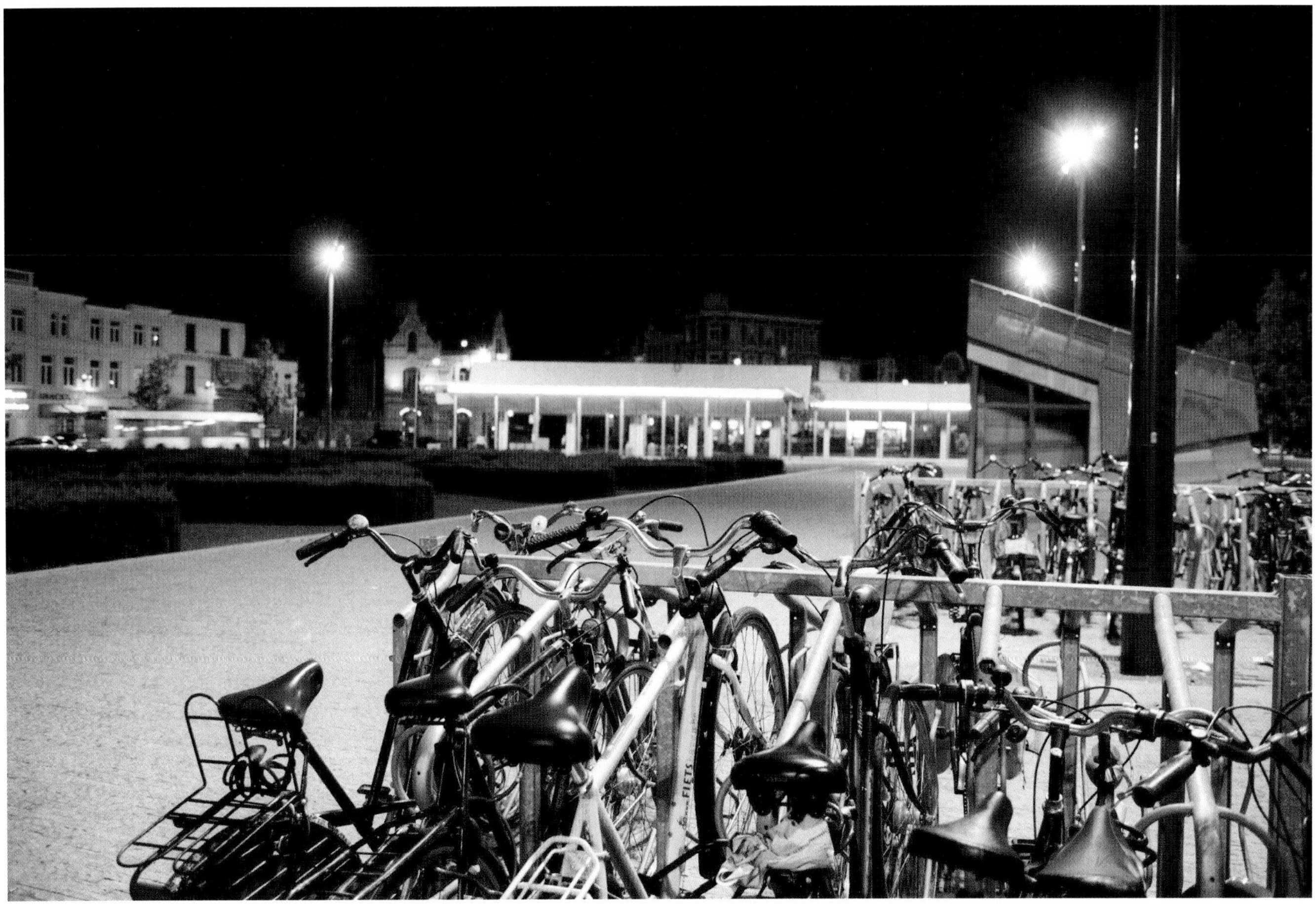

26

27

28

24–28: Bicycle racks

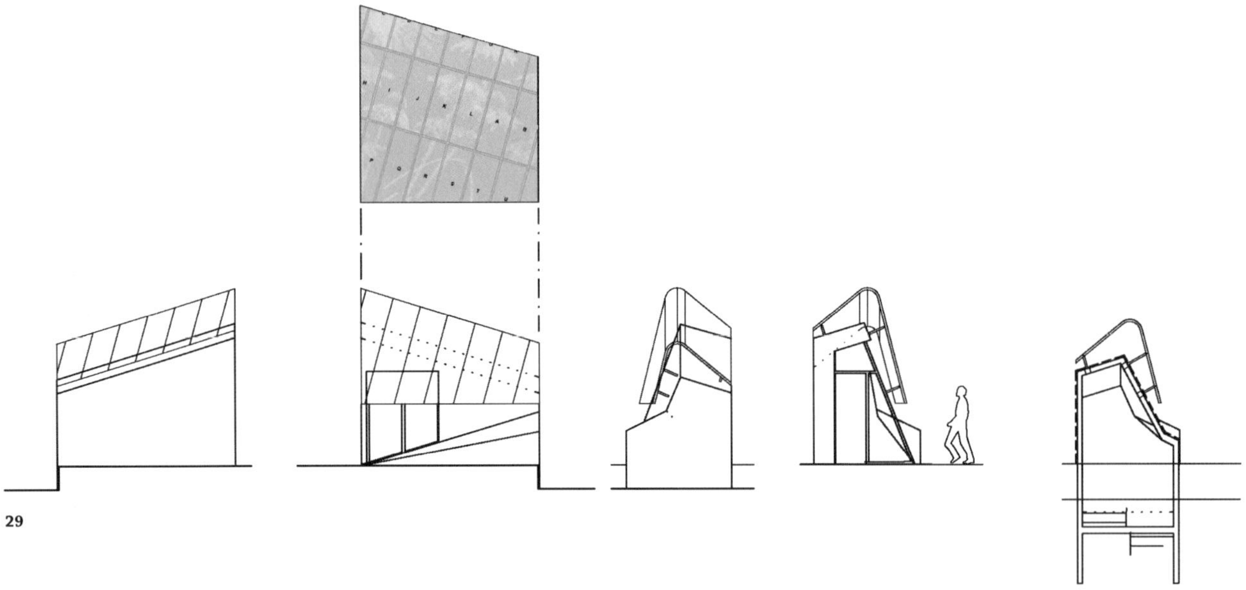

29

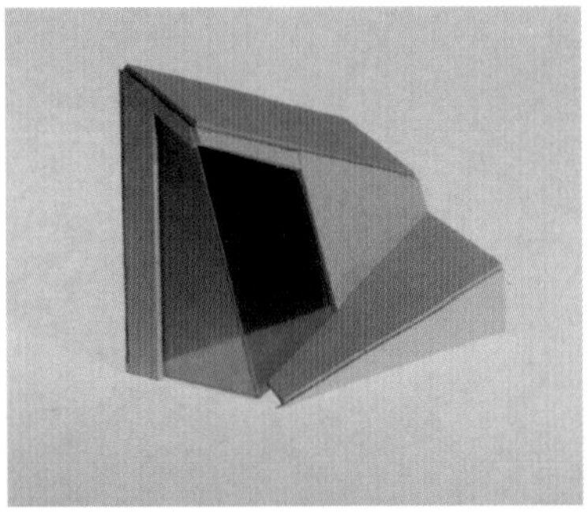

30

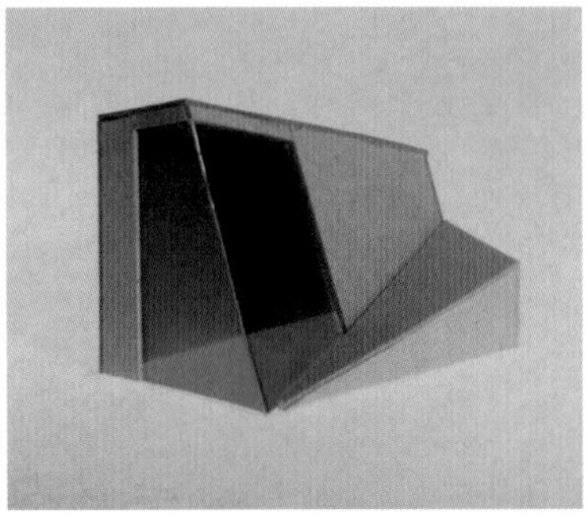

31

CAR PARK ENTRANCES

29: Sections
30–31: Models
32–33: Situation
34: Perforated copper, detail

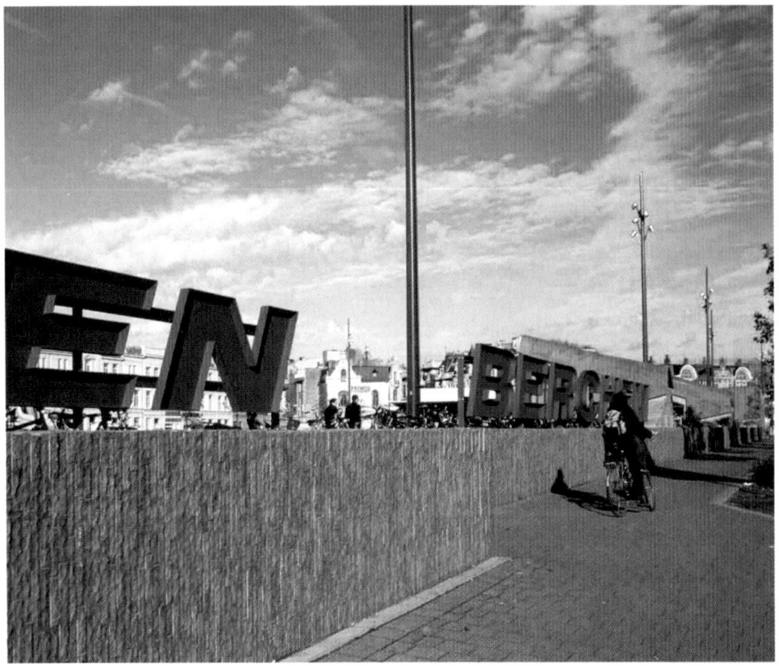

32

33

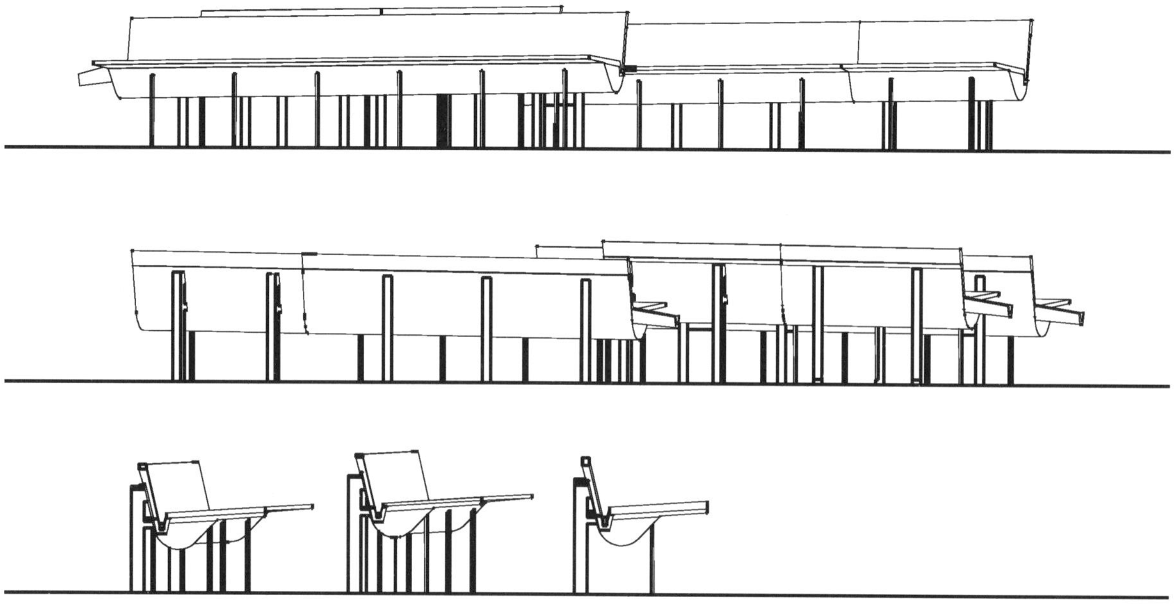

35

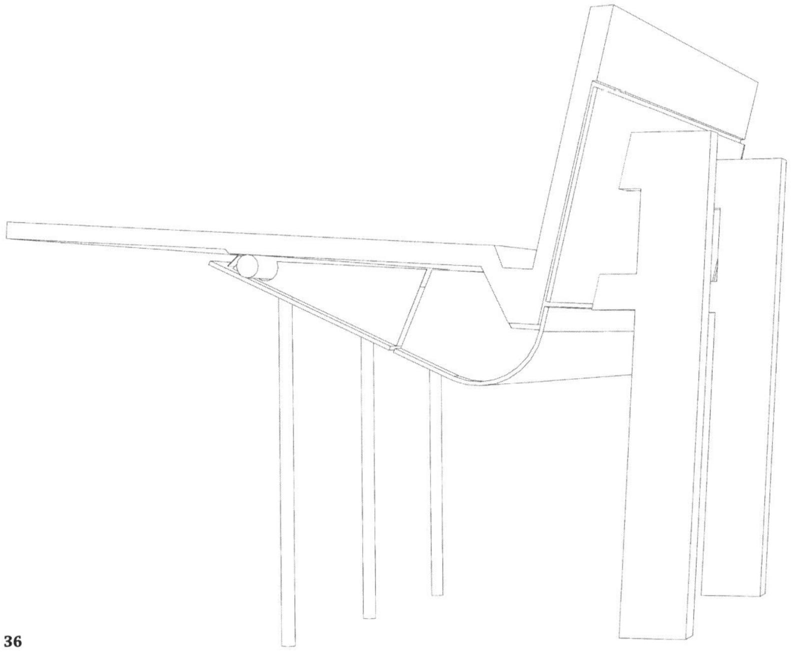

36

TRAM STOP SHELTERS

35–36: Elevations

37: Concrete and copper construction, technical drawing

38–39: Design, perforation pattern

37

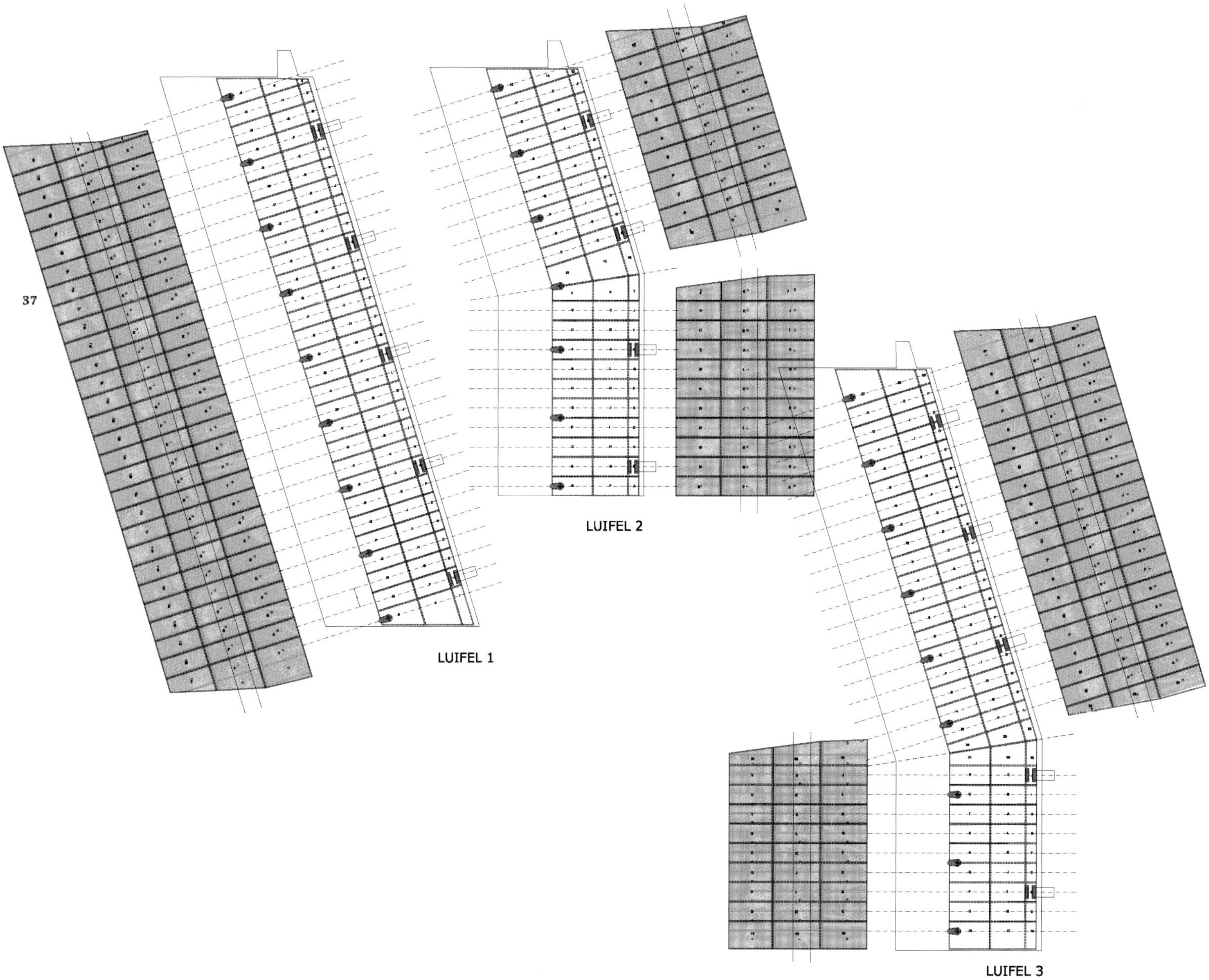
LUIFEL 1
LUIFEL 2
LUIFEL 3

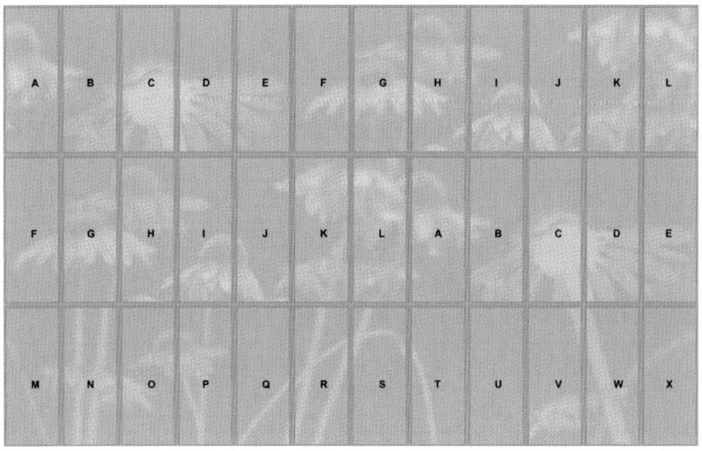
A B C D E F G H I J K L
F G H I J K L A B C D E
M N O P Q R S T U V W X

38

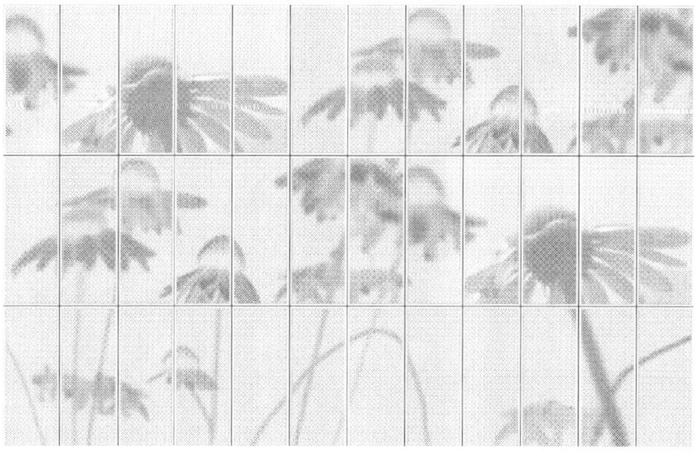

39

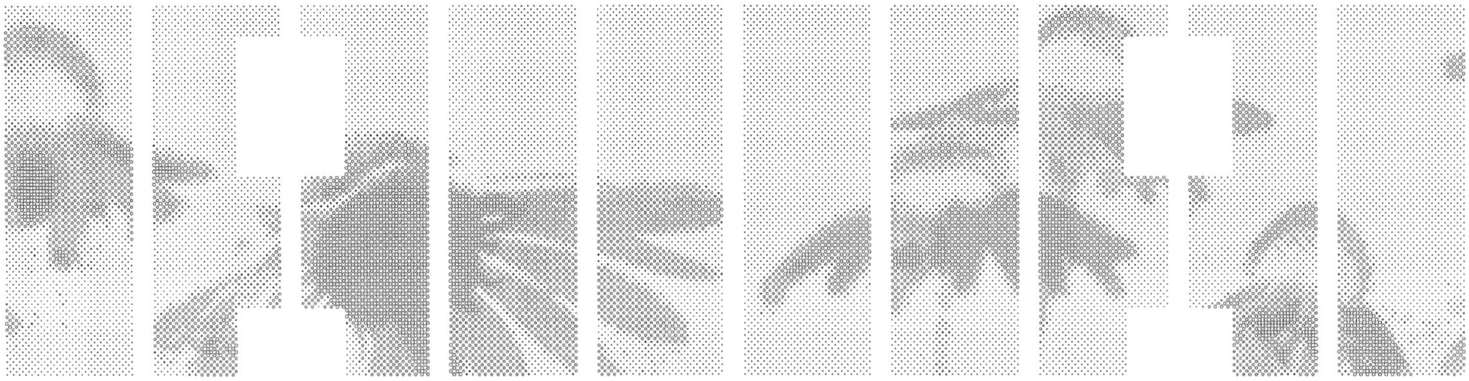

40

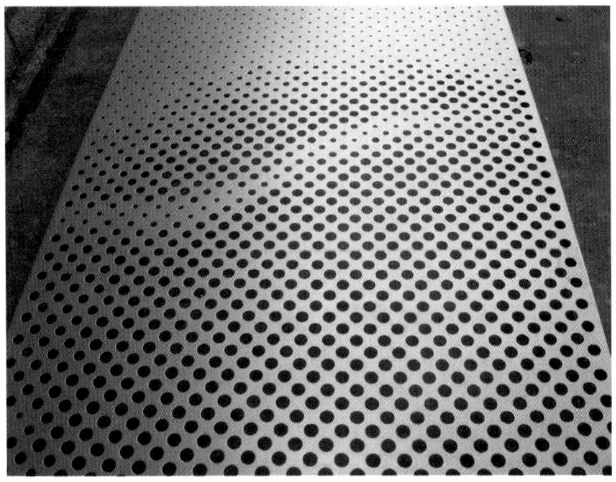

41

42

40: Design, perforation pattern
41: Copper panel
42: Mock-up
43–46: Situation

43

44

45

46

LENSVELT GARDEN

BREDA, THE NETHERLANDS

A furniture company whose headquarters are a tautly designed box, set in an ecological garden with swamps and marshes. A gravel moat surrounds the building, while inside a patio entrance was created with a large, sail-like tent under which employees can take their lunch. This was detailed as a still life in wood, slate and ginkgo trees. The tarmac of the parking areas and the loading docks came to life through a linear pattern of white stripes that organises the trucks and cars.

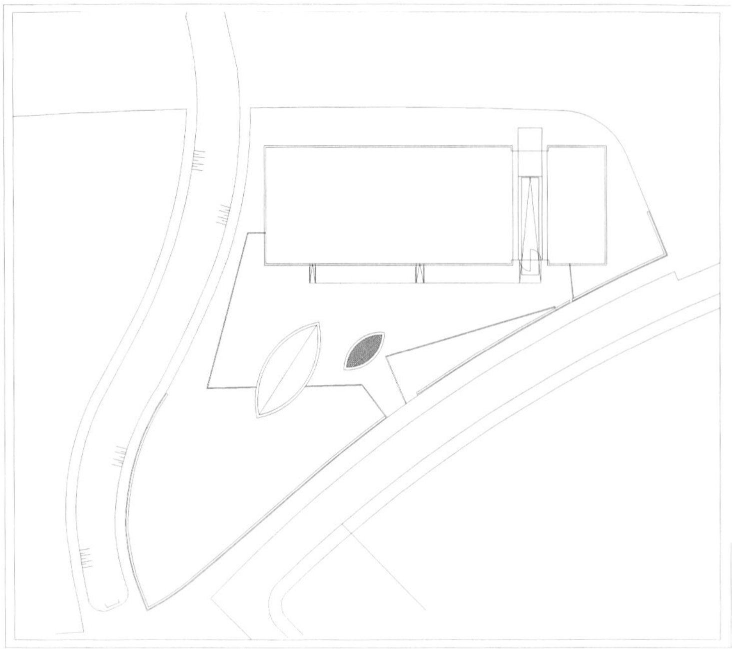

1

1: Master plan
2: Sketch drawing
3: Patio, through the glass
4: Patio, situation

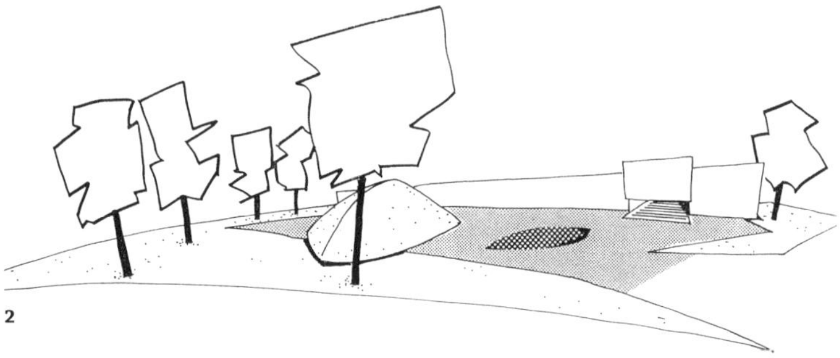

2

3

5

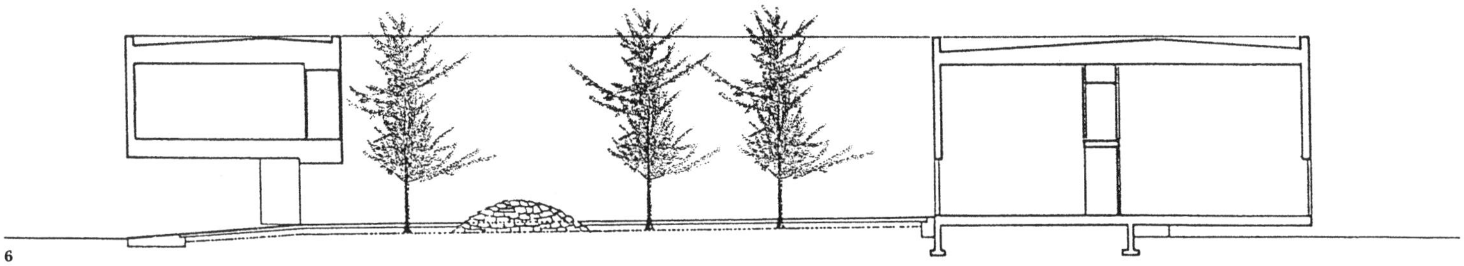

6

7a

b

c

5: Situation
6: Section
7a–c: Sunscreen
8–9: Entrance, slope

8

9

10

11

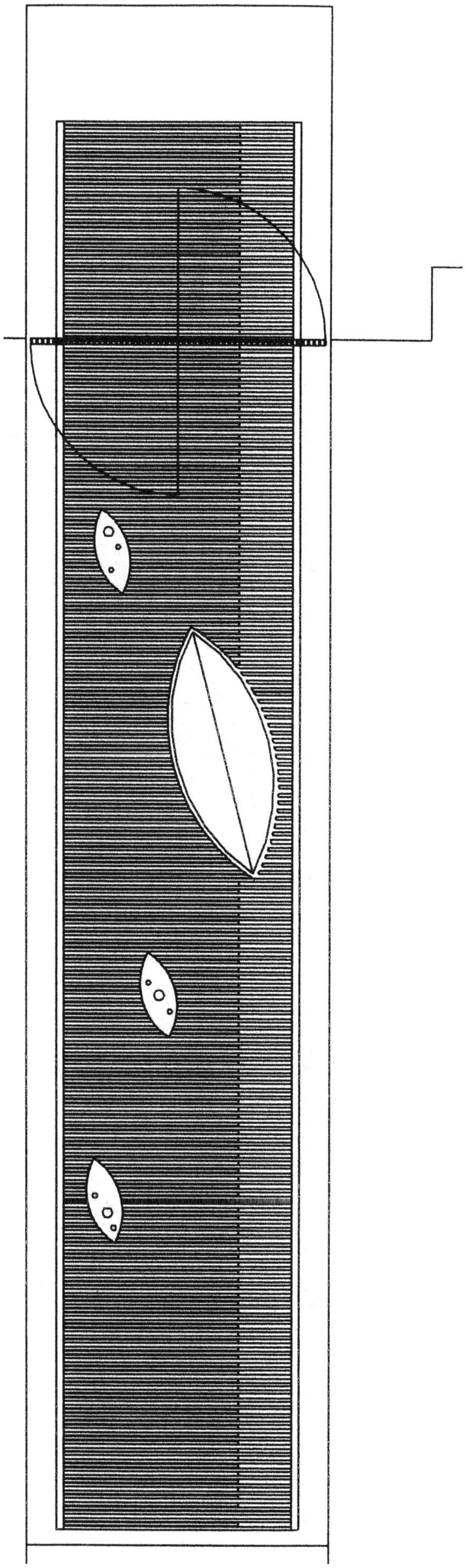

12

10: Bird's nest
11: Detail
12: Wood structure, technical drawing

13

14

13–14: Swamp
15: Parking
16: Fountain

15

16

17

18

17–18: Swamp
19: Hill in car park

19

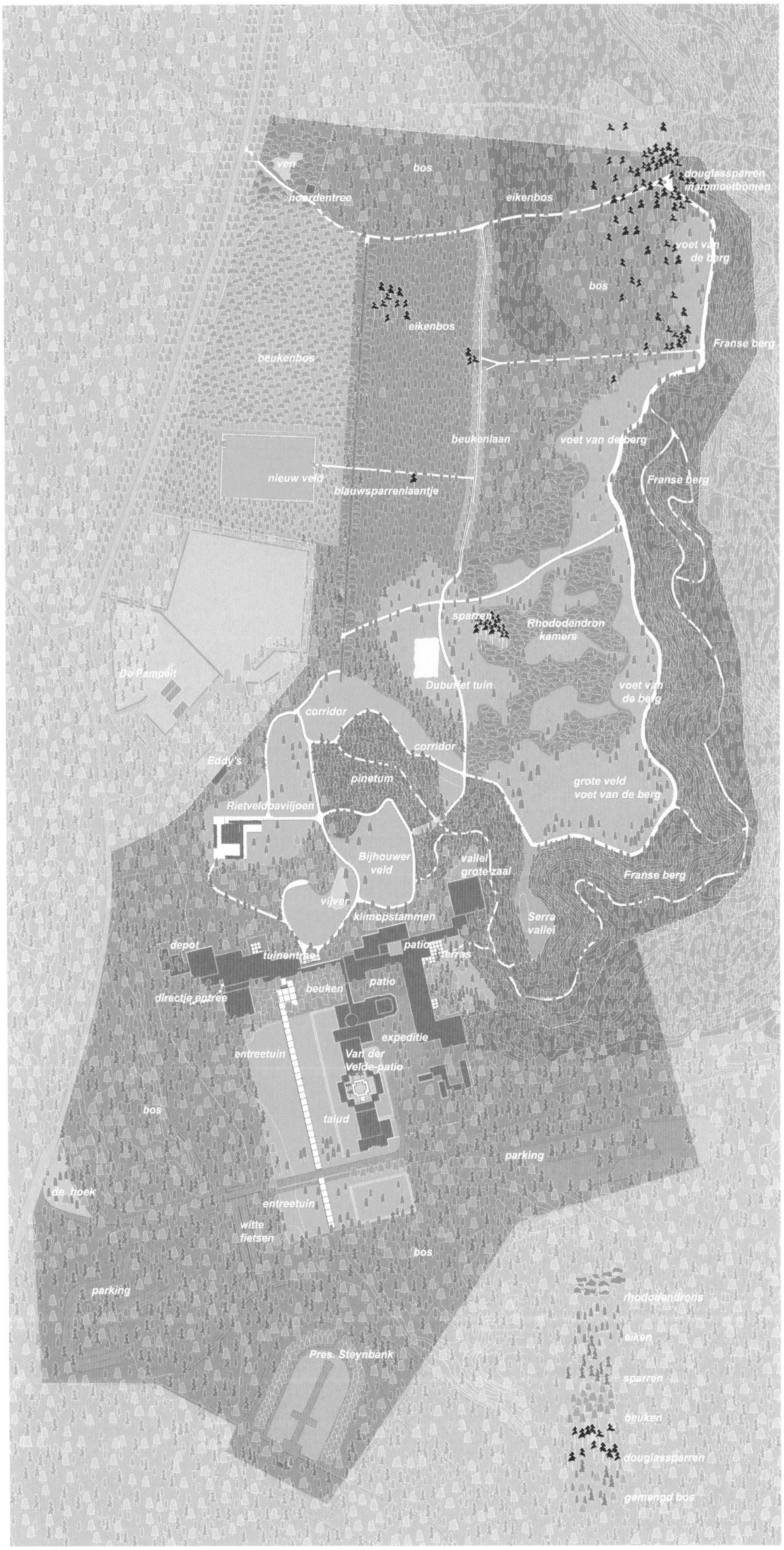

1

1: Master plan
2: New paths, woods
3: Extension of entrance area
4–7: Transformations of the woods in winter

2

3

KRÖLLER-MÜLLER MUSEUM SCULPTURE GARDEN

OTTERLO, THE NETHERLANDS

Kröller-Müller is a key design in West 8's oeuvre. West 8 designed a new entrance with the team of curators and gardeners and divided up the surroundings and woodlands according to different contexts: the Bijhouwer garden, the French Mountain, the rhododendron garden, the beech wood, various lawns and meadows, the Rietveld and the Van Eyck pavilion.

The sculpture garden is a national heritage site. The main motive for the design was the museum's wish to vary the contexts in which its huge collection of sculpture was presented, and to make the garden accessible in all seasons.

4

5

6

7

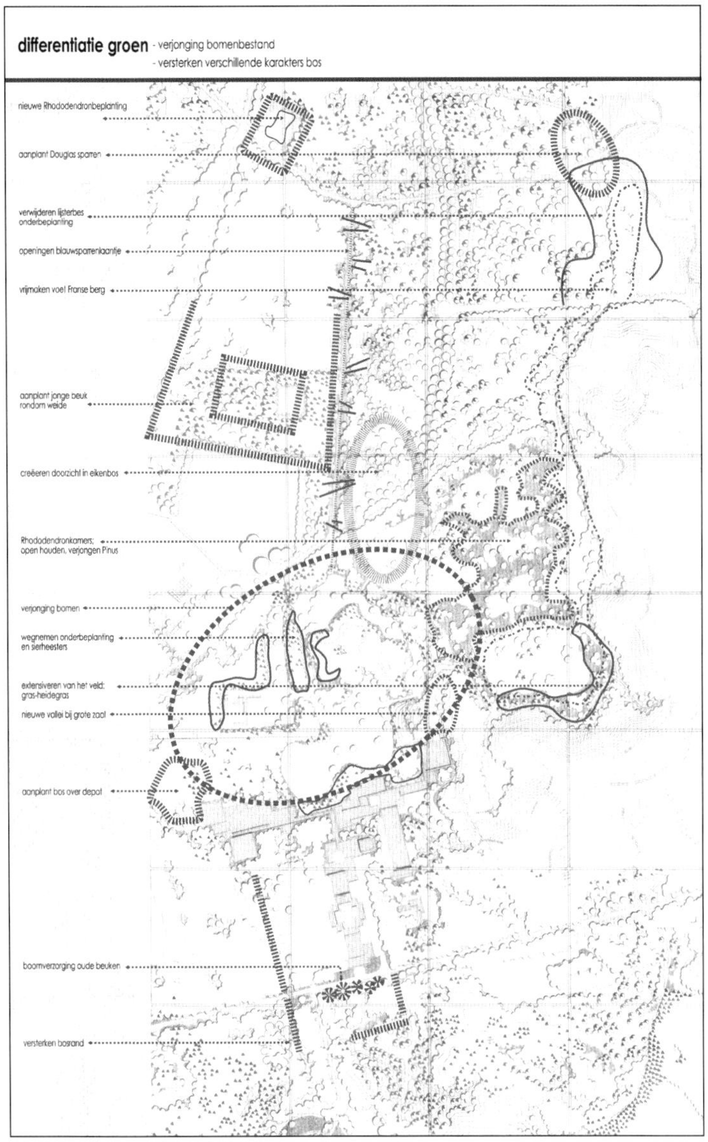
differentiatie groen
- verjonging bomenbestand
- versterken verschillende karakters bos
nieuwe Rhododendronbeplanting
aanplant Douglas sparren
verwijderen lijsterbes onderbeplanting
openingen blauwsparrenlaantje
vrijmaken voet Franse berg
aanplant jonge beuk rondom weide
creëeren doorzicht in eikenbos
Rhododendronkamers; open houden, verjongen Pinus
verjonging bomen
wegnemen onderbeplanting en sierheesters
extensiveren van het veld: gras-heidegras
nieuwe vallei bij grote zaal
aanplant bos over depot
boomverzorging oude beuken
versterken bosrand

8

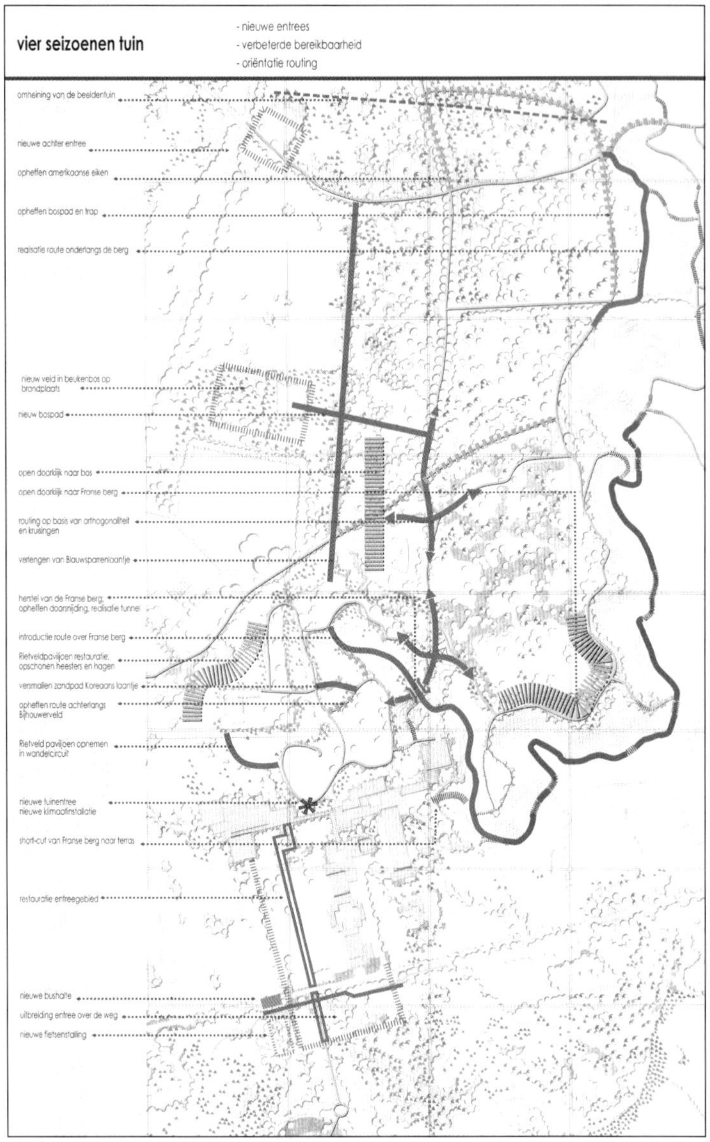
vier seizoenen tuin
- nieuwe entrees
- verbeterde bereikbaarheid
- oriëntatie routing
omheining van de beeldentuin
nieuwe achter entree
opheffen amerikaanse eiken
opheffen bospad en trap
realisatie route onderlangs de berg
nieuw veld in beukenbos op brandplaats
nieuw bospad
open doorkijk naar bos
open doorkijk naar Franse berg
routing op basis van orthogonaliteit en kruisingen
verlengen van Blauwsparrenlaantje
herstel van de Franse berg; opheffen doorsnijding, realisatie tunnel
introductie route over Franse berg
Rietveldpaviljoen restauratie; opschonen heesters en hagen
versmallen zandpad Koreaans laantje
opheffen route achterlangs Bijhouwerveld
Rietveld paviljoen opnemen in wandelcircuit
nieuwe tuinentree
nieuwe klimaatinstallatie
short-cut van Franse berg naar terras
restauratie entreegebied
nieuwe bushalte
uitbreiding entree over de weg
nieuwe fietsenstalling

9

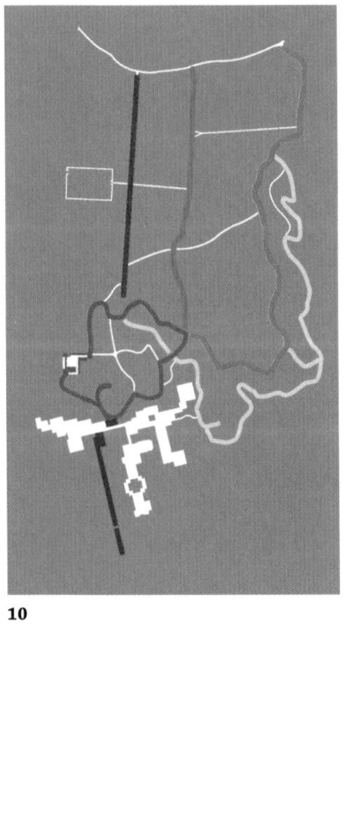

10

8: Interventions
9: New path structure
10: Routeing for public
11: Regrouping of the collection
12: Designated areas

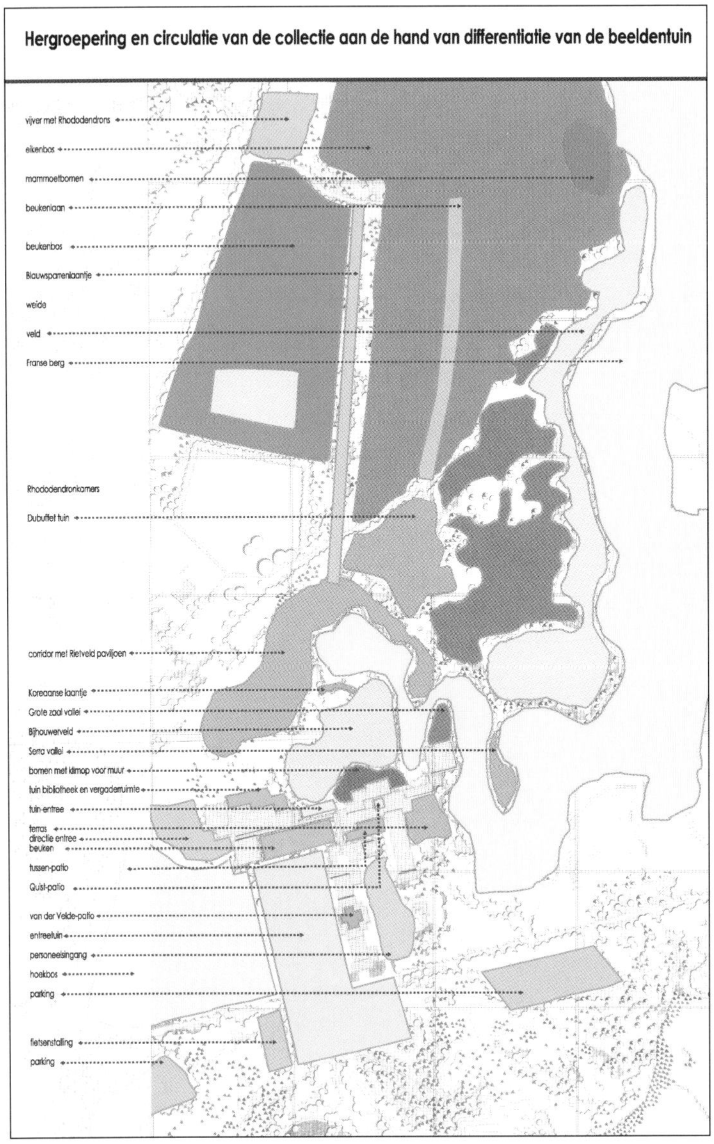

Hergroepering en circulatie van de collectie aan de hand van differentiatie van de beeldentuin
vijver met Rhododendrons
eikenbos
mammoetbomen
beukenlaan
beukenbos
Blauwsparrenlaantje
weide
veld
Franse berg
Rhododendronkamers
Dubuffet tuin
corridor met Rietveld paviljoen
Koreaanse laantje
Grote zaal vallei
Bijhouwerveld
Serra vallei
bomen met klimop voor muur
tuin bibliotheek en vergaderruimte
tuin-entree
terras
directie entree
beuken
tussen-patio
Quist-patio
van der Velde-patio
entreetuin
personeelsingang
hoekbos
parking
fietsenstalling
parking

11

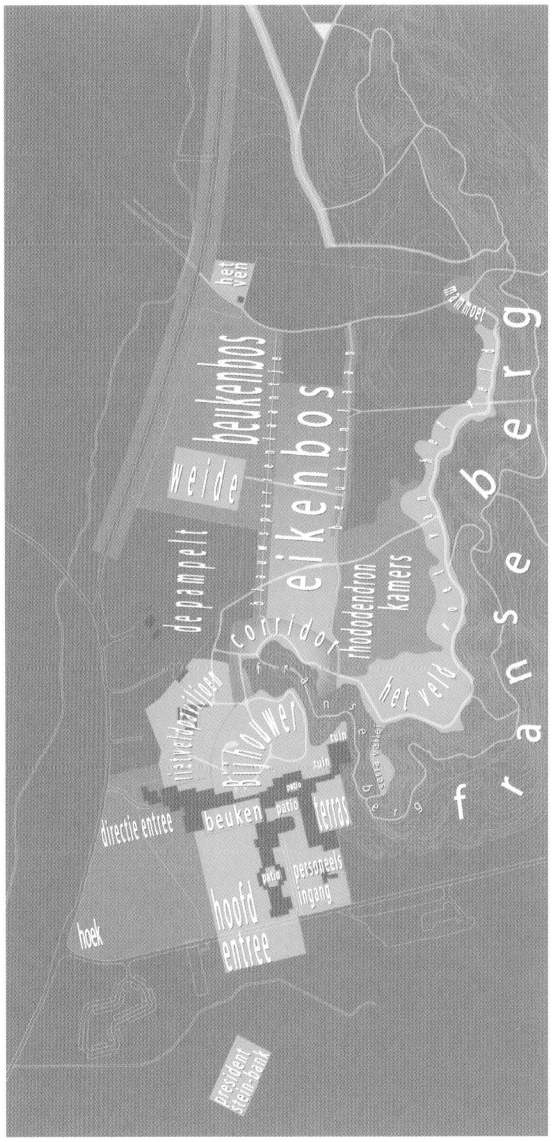

het ven
mammoet
beukenbos
weide
eikenbos
depampelt
corridor
rhododendron kamers
het veld
franse berg
Bijhouwer
directie entree
beuken
patio
terras
tuin
personeels ingang
hoofd entree
hoek
president Stein-bank

12

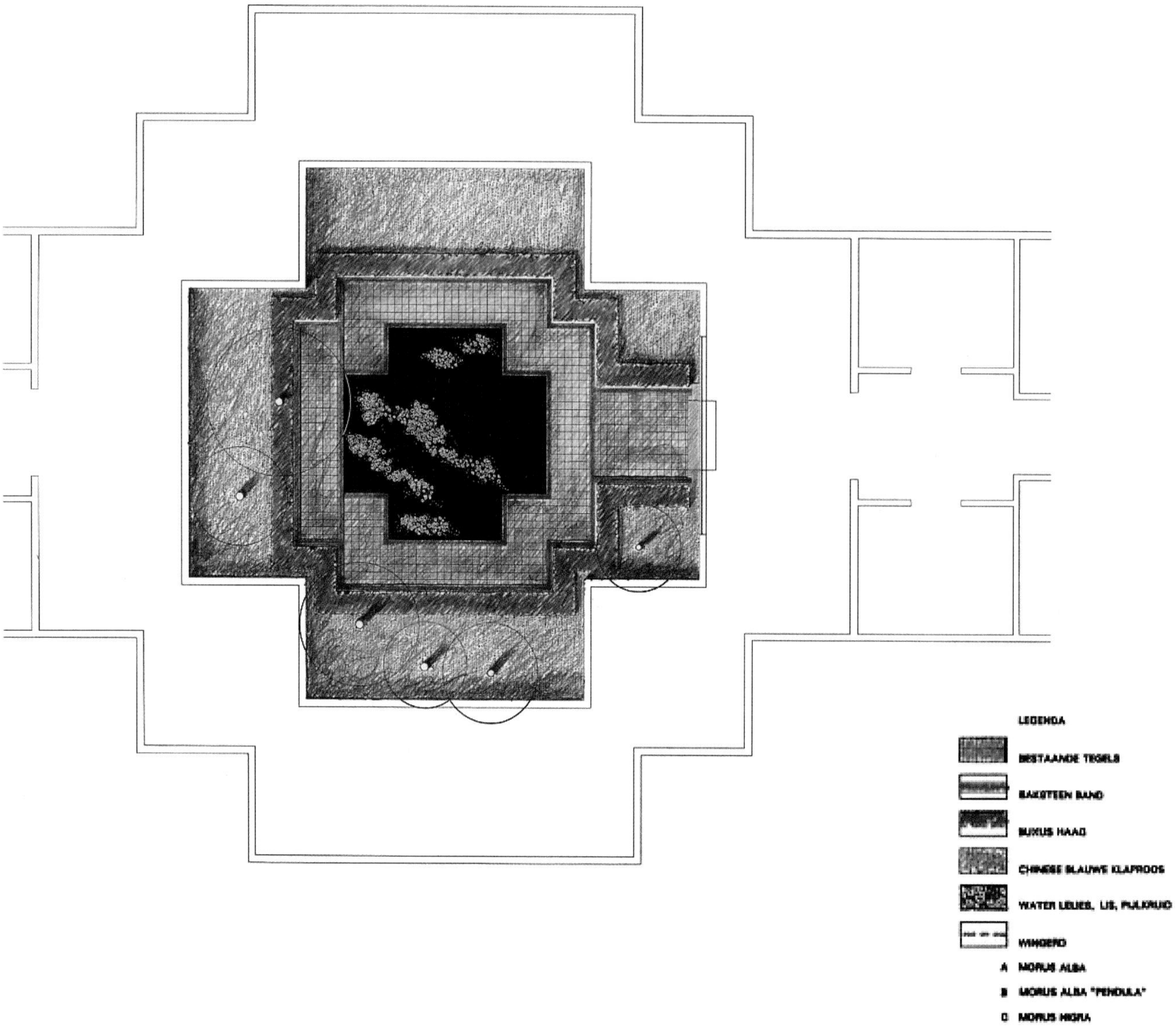
LEGENDA
BESTAANDE TEGELS
BAKSTEEN BAND
BUXUS HAAG
CHINESE BLAUWE KLAPROOS
WATER LELIES, LIS, PIJLKRUID
WINGERD
A MORUS ALBA
B MORUS ALBA "PENDULA"
C MORUS NIGRA

13

14

15

PATIO

13: Blue garden design

14: Blue poppies

15: View from the museum

16

17

16–17: Dubuffet sculpture in a woodland clearing

18–19: Rietveld pavilion

18

19

20: Rhododendron garden
21–22: Corridor with bronzes
23: Field at the foot of Franse Berg ('French mountain')

20

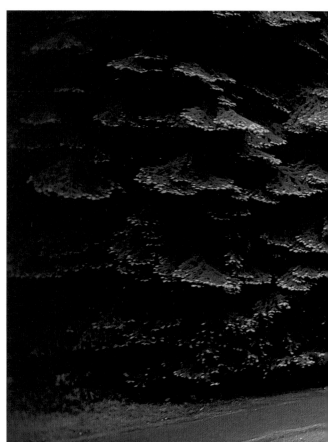
22

21

23

24

Pond with Marta Pan sculpture

25

26

27

25: Still-life of trees in the moss
26: New entrance to the garden
27: Marta Pan pond
28: Bicycle racks, white bicycles

29

30

31

32

THE FIELD IN THE BEECH WOOD

29: Realisation
30–31: Situation
32: Installations by Joep van Lieshout

33

34

STEINBANK

33: In winter

34: Detail, paving

1

2

3

4

1–4: Situation
5: Artist's impression

5

MOSCOW LUXURY VILLAGE
MOSCOW, RUSSIA

Mercury, a top-segment retail enterprise, ventured into developing a luxury housing estate in the woods west of Moscow. The proposed one-mile strip, built to a master plan by Meganom, needed a strong identity expressed through its public space. West 8 filled the space between the buildings with a mosaic floor, which encloses islands and pockets of lawns, flower beds, design, art and advertising. Special seating and unique orange lighting were added. The mosaic surface is made up of miniature bricks and was built by craftsmen from Armenia, ex-Yugoslavia and the Ukraine.

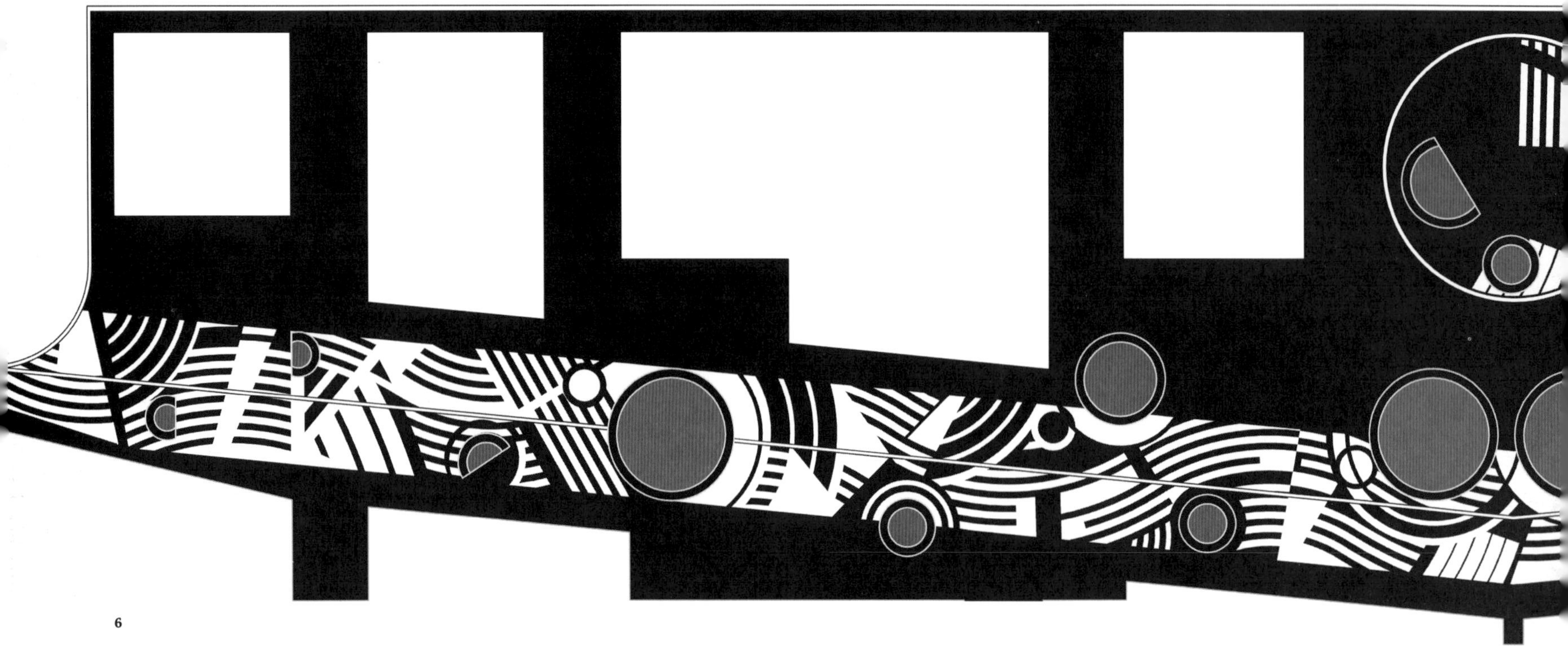

6

7

6: Mosaic design, west

7–10: Situation, paving detail

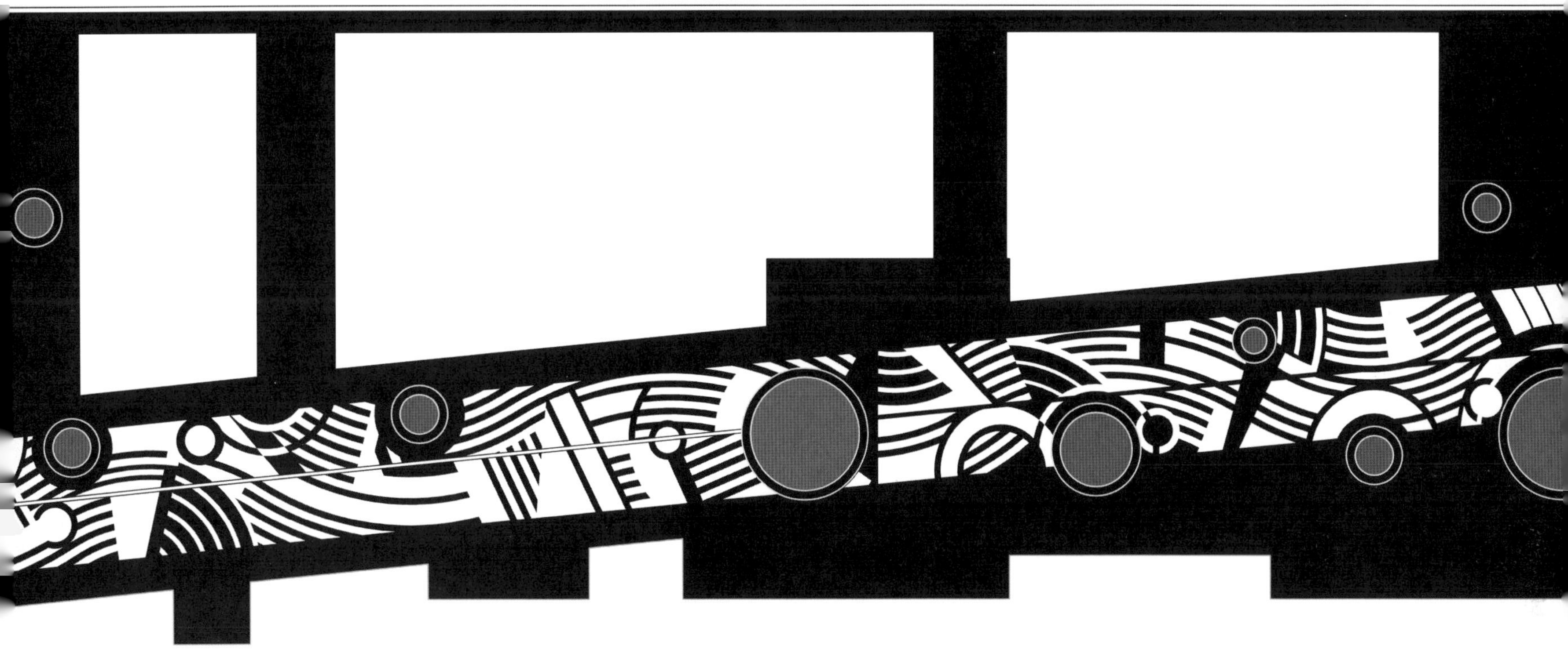

8

9

10

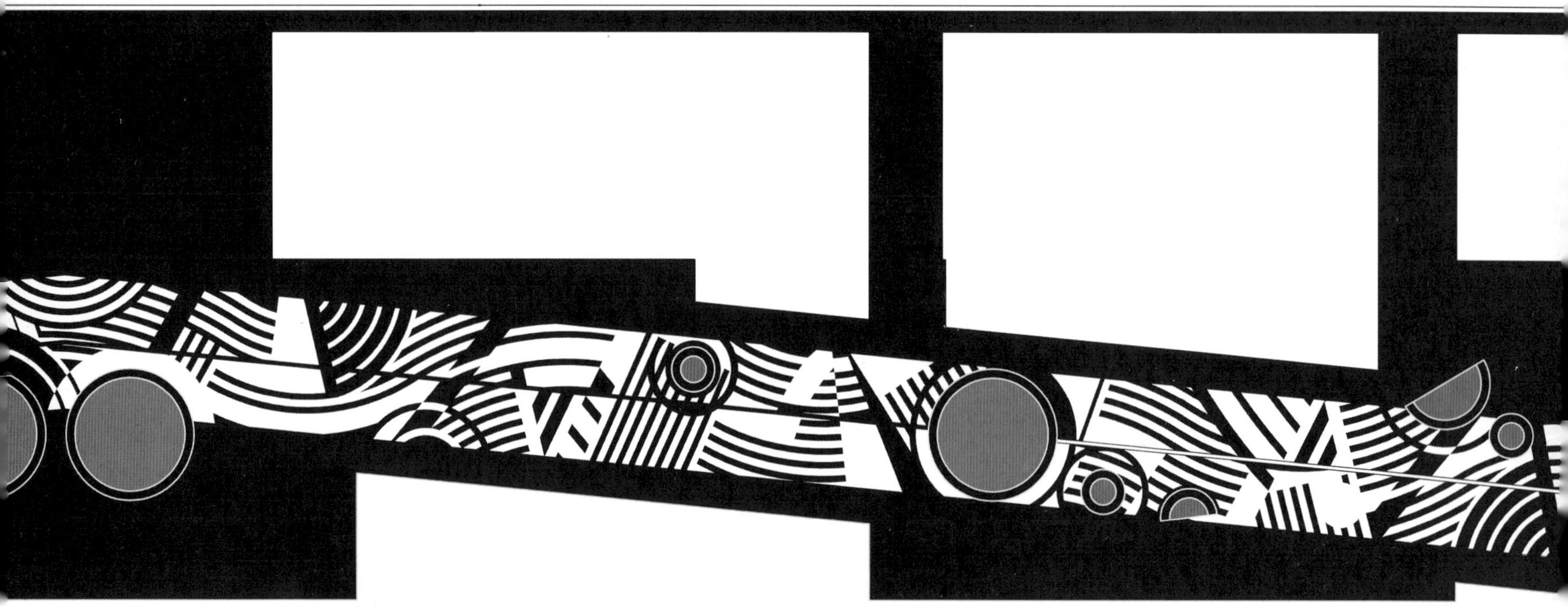

11

12

13

14

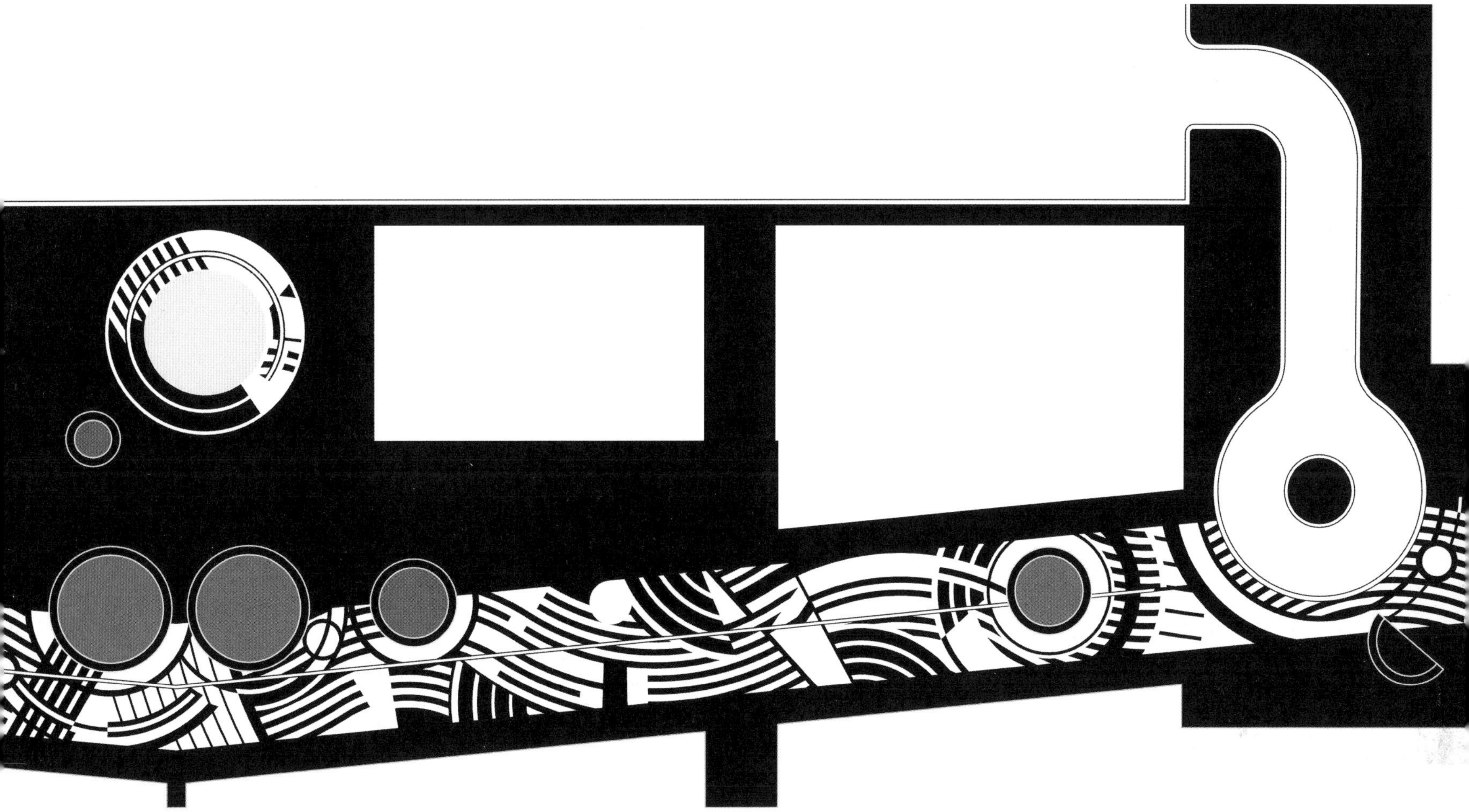

5

11: Mosaic design, east

12–15: Situation

16

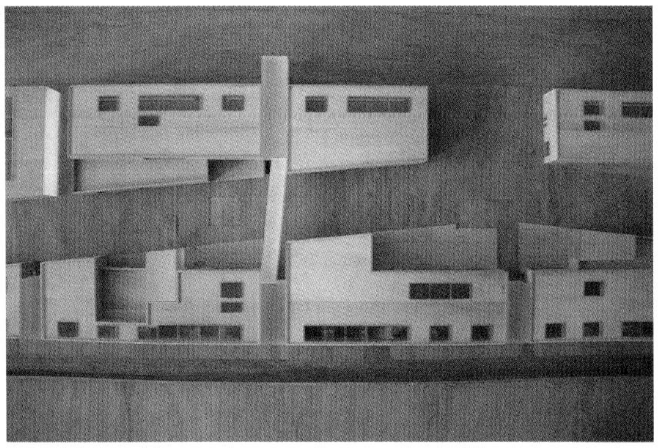

17

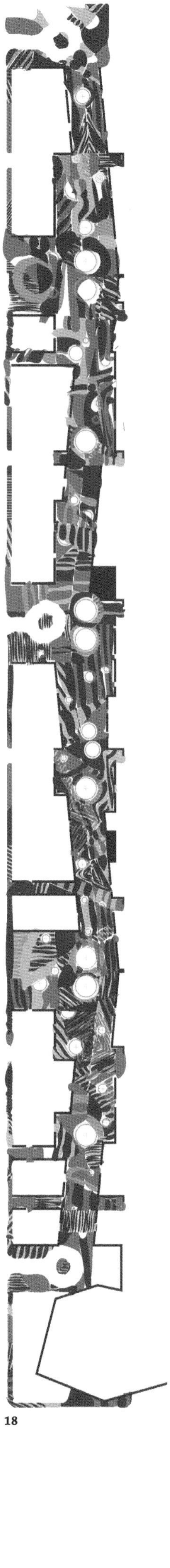

18

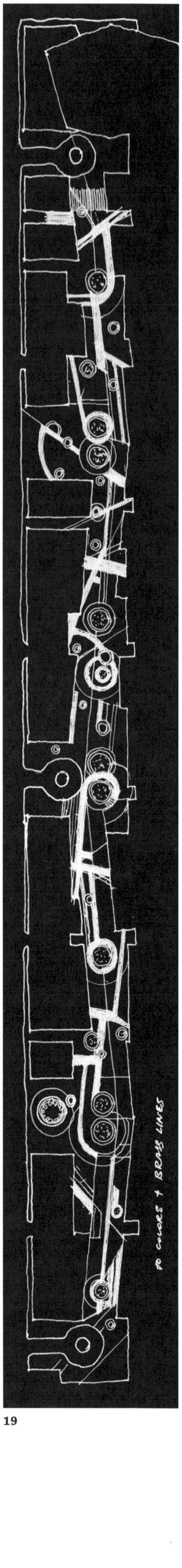

19

16–17: Master plan, model
18–20: Design studies

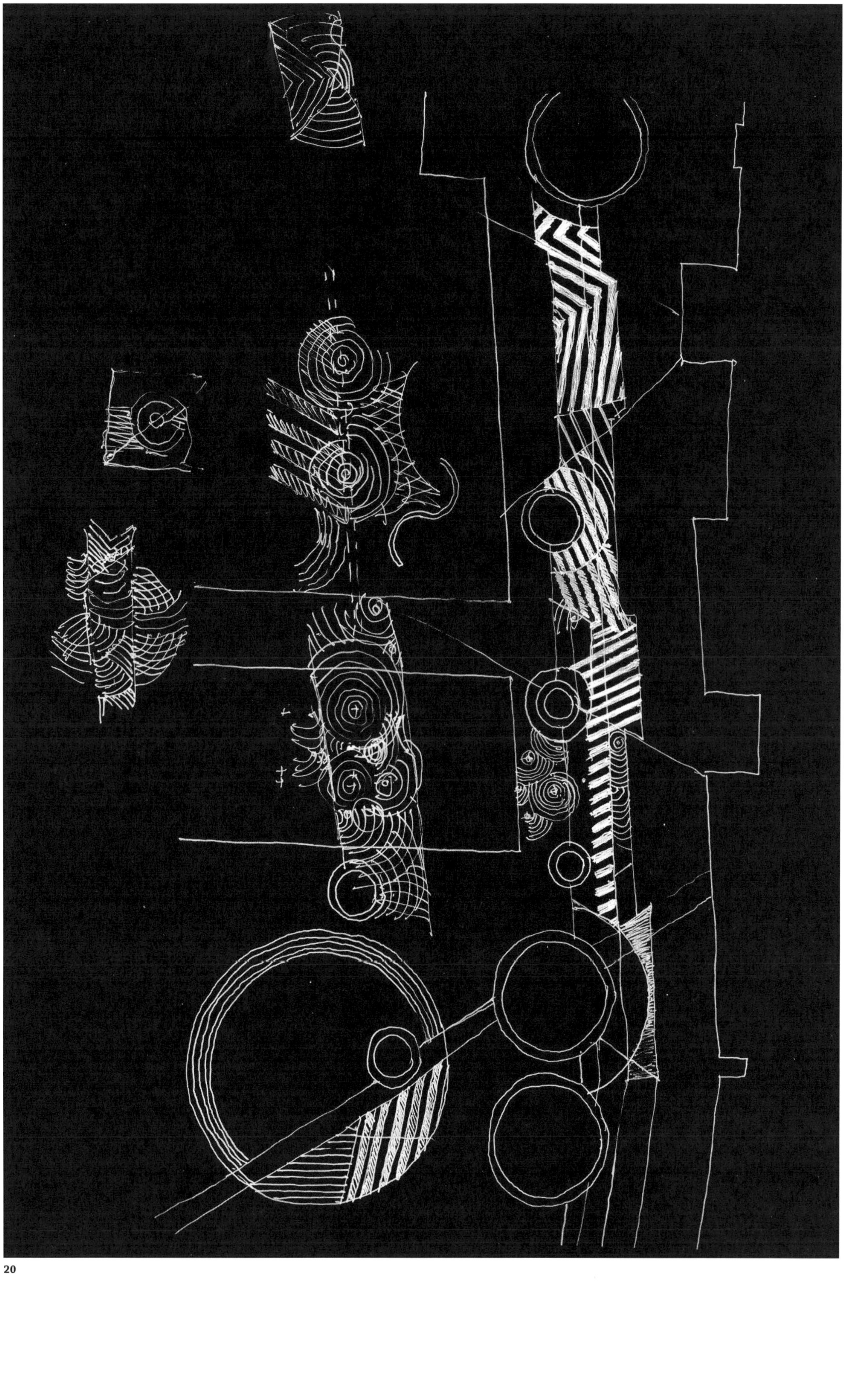

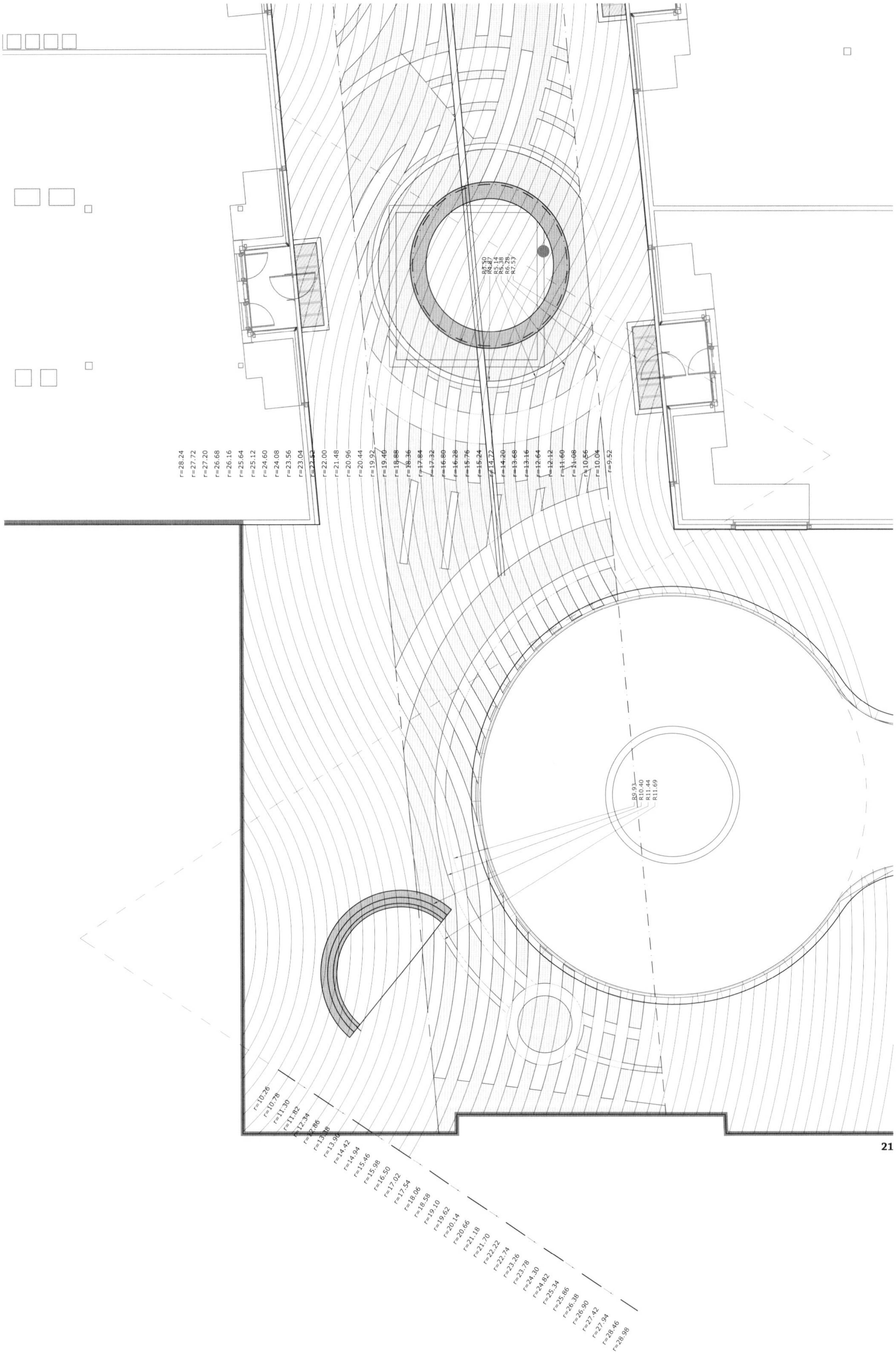
R3.50
R4.37
R5.14
R5.38
R6.28
R7.53
r=28.24
r=27.72
r=27.20
r=26.68
r=26.16
r=25.64
r=25.12
r=24.60
r=24.08
r=23.56
r=23.04
r=22.52
r=22.00
r=21.48
r=20.96
r=20.44
r=19.92
r=19.40
r=18.88
r=18.36
r=17.84
r=17.32
r=16.80
r=16.28
r=15.76
r=15.24
r=14.72
r=14.20
r=13.68
r=13.16
r=12.64
r=12.12
r=11.60
r=11.08
r=10.56
r=10.04
r=9.52
R9.93
R10.40
R11.44
R11.69
r=10.26
r=10.78
r=11.30
r=11.82
r=12.34
r=12.86
r=13.38
r=13.90
r=14.42
r=14.94
r=15.46
r=15.98
r=16.50
r=17.02
r=17.54
r=18.06
r=18.58
r=19.10
r=19.62
r=20.14
r=20.66
r=21.18
r=21.70
r=22.22
r=22.74
r=23.26
r=23.78
r=24.30
r=24.82
r=25.34
r=25.86
r=26.38
r=26.90
r=27.42
r=27.94
r=28.46
r=28.98

21

22

23

21: Paving, technical drawing
22–23: Construction of the mosaic

24

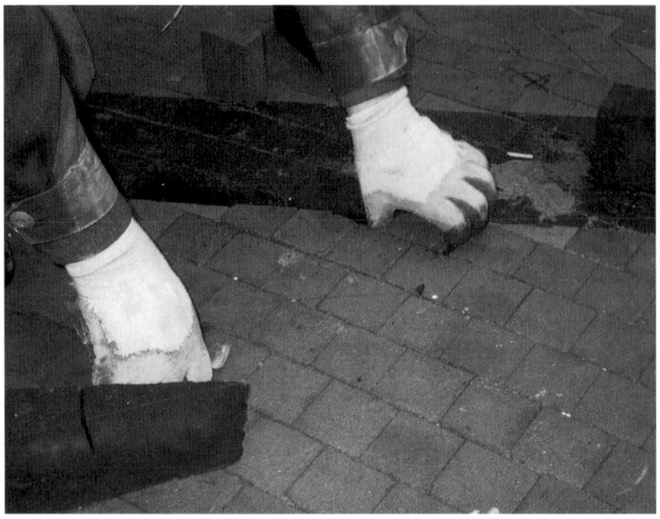

25

26

27

24–25: Cutting and laying of stones at minus 20°C

26: Protection for workers

27: Temporary accommodation on the site

28

29

30

31

28–31: Work meeting with client team

32

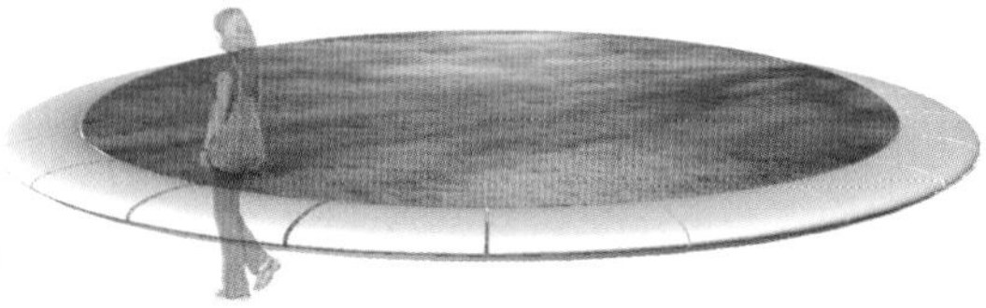

33a

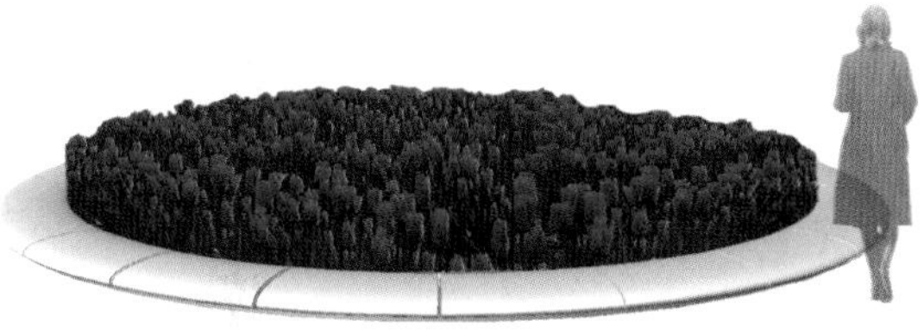

b

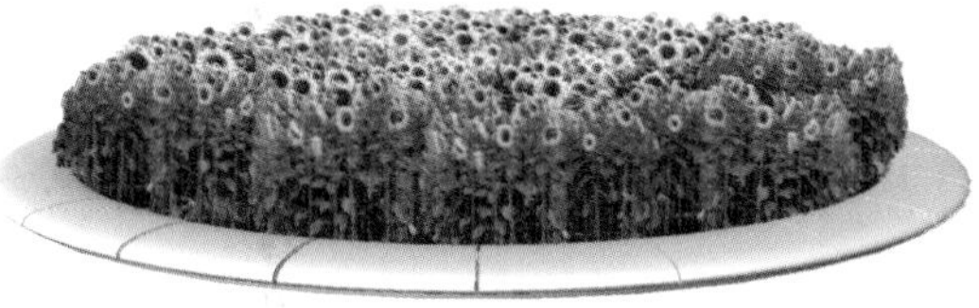

c

d

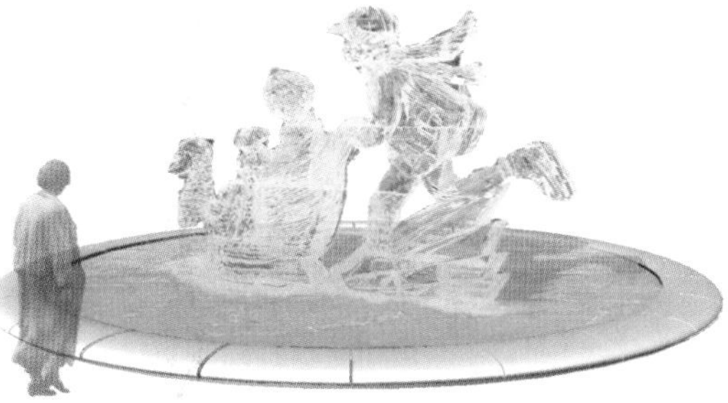

e

34

35

32: Plan fragment, artist's impression
33a–e: Pockets, seasonal
34: Pockets, temporary border
35: Doughnut bench

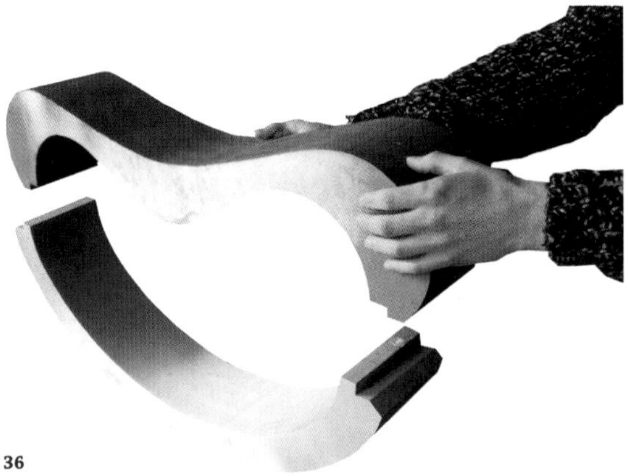

36

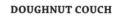

DOUGHNUT COUCH

36: Foam model

37: Computer models

38: Test model

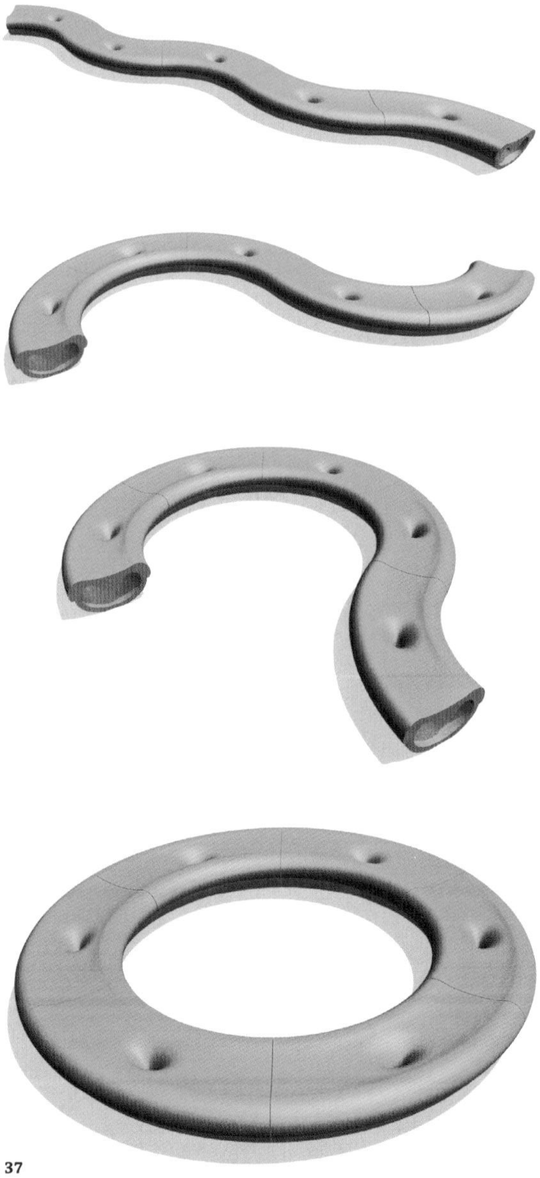

37

38

39

40

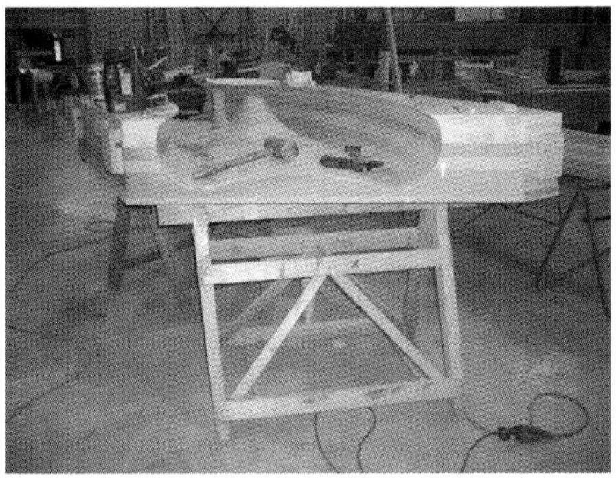

41

42

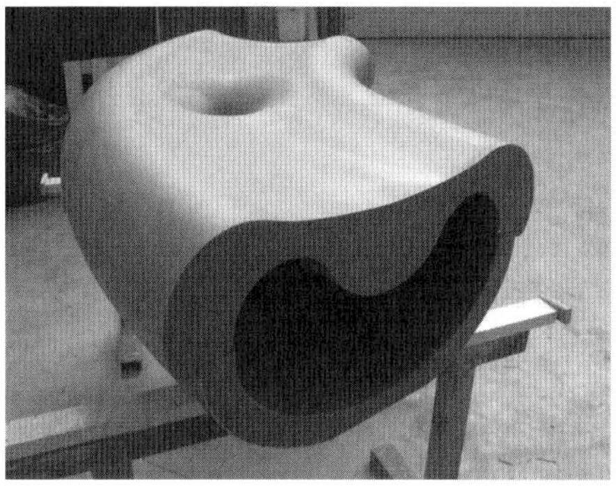

43

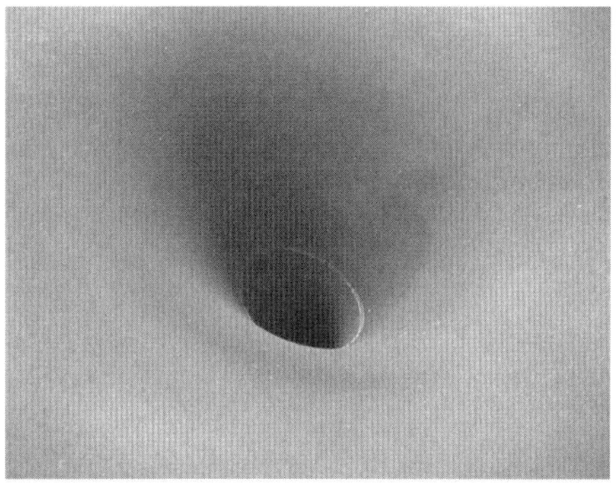

44

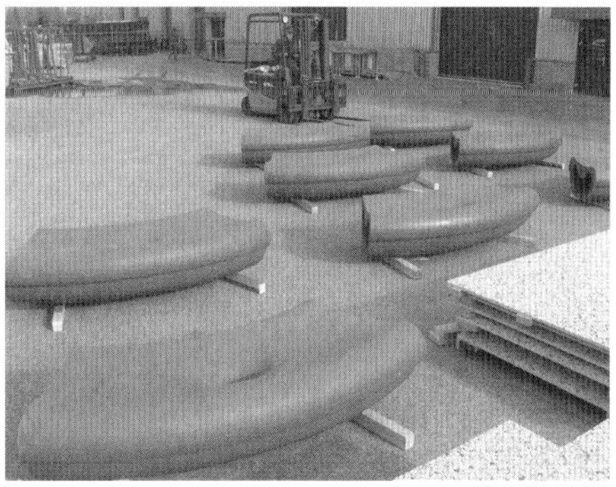

45

39–41: MDF moulds

42–45: First copies

46

47

48

46–49: Parking zone, situation

49

50

51

52

LIGHTING

50: 1.000 small lights

51–52: Cast steel gutter

53: Situation

54

55

56

57

PLANTING POCKET #3

54: Plant pocket #3, Autumn 2004

55: Tree #16

56: Tree #47

57: Pocket #3, trees #16 and #47

58: Pocket #3, Winter 2005

1

2

1–2: People in contemplation
3: Pinecones with light, detail

PINECONE GARDEN

PADUA, ITALY

The monastery of Padua, dating back to the 11th century, has a tranquil patio garden shaded by an old pine. This tree is extremely virile and continuously sheds an uninterrupted flow of pinecones.

The monastery and the patios are covered with these cones. They pile up against the walls. Many believe that it represents a miracle and pilgrims come to witness this unique experience and to meditate. The fragrance of the resin and the crackling sound of the cones stimulate the senses. In several places the cones are glowing, reflecting red light. The pinecones lose their seeds, causing seedlings to germinate everywhere.

4

5

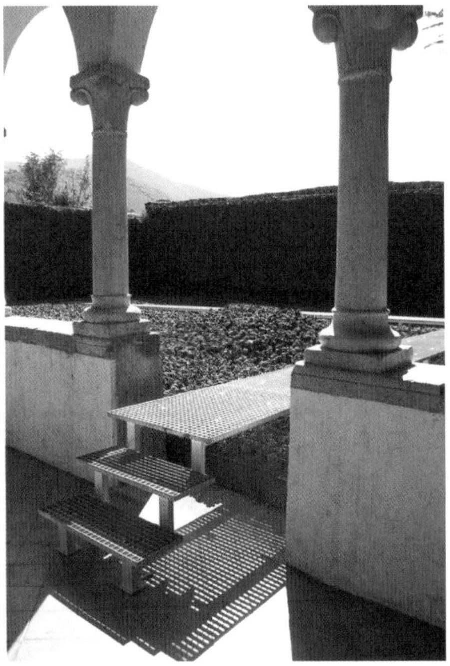
6

7

4: Young pine sprouts
5: Wall
6–7: Elevated path
8: Gabion, 3D visual
9–11: Potency: pine with endless production

9

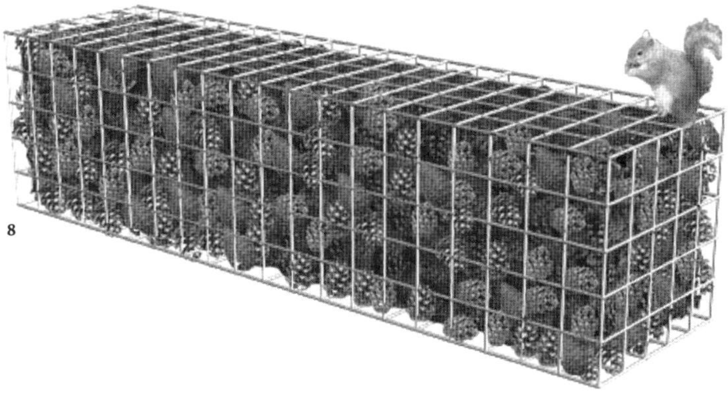
8

10

11

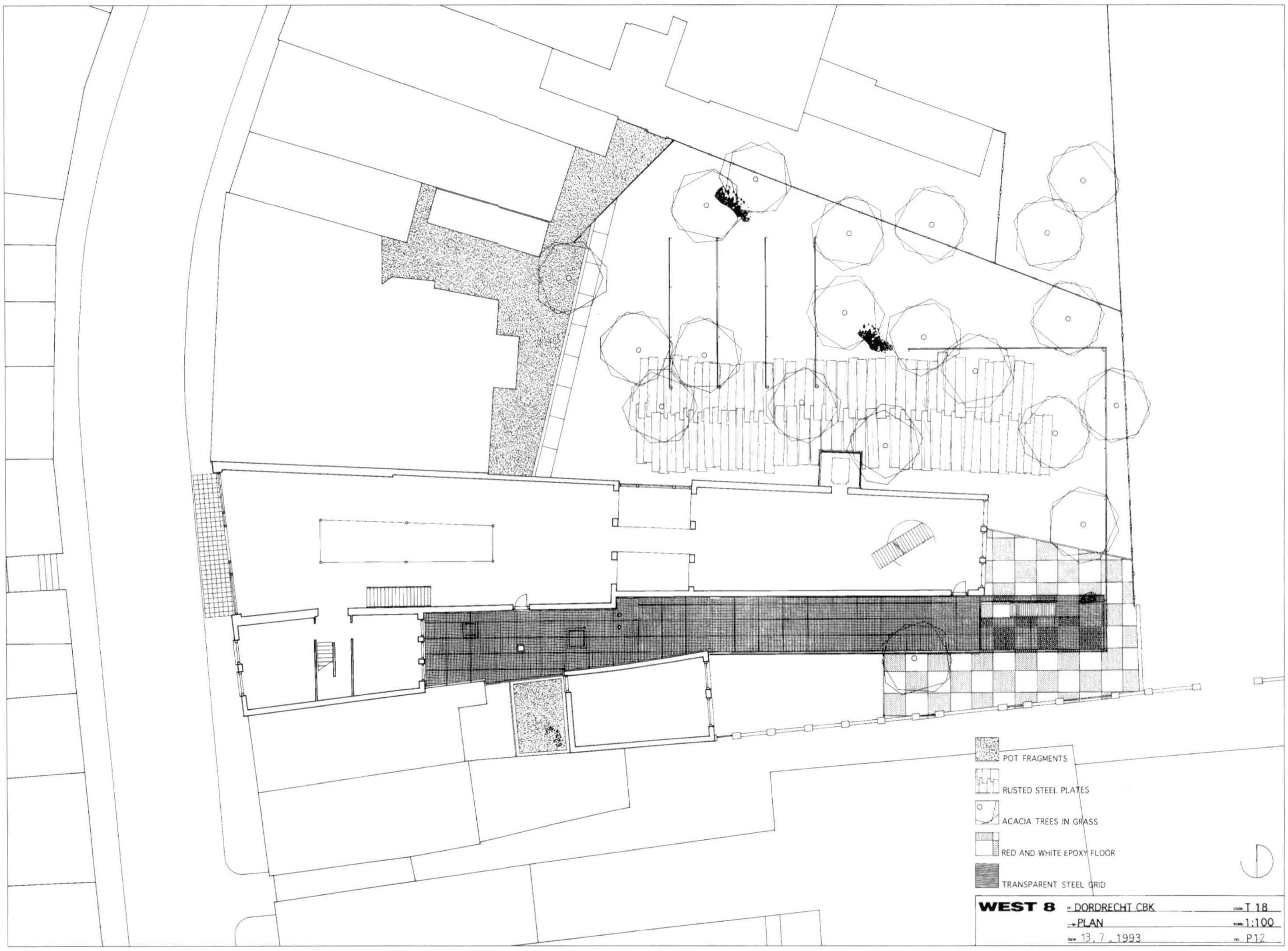

1

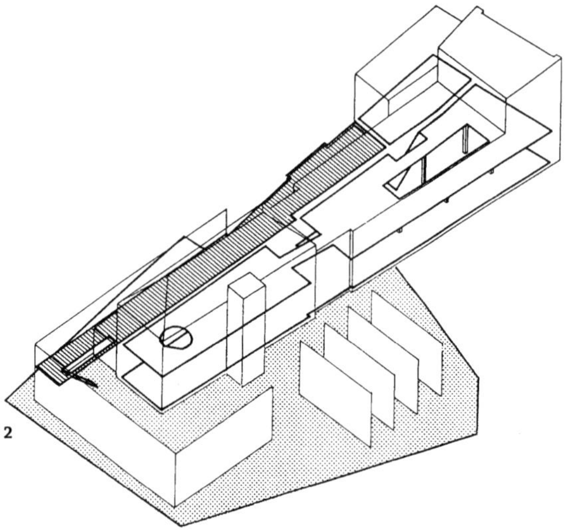

2

1: Master plan
2: Isometric view
3: Cabinets

CBK SCULPTURE GARDEN

DORDRECHT, THE NETHERLANDS

The Dordrecht Centre for Contemporary Art, located in an old Art Nouveau building, needed an outdoor exhibition space. West 8 designed a sculpture garden around the museum building, also extending over one of the roofs. Six-metre-tall fences enclose the garden and create a series of outdoor 'galleries'. Wisteria and Robinia were planted to grow over the wire mesh. The upper exhibition space on the roof can be reached via a folding ladder. In the garden, a terrace made of steel plates from dismantled ships underscores the maritime history of the city of Dordrecht.

3

4

5

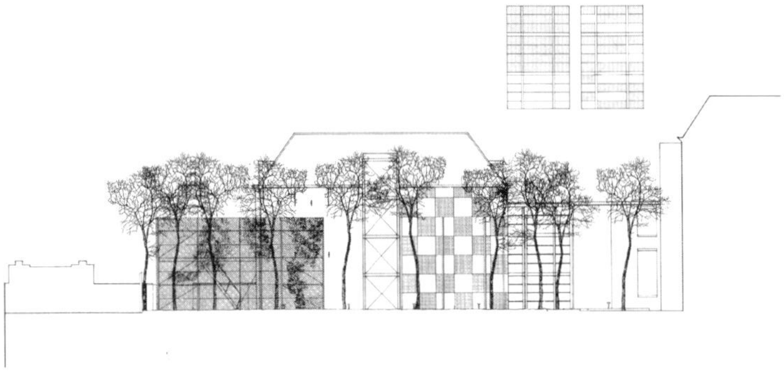

7

8

6

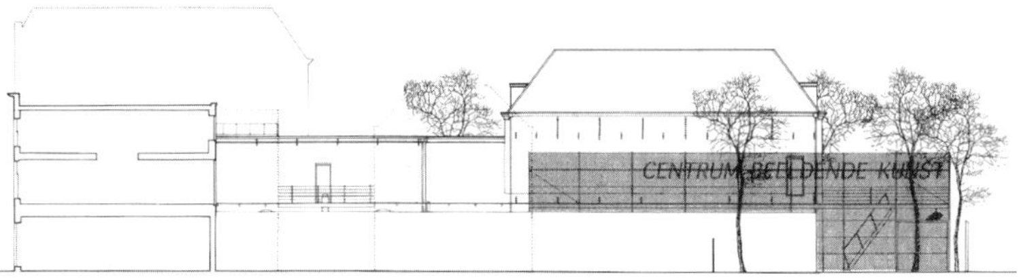

9

10

4–6, 10: Moiré pattern of gates
7–9: Elevations

11

12

13

14

11, 13–14: Acacia through the gate
12: Overview

15

16

15–17: Wisteria through the gate

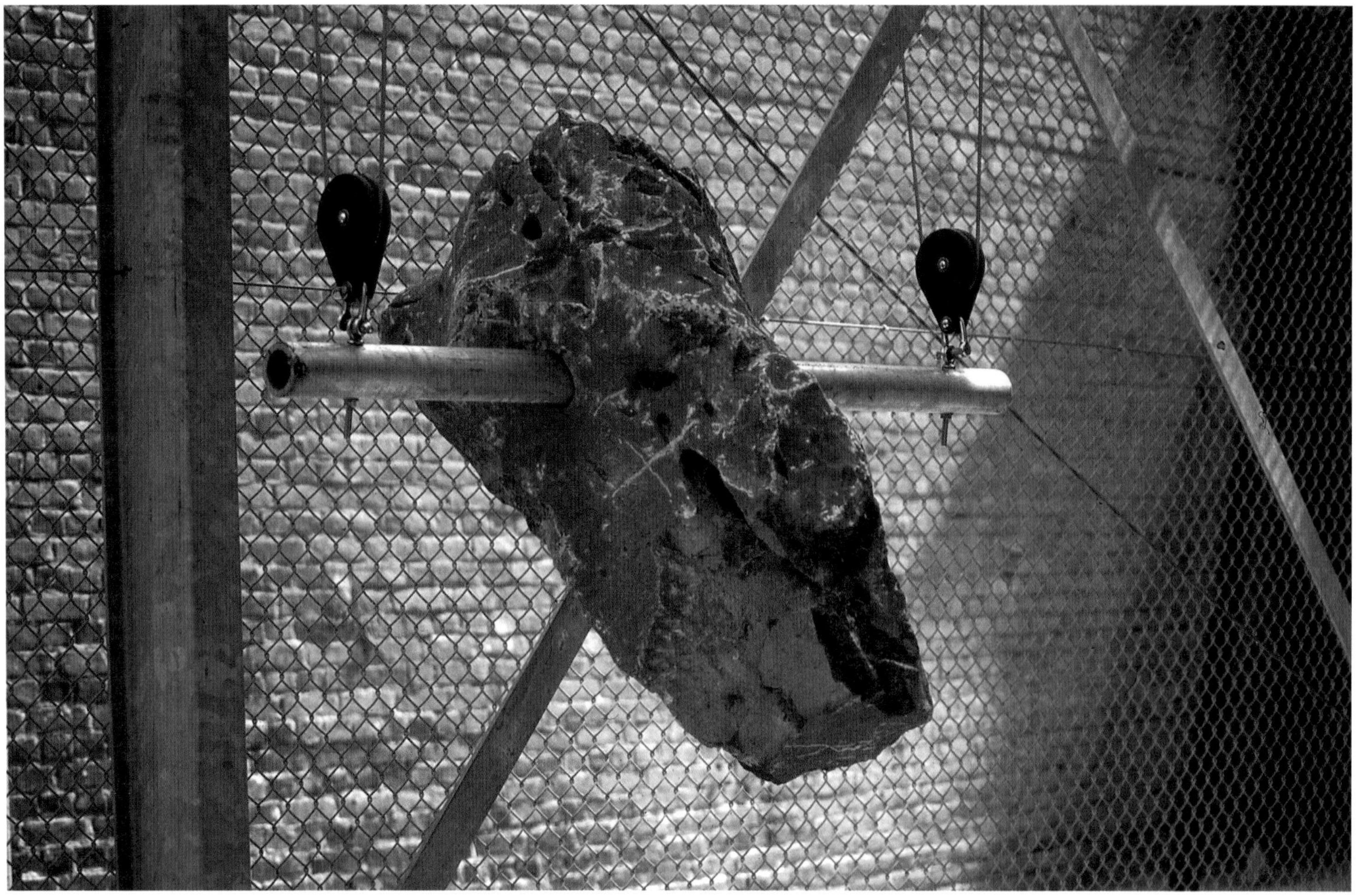

18

19

20

FOLDING LADDER

18: Counterweight

19: Deck

20: Foot of stairway

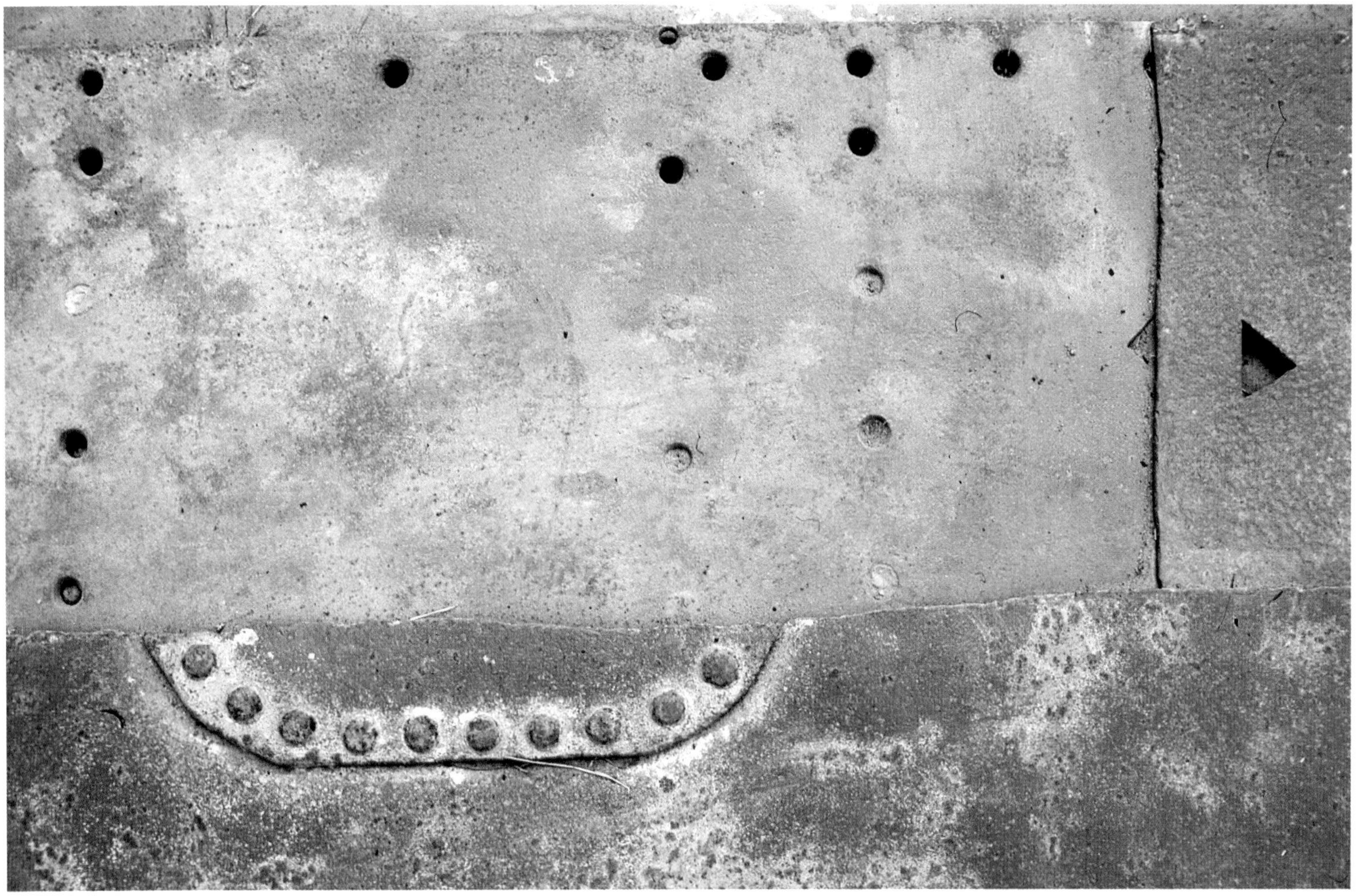

21

22

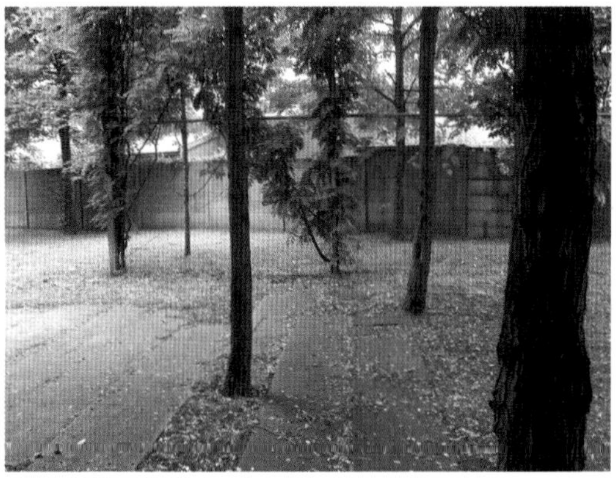

23

24

TERRACE

21: Old ship's hull, detail
22–23: Situation
24: Plan

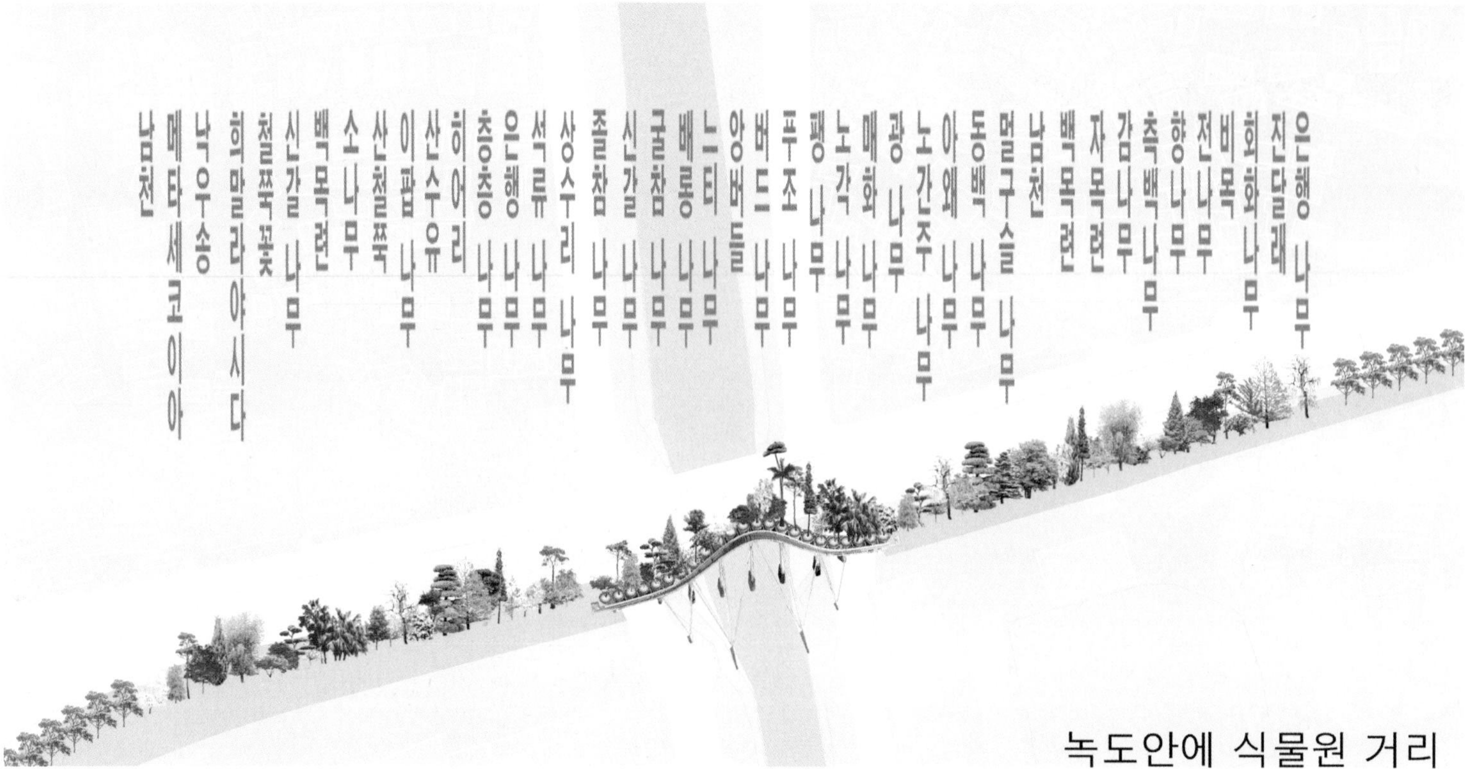

1

광주천을 넘어가는 식물원

2

HIGH BOTANIC BRIDGE

GWANGJU, SOUTH KOREA

West 8 was invited to investigate the development potential of an obsolete railway track around the centre of the city of Gwangju. West 8 suggested creating a green ribbon that would form a safe link between more than twenty public schools.

At the crossing with the Gwangju River, a botanic bridge was planned to pay homage to nature. This iconic bridge would become a landmark in the rapidly modernising city.

The pedestrian bridge, parabolic in shape and 35 metres in height, was lined with 24 concrete pots containing a variety of tree species, up to 7 metres in height. For pedestrians, crossing the bridge would entail a steep climb; however, its functionality was not a considered to be important in the design.

1: Poster
2: Sketch drawing
3: 3D pot models
4–5: Construction, model

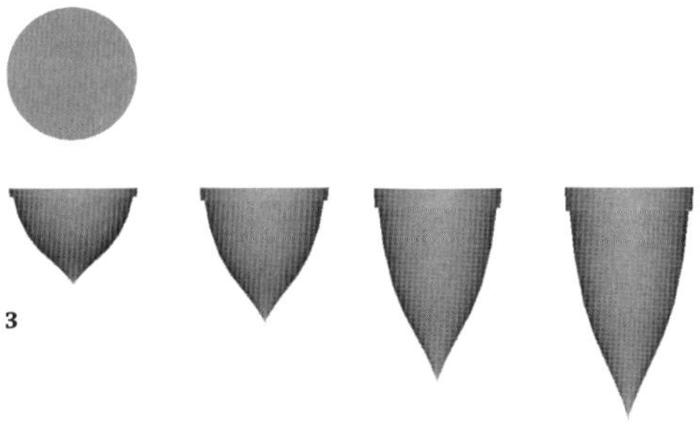

3

4

5

6

7

8

9

6, 9: Artist's impressions

7: Situation

8: View from the river

10

11

10–11: Model, gold and velvet

1

MÖBIUS HOUSE

BUSSUM, THE NETHERLANDS

This garden is a continuation of the virtuoso line-play found in the architecture of the Möbius house (designed by UN Studio), which stands on a plot of woodland. The garden was not treated as an independent space but as a means of connecting the house to the woods. Several subtle designed elements were introduced: a greenhouse, grassy paths and a dark, reflecting pool.

The black pool reflects the trees and sky. The winding paths of Wimbledon grass bridge various levels of the garden. They turn and double back before vanishing into thick undergrowth. The textures of the wood and the changing of the seasons are captured in the Möbius garden. The garden evaporates in the forest.

1: Terrace
2: Master plan
3–4: Path through the woods

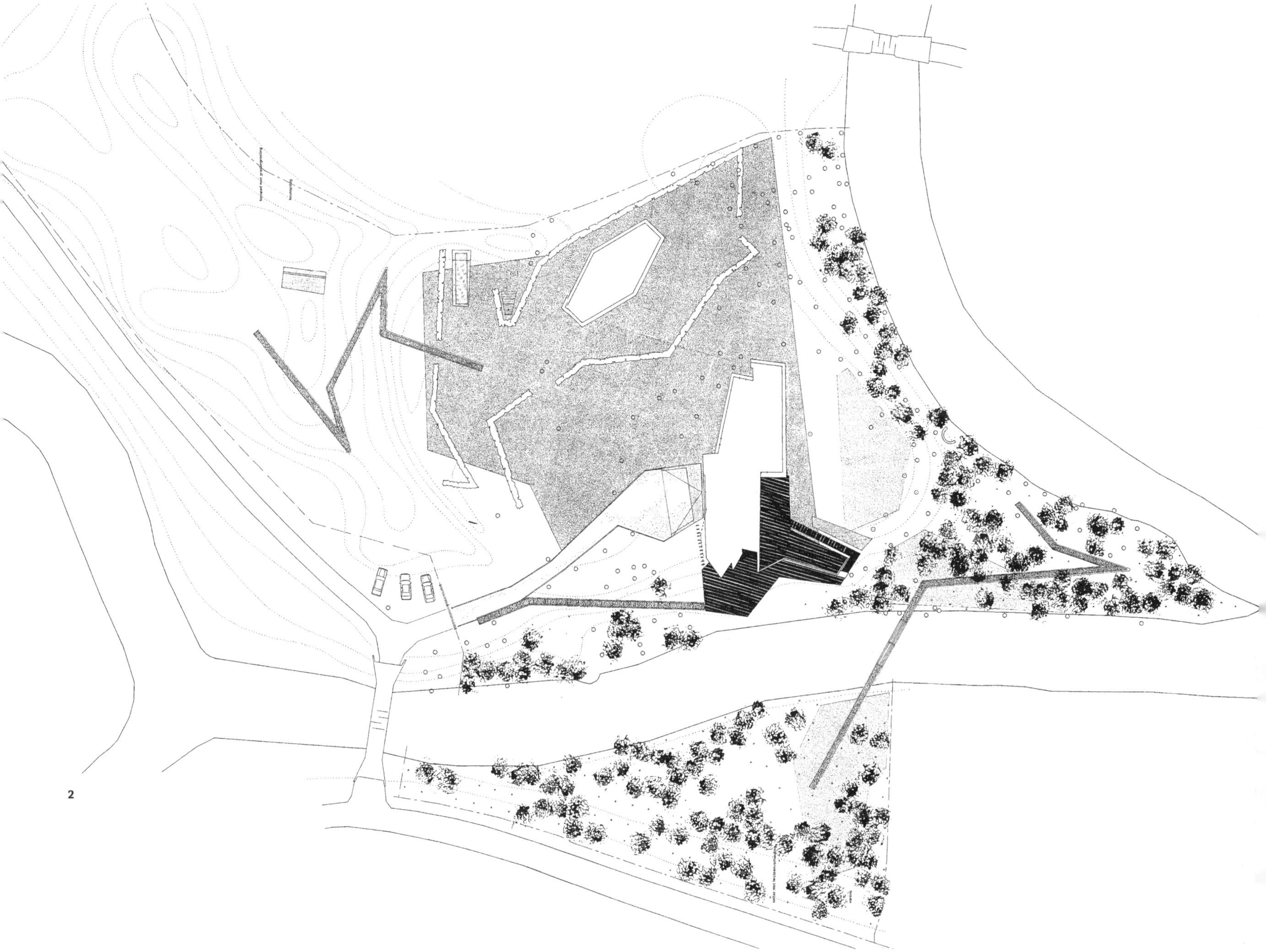

2

3

4

5

5: Reflecting pool
6: Greenhouse
7: Path through the woods

6

7

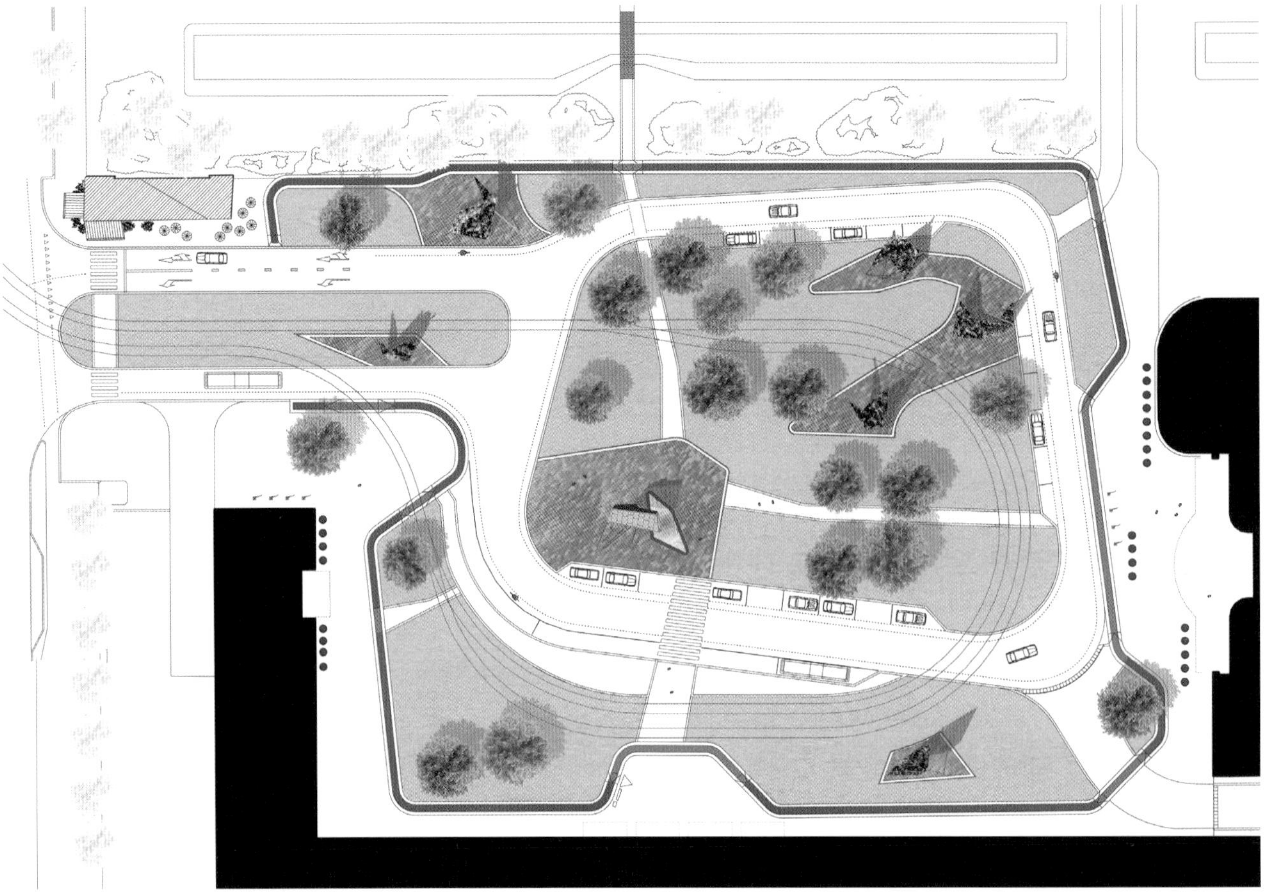

1

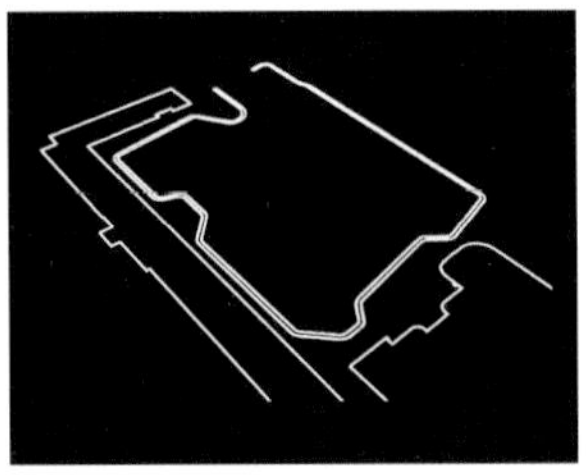

2a

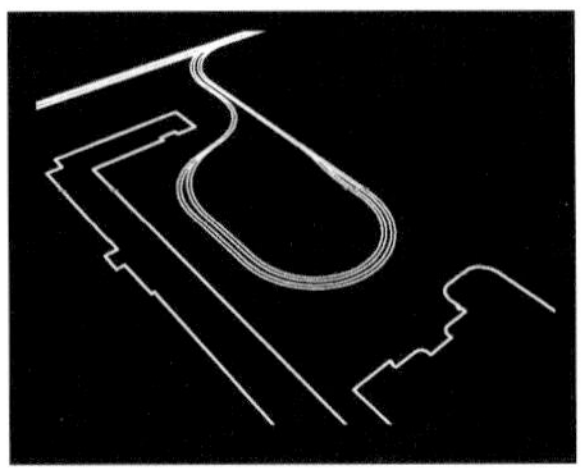

b

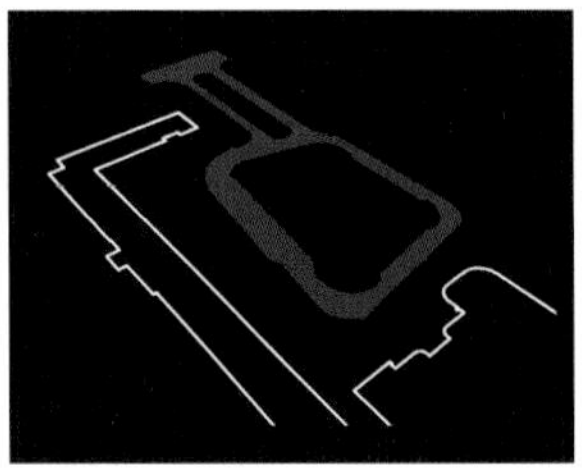

c

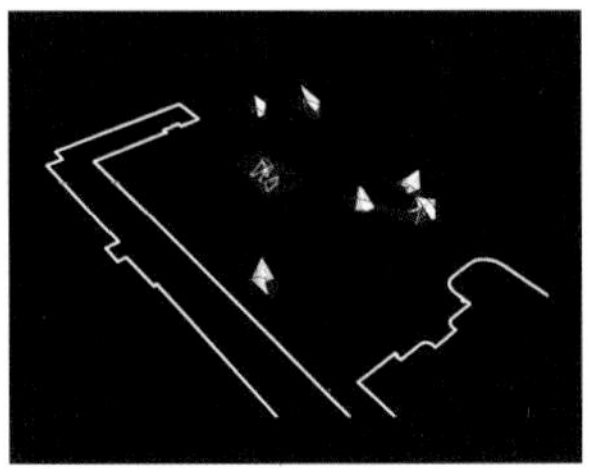

d

3

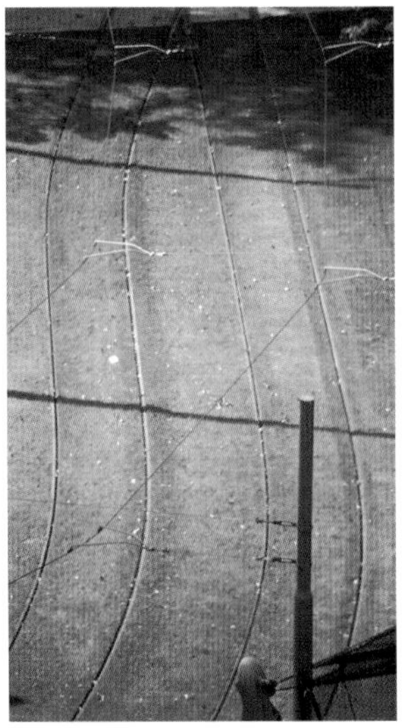

4

1: Master plan
2a: Border, detail
b: Tram
c: Bus and taxi
d: Seven follies
3: Pavement
4: Tram tracks

5

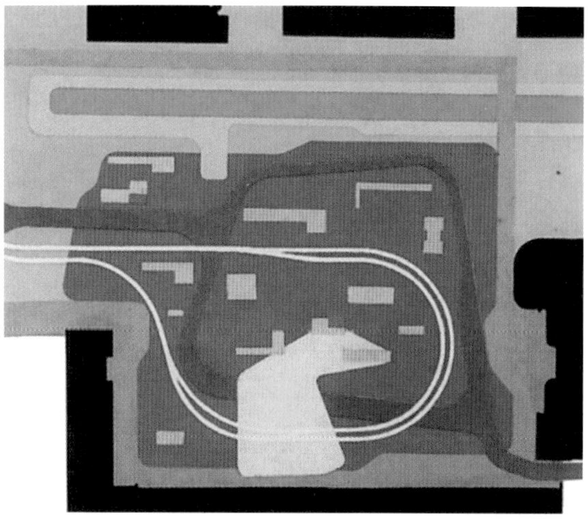

6

AEGONPLEIN

THE HAGUE, THE NETHERLANDS

A public square between a local railway station and the headquarters of the Aegon insurance group. The company offered the redesigned square, including its upkeep, as a gift to the city of The Hague. West 8's design for the square is a still-life composition of asphalt, gravel and grass, within which eight follies are placed. Six of these are ivy structures, one is a water installation, and the last incorporates a florist's shop and a bar.

5: Collage
6: Early plan
7: Computer visual

7

8

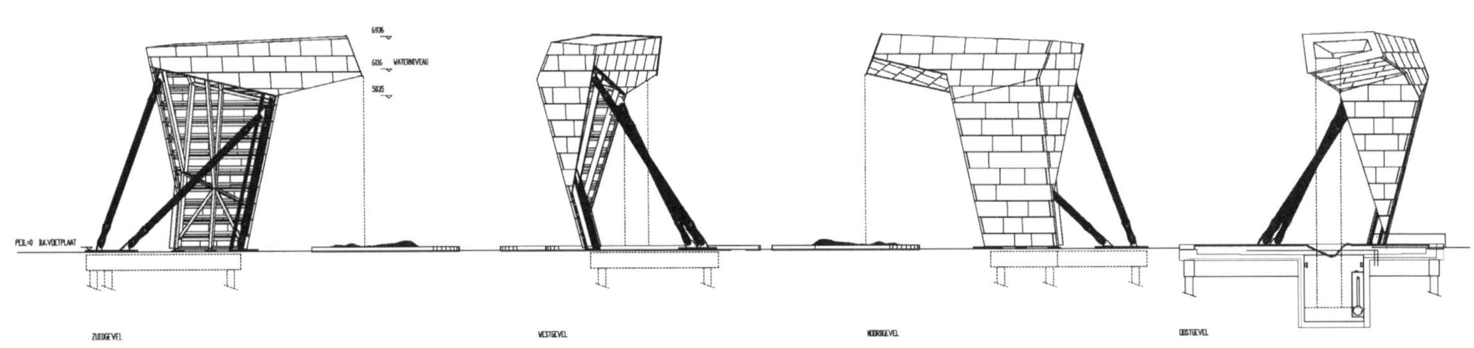
GEVELS
6936
6136 WATERNIVEAU
5035
PEIL=0 B.K.VOETPLAAT
ZUIDGEVEL
WESTGEVEL
NOORDGEVEL
OOSTGEVEL

9

FOLLIES

8: Water folly, artist's impression
9: Water folly, views
10: Corner, artist's impression
11a-f: Follies seen from four corners
12: Folly #5

10

11a
b
c
d
e
f

North West South East

12

13

14

15

FOLLY # 2

13–15: Folly #2

16: Water folly

17: Aegonplein from main building

16

17

18

Aegonplein from north-east

P

19, 21: Grille
20: Water folly

20

21

22

23

24

25

KIOSK

22–23: Flower kiosk, open and closed

24: Artist's impression

25–26: Situation

26

1

Le Monde

MERCREDI 8 NOVEMBRE 2000

FONDATEUR : HUBERT BEUVE-MÉRY

La grande peur de la vache folle

● La méfiance s'installe envers la viande de bœuf ● De nombreux maires l'interdisent dans les cantines scolaires ● Que faut-il vraiment craindre ? ● Notre dossier et un entretien avec le directeur général de la santé

UN DÉBUT de panique a saisi les consommateurs français sur les risques liés à la maladie de la « vache folle ». La polémique sur l'interdiction des farines animales et sur la qualité de la viande de bœuf alimentent ces craintes et obligent les pouvoirs publics à rassurer. Dans un entretien au *Monde*, le professeur Lucien Abenhaïm, directeur général de la santé, annonce qu'il saisit l'Agence française de sécurité sanitaire des aliments sur la question des cantines scolaires et des aliments bovins que les Français peuvent consommer. Il demande parallèlement *« une nouvelle expertise »* sur les risques liés aux produits sanguins. Au nom du principe de précaution, de nombreux maires ont retiré le bœuf du menu des cantines des écoles primaires. La filière bovine craint une forte baisse des ventes de bœuf, accrue par la décision de certains pays européens de restreindre l'entrée de la viande bovine sur leur territoire.

Lire notre dossier pages 10 et 11

JEFF MITCHELL/AFP

2

FESTIVAL GARDEN

CHAUMONT, FRANCE

This model garden is a still-life made up of bones, pot shards and pumpkins. Visitors to the garden are invited to contemplate on the transient nature of our existence. The cattle bones and the pot shards literally refer to death. Amongst these the pumpkins grow with their large orange fruits. The garden was realised at the peak of the mad cow disease epidemic in France.

1: Overall view of the garden
2: Newspaper cutting of the French beef crisis
3–4: Details showing pot shards, pumpkins and bones

3

4

GRAND EGYPTIAN MUSEUM

CAIRO, EGYPT

The Irish architecture firm Heneghan Peng won the prestigious competition for the Grand Egyptian Museum in Giza, Cairo. Following the competition, an international team of advisers was formed to build the structure. West 8 joined the team to refine the concept of the museum, to prepare a design for the garden and to develop a master plan for the museum environs in relation to the pyramids of Giza. The project, which falls under the aegis of the Egyptian Minister of Culture and is supported by UNESCO, involves building the 800-metre-long museum in the flank of the plateau of Giza. West 8 contributed by integrating the original landscape of the Nile delta and flood plain into the museum concept. The huge building gained a series of gardens and outdoor spaces with greenery, referring to the source of Egyptian civilisation – the Nile – its fertile fields, its water, the abundance of food and the temple gardens. The design of the outdoor spaces is fully coordinated with the triangular grid of the museum. The climax is the Nile Park, a monumental series of water attractions that embrace the entire space in a zigzag formation. Behind the museum lies the triangular Land of Egypt, a cluster of fields with small irrigation channels. Lying to the south of this are the thematic gardens and Temple Gardens. The research centre, for which West 8 designed the long patio space, is under construction.

1

2

3

4

5

SITE

1: East view

2: West view

3: Giza plateau satellite photograph

4: Master plan

5: View towards desert plateau

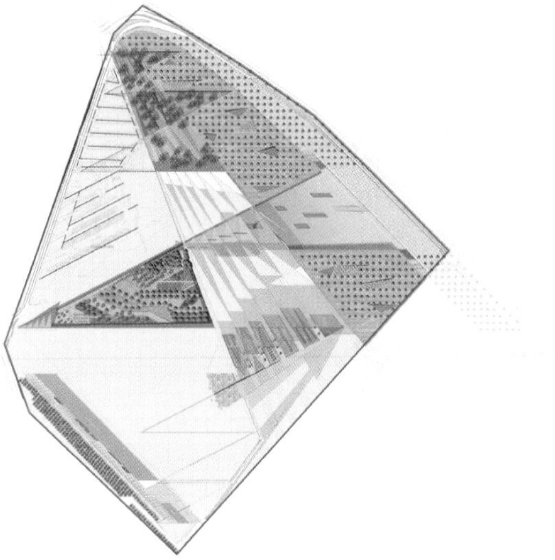

6

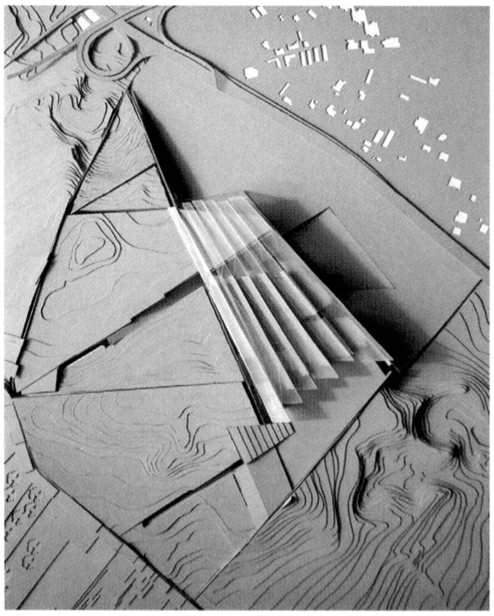

7

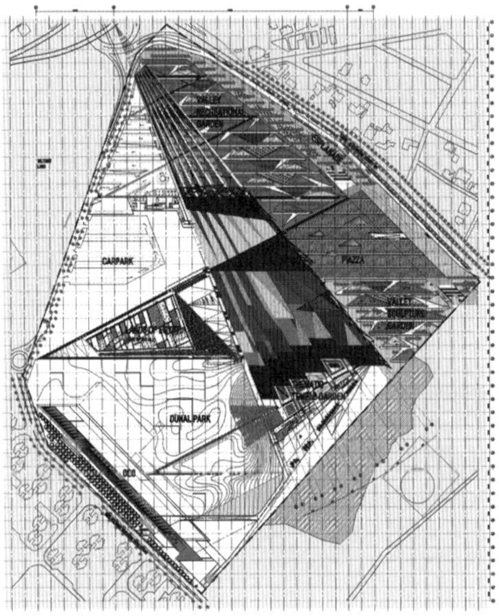

8

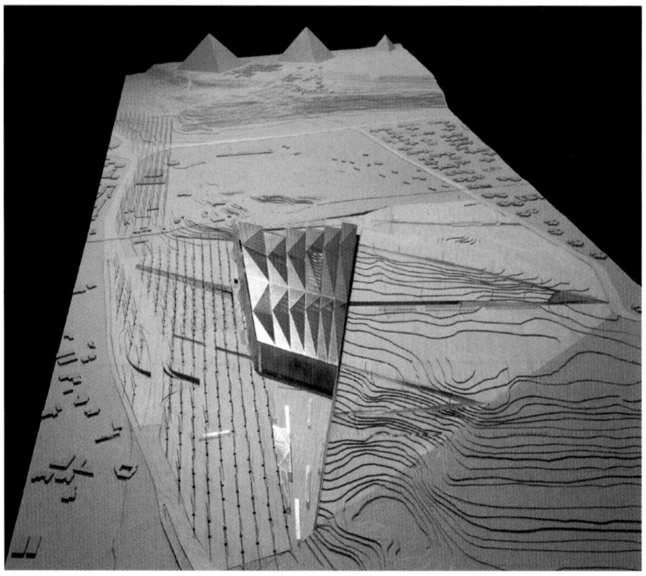

9

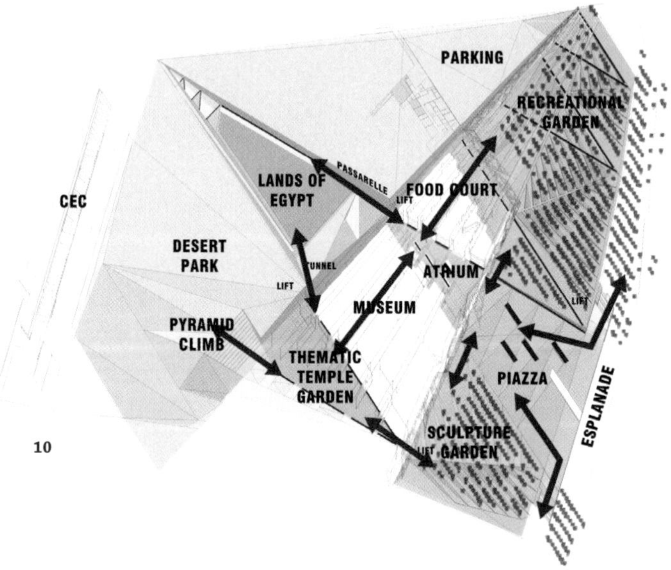

10

MASTER PLAN

6, 8: Conceptual diagram
7: Model showing museum on edge of desert plateau
9: Model
10: Conceptual diagram of outdoor routeing
11: Master plan

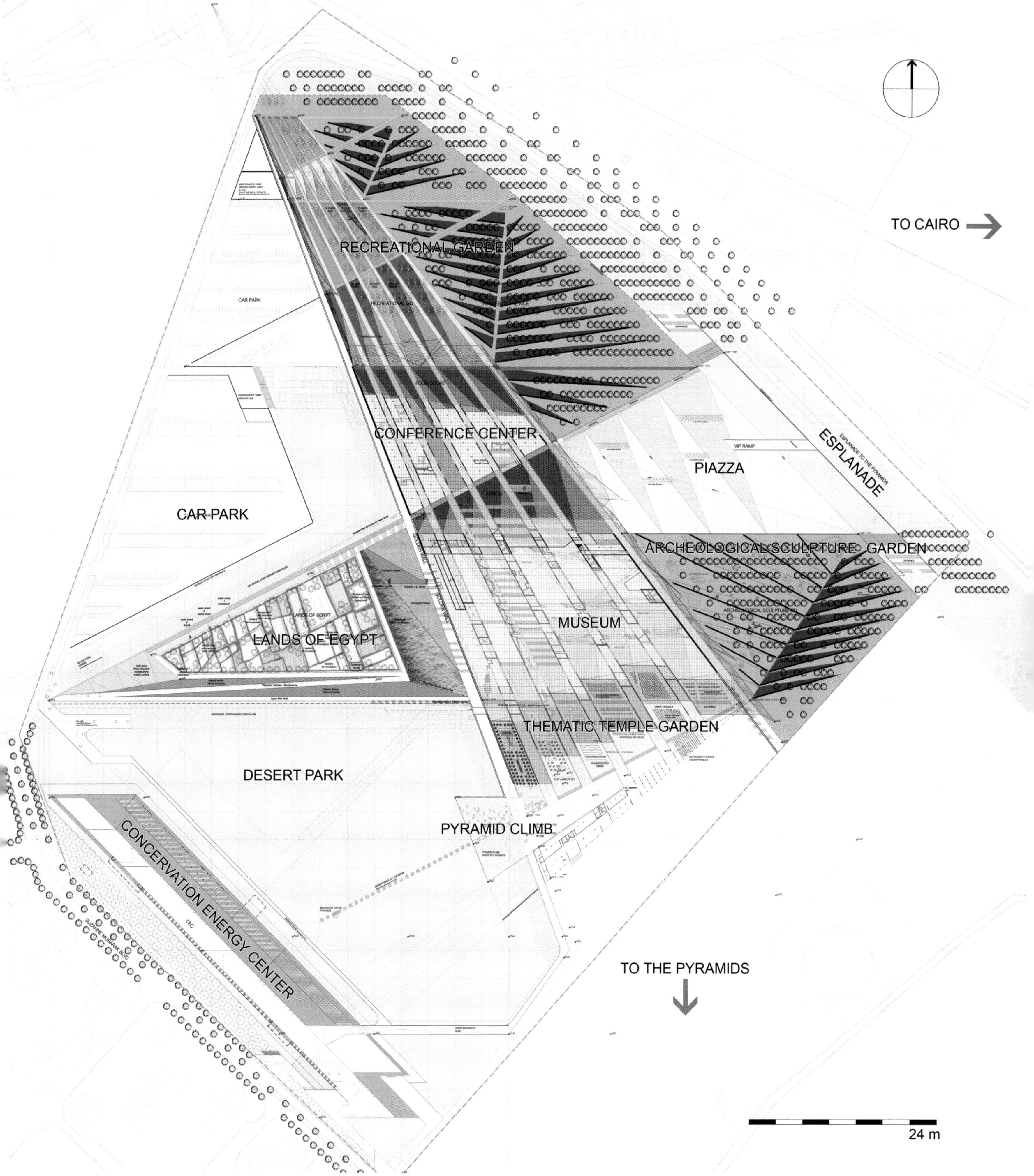
TO CAIRO
RECREATIONAL GARDEN
CAR PARK
CONFERENCE CENTER
PIAZZA
ESPLANADE
VIP RAMP
CAR PARK
ARCHEOLOGICAL SCULPTURE GARDEN
MUSEUM
LANDS OF EGYPT
THEMATIC TEMPLE GARDEN
DESERT PARK
PYRAMID CLIMB
CONCERVATION ENERGY CENTER
TO THE PYRAMIDS
24 m

12

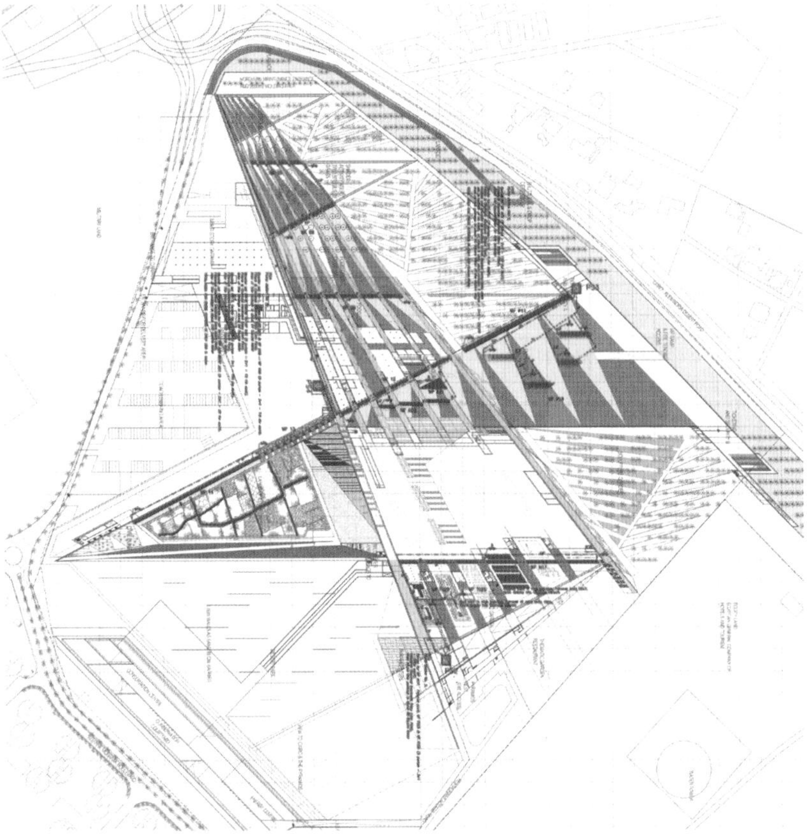

13

14

NILE PARK

12: Nile Park diagram

13: Nile Park water features diagram

14: Nile Park water cascade impression

15

16

17

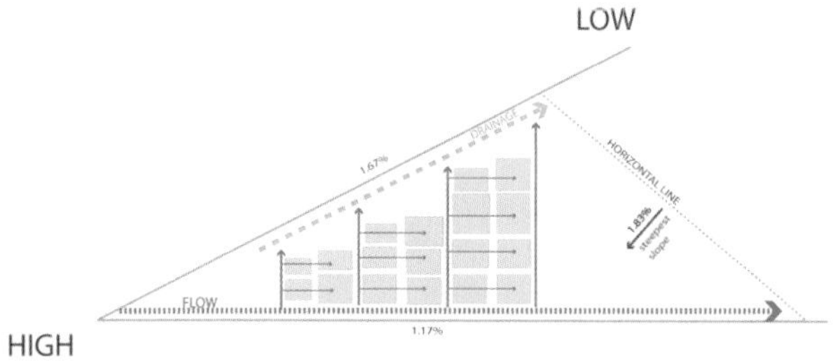

18

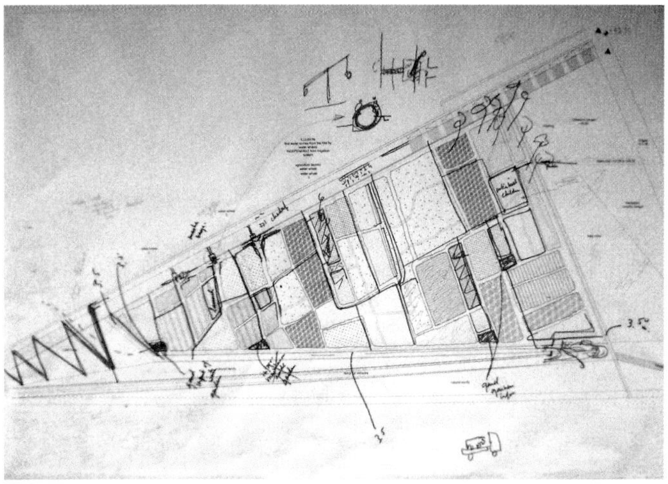

19

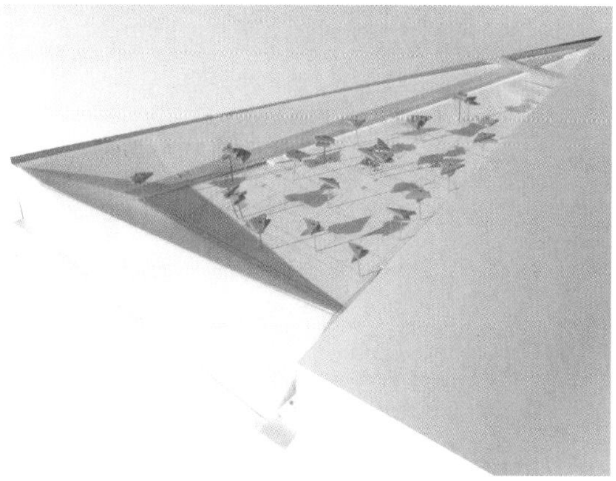

20

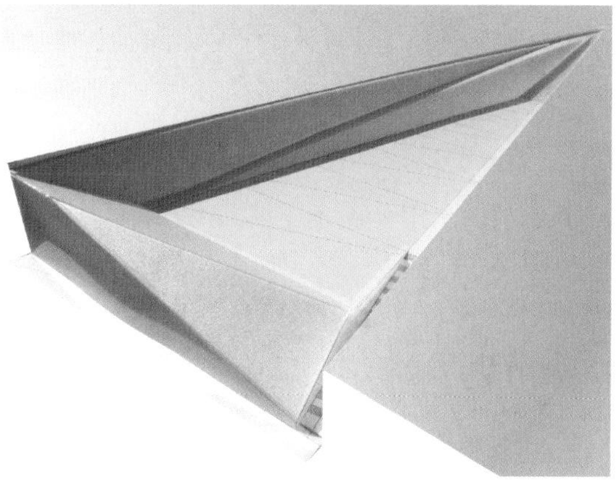

21

22

LANDS OF EGYPT

15–16: Traditional fields and vegetation of Egypt

17: Wall painting showing ancient Egyptian irrigation technique

18: Irrigation diagram

19: Sketch

20–22: Study models

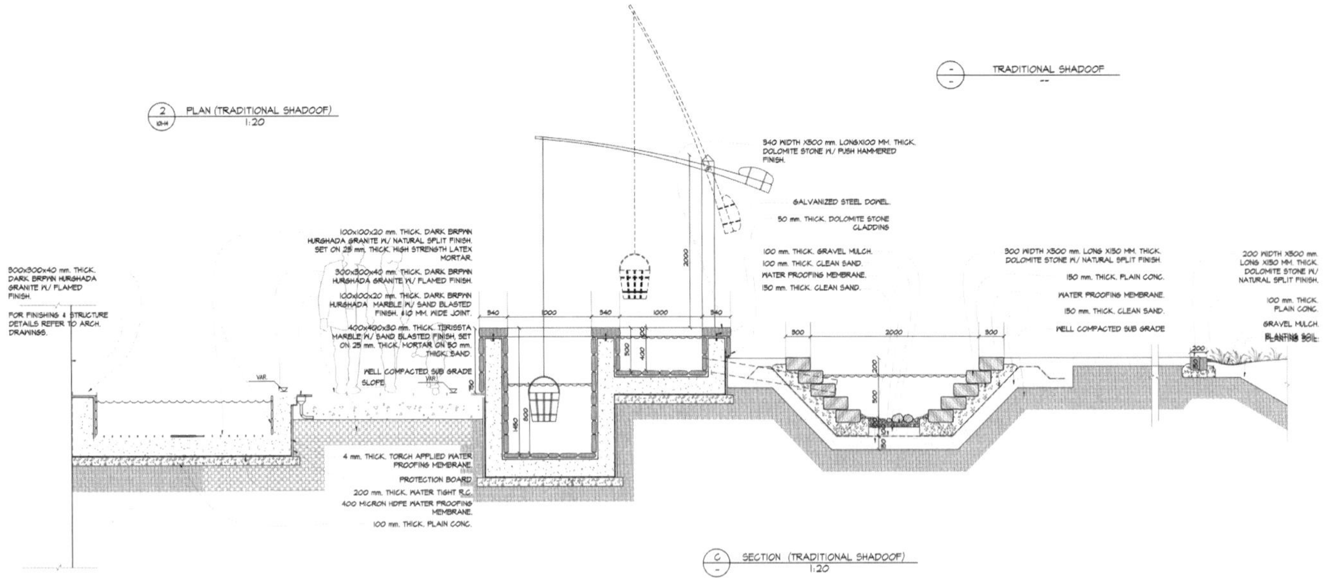

PLAN (TRADITIONAL SHADOOF)
1:20
TRADITIONAL SHADOOF
340 WIDTH X500 mm. LONGX100 MM. THICK. DOLOMITE STONE W/ PUSH HAMMERED FINISH.
GALVANIZED STEEL DOWEL.
50 mm. THICK. DOLOMITE STONE CLADDING
100 mm. THICK. GRAVEL MULCH.
100 mm. THICK. CLEAN SAND.
WATER PROOFING MEMBRANE.
150 mm. THICK. CLEAN SAND.
100x100x20 mm. THICK. DARK BRPWN HURGHADA GRANITE W/ NATURAL SPLIT FINISH. SET ON 25 mm. THICK. HIGH STRENGTH LATEX MORTAR.
300x300x40 mm. THICK. DARK BRPWN HURGHADA GRANITE W/ FLAMED FINISH.
100x100x20 mm. THICK. DARK BRPWN HURGHADA MARBLE W/ SAND BLASTED FINISH. ⌀10 MM. WIDE JOINT.
400x400x30 mm. THICK. TERISSTA MARBLE W/ SAND BLASTED FINISH, SET ON 25 mm. THICK. MORTAR ON 50 mm. THICK. SAND.
WELL COMPACTED SUB GRADE
SLOPE
300x300x40 mm. THICK. DARK BRPWN HURGHADA GRANITE W/ FLAMED FINISH.
FOR FINISHING & STRUCTURE DETAILS REFER TO ARCH. DRAWINGS.
4 mm. THICK. TORCH APPLIED WATER PROOFING MEMBRANE.
PROTECTION BOARD
200 mm. THICK. WATER TIGHT R.C.
400 MICRON HDPE WATER PROOFING MEMBRANE.
100 mm. THICK. PLAIN CONC.
300 WIDTH X500 mm. LONG X150 MM. THICK. DOLOMITE STONE W/ NATURAL SPLIT FINISH.
150 mm. THICK. PLAIN CONC.
WATER PROOFING MEMBRANE.
150 mm. THICK. CLEAN SAND.
WELL COMPACTED SUB GRADE
200 WIDTH X500 mm. LONG X150 MM. THICK. DOLOMITE STONE W/ NATURAL SPLIT FINISH.
100 mm. THICK. PLAIN CONC.
GRAVEL MULCH.
PLANTING SOIL.
SECTION (TRADITIONAL SHADOOF)
1:20

23

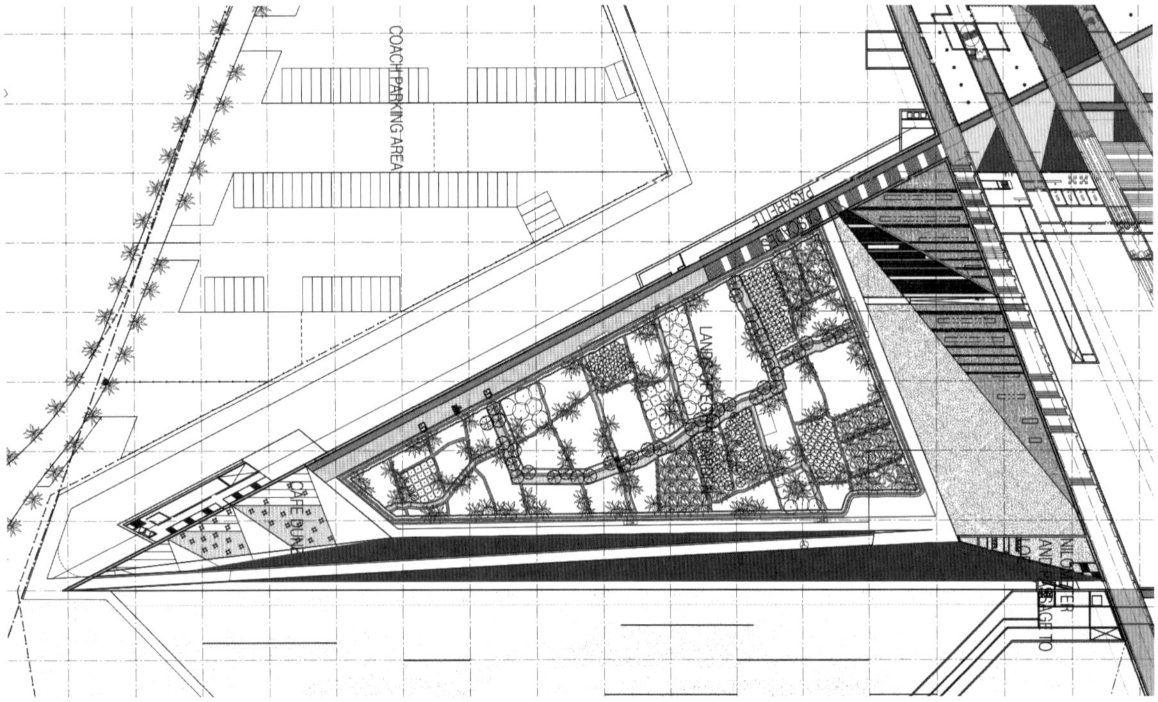

COACH PARKING AREA

24

23: Technical section irrigation system
24: Technical plan drawing
25: Artist's impression
26: Model showing 'the Golden Wall'
27: Section

25

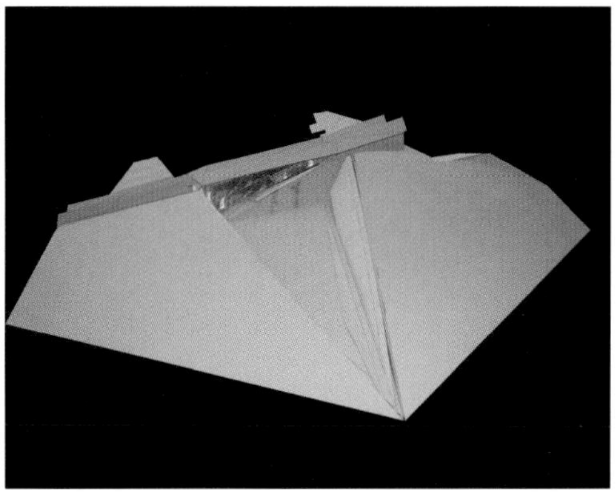

26

27

FRONT SPACE

28–29: Conceptual diagram
30: Recreational Garden, perspective view
31: Recreational Garden, isometric view
32: Museum façade, detail (Hparc and ARUP)
33: Elevation of museum Sierpinski façade
34–35: Artist's impression showing entrance piazza
36: Recreational Garden, technical drawing

30

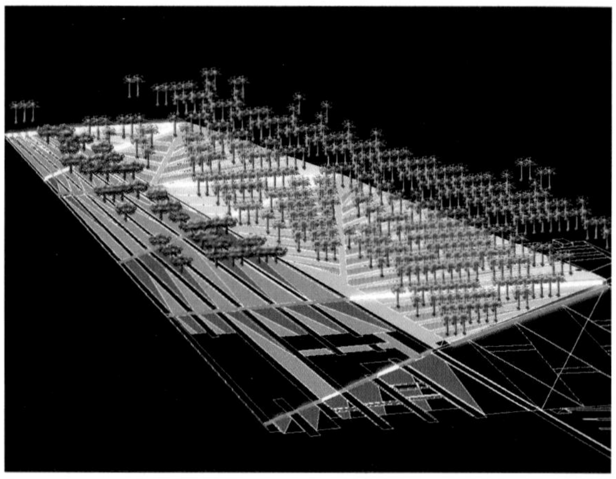

31

28

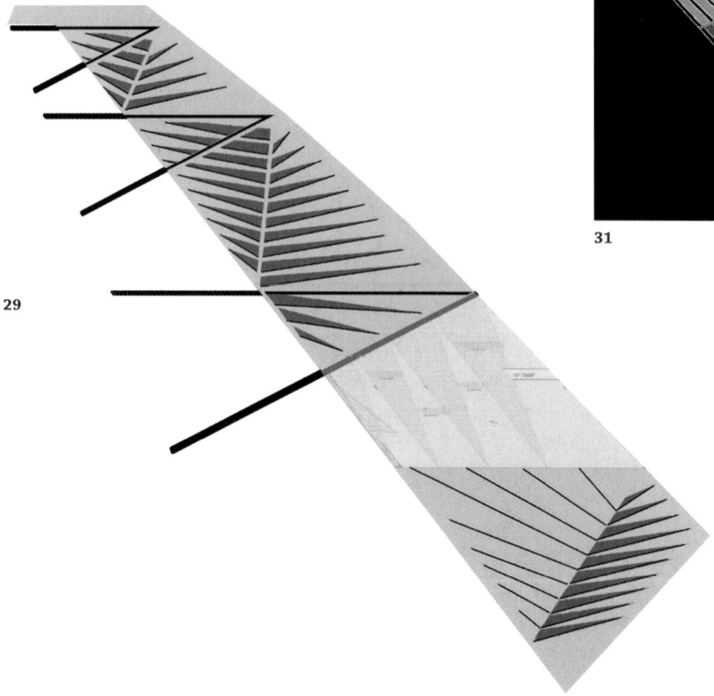

29

32

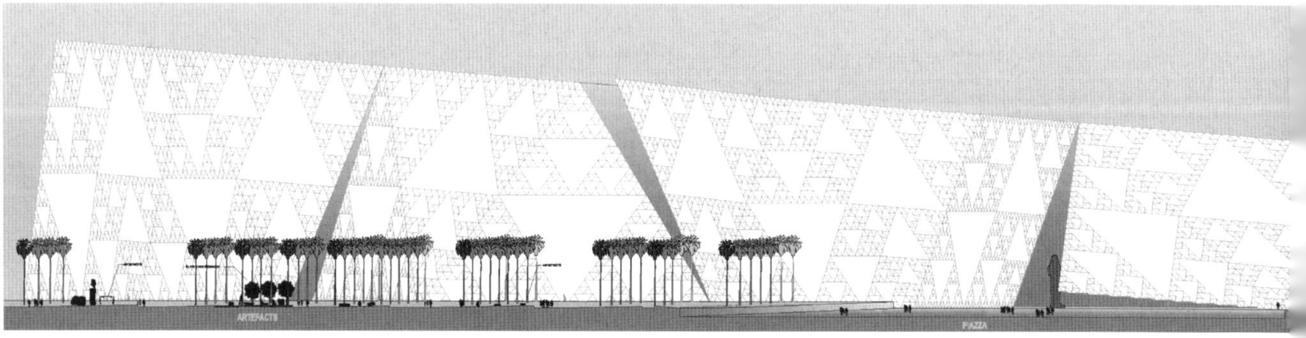

33

34

35

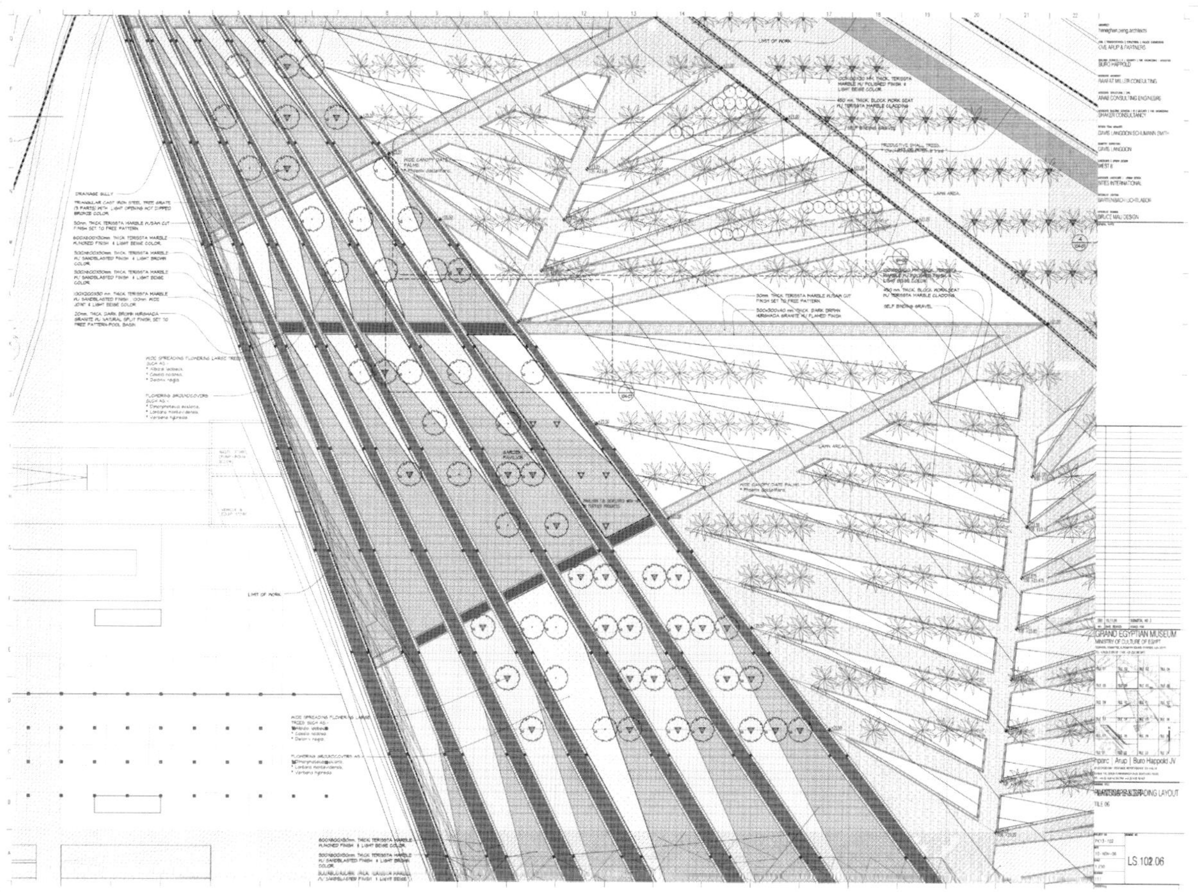
GRAND EGYPTIAN MUSEUM
MINISTRY OF CULTURE OF EGYPT
LS 102.06

36

OLIVE TREE GD
OLIVE TREE GD
FLOWERPAVILLION
WATERPAVILLION

37

37: View over Cairo through the façade
38: Archeological Sculpture Garden elevation
39: Archeological Sculpture Garden plan

38

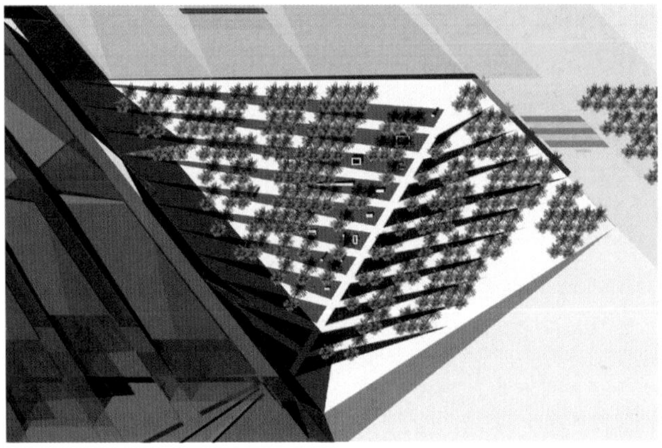

39

40

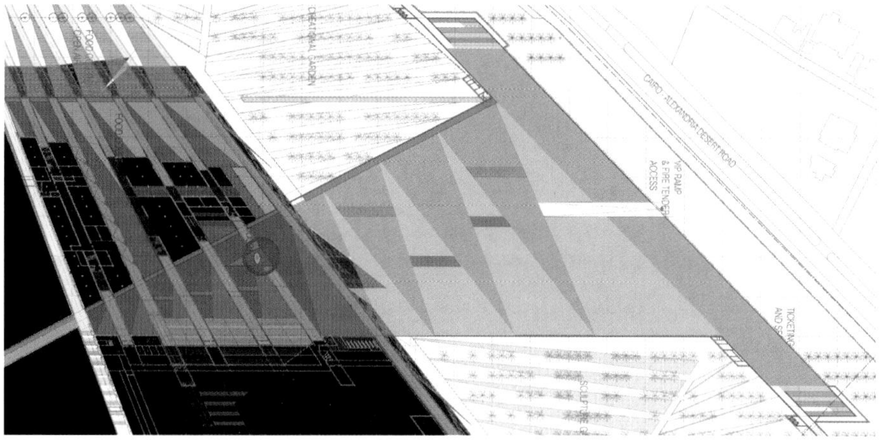

41

42

RAMSES II

40–41: Ramses II statue in the atrium

42: Ramses II statue route moving from city center to GEM site

43–46: Ramses II statue moved from Cairo Central Station to Giza, August 24, 2006

43

44

45

46

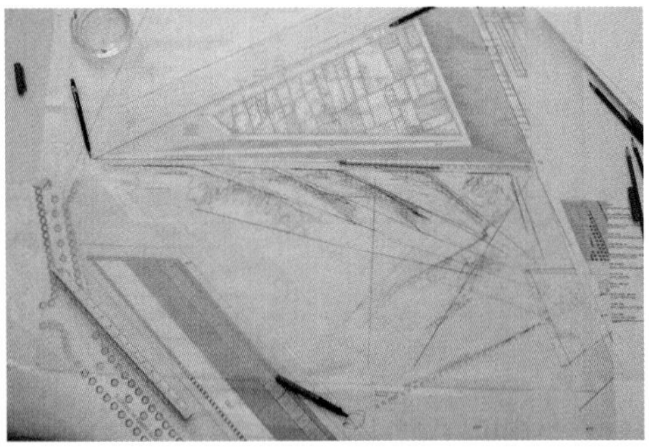
47

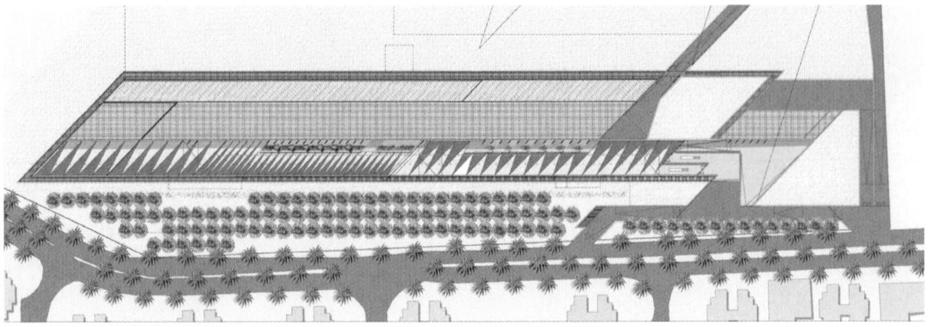
48

49

50

CONSERVATION ENERGY CENTER

47: Desert Park sketch
48: Conservation Energy Center, plan of the courtyard
49: Billboard
50: Construction site
51: Theme gardens
52: Perspective view
53: View onto the pyramids from the Museum
54: View from pyramid climb

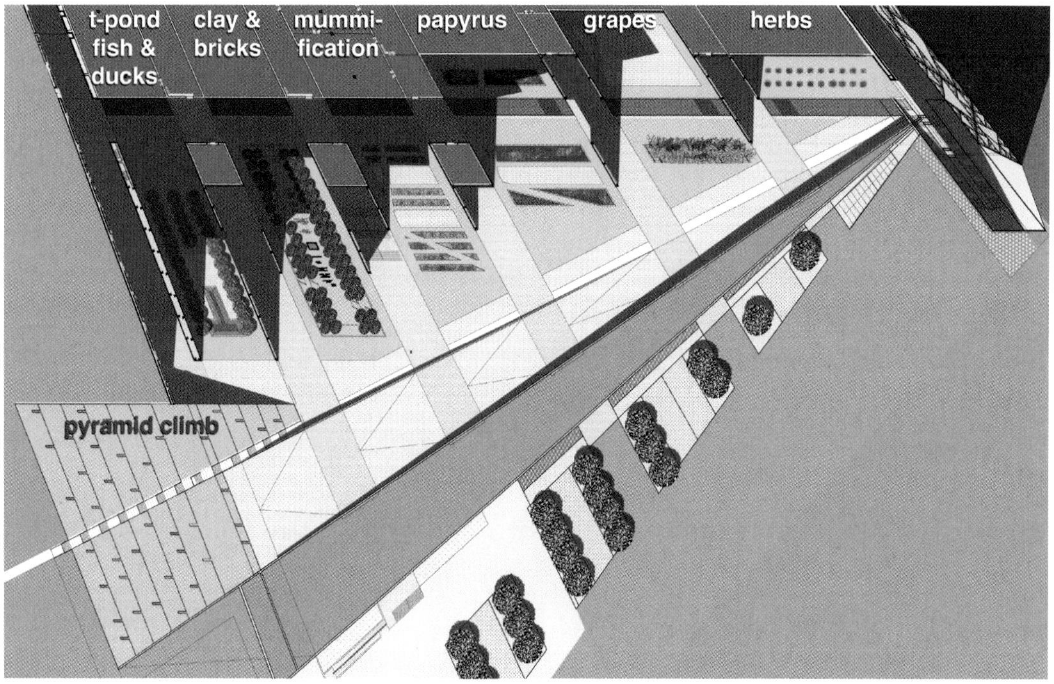
t-pond
fish &
ducks
clay &
bricks
mummi-
fication
papyrus
grapes
herbs
pyramid climb

51

52

53

54

1

2

3

SANTA GIULIA

MILAN, ITALY

A private developer has planned the development of a new town on the heavily polluted former industrial estate of Santa Giulia. Sir Norman Foster designed the master plan for this Montecity project, which is situated adjacent to Linate Airport.

West 8 was asked to create a master plan of the landscape areas and public spaces.

The work focused on establishing a large public park covering polluted landfill areas, and on creating of communal gardens within the oval shaped built area. The park provides links between several urban areas and, with its gently undulating and decorative surface, offers a green oasis within the overall development.

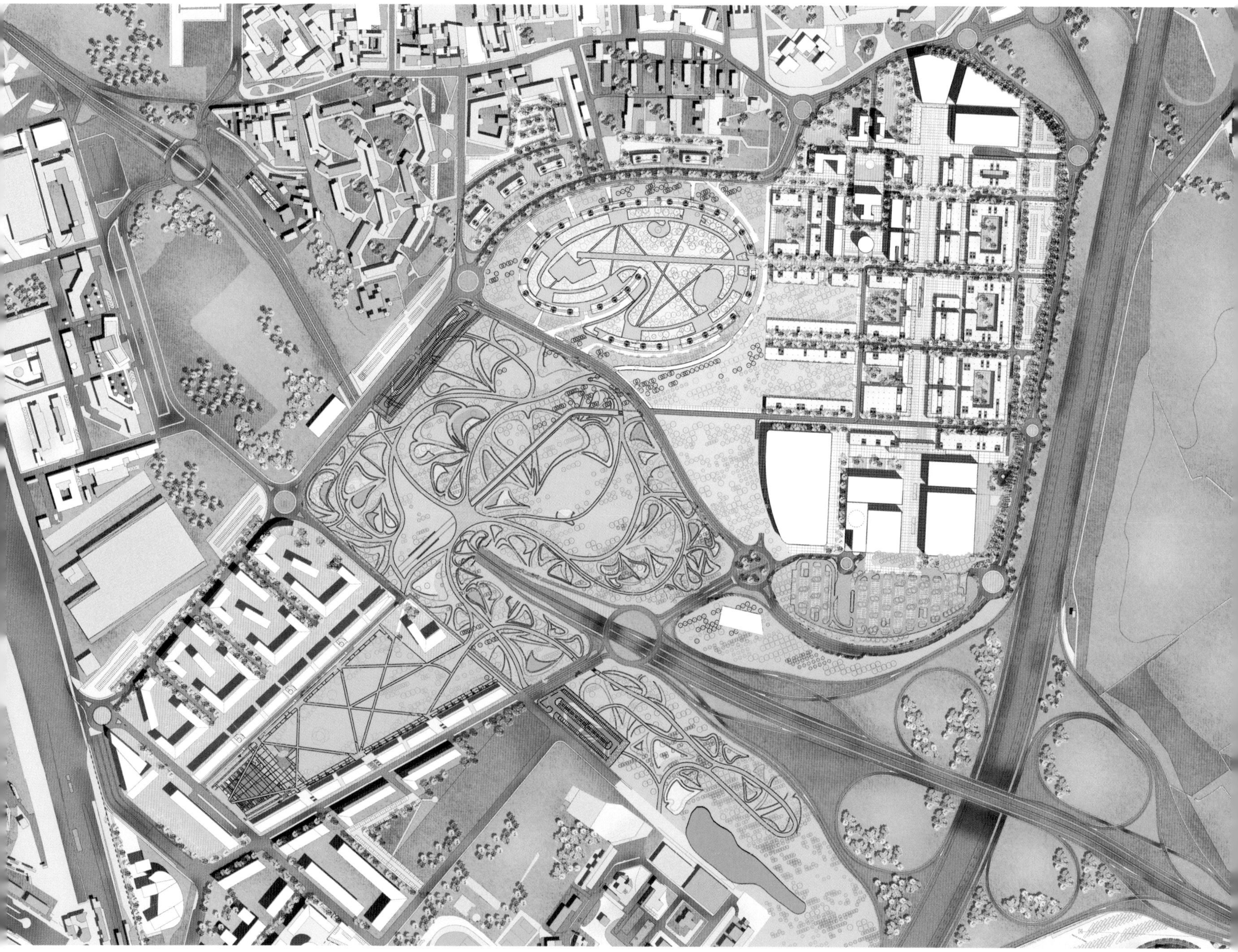

4

1–3: Situation, site
4: Master plan

5

6

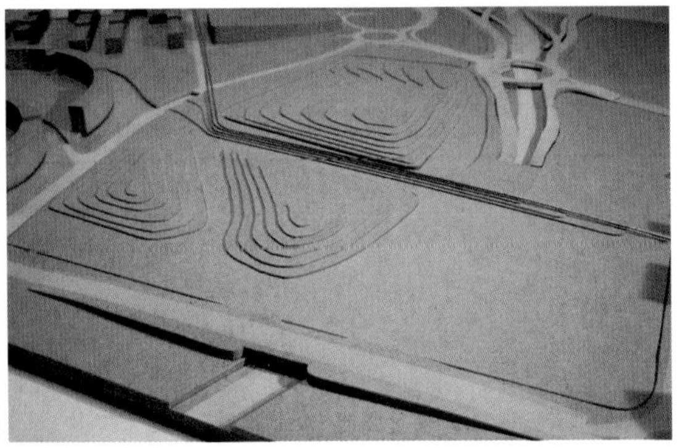

7

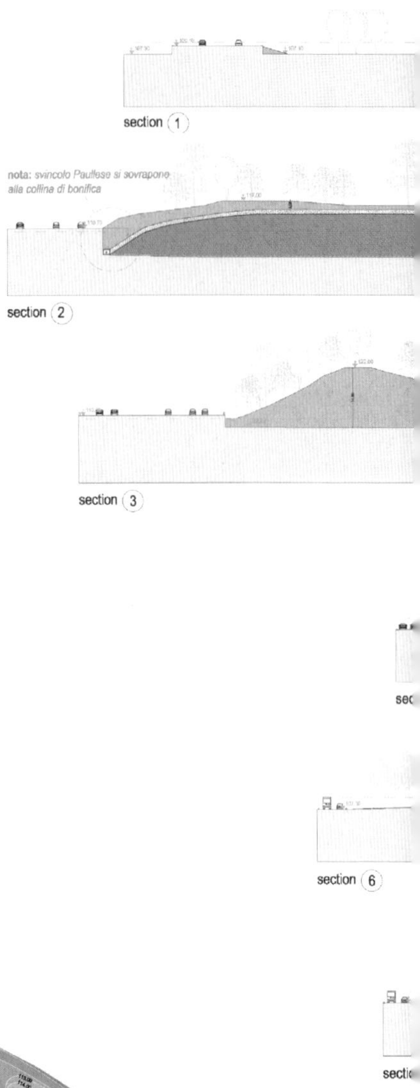

5: Hill, contaminated soil
6: Foil covering
7: Poison hills, models
8: New topography, 3D visual
9: New topography, sections
10–11: Models

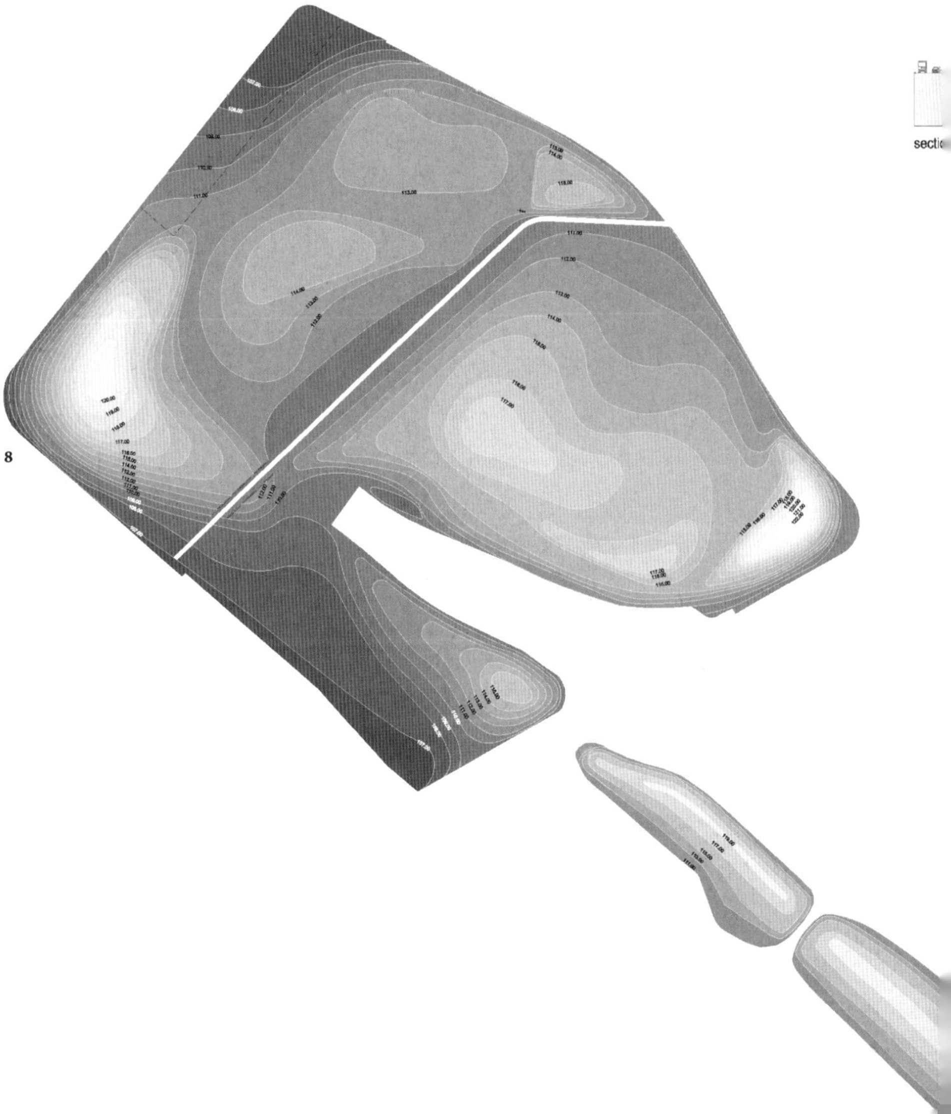

8

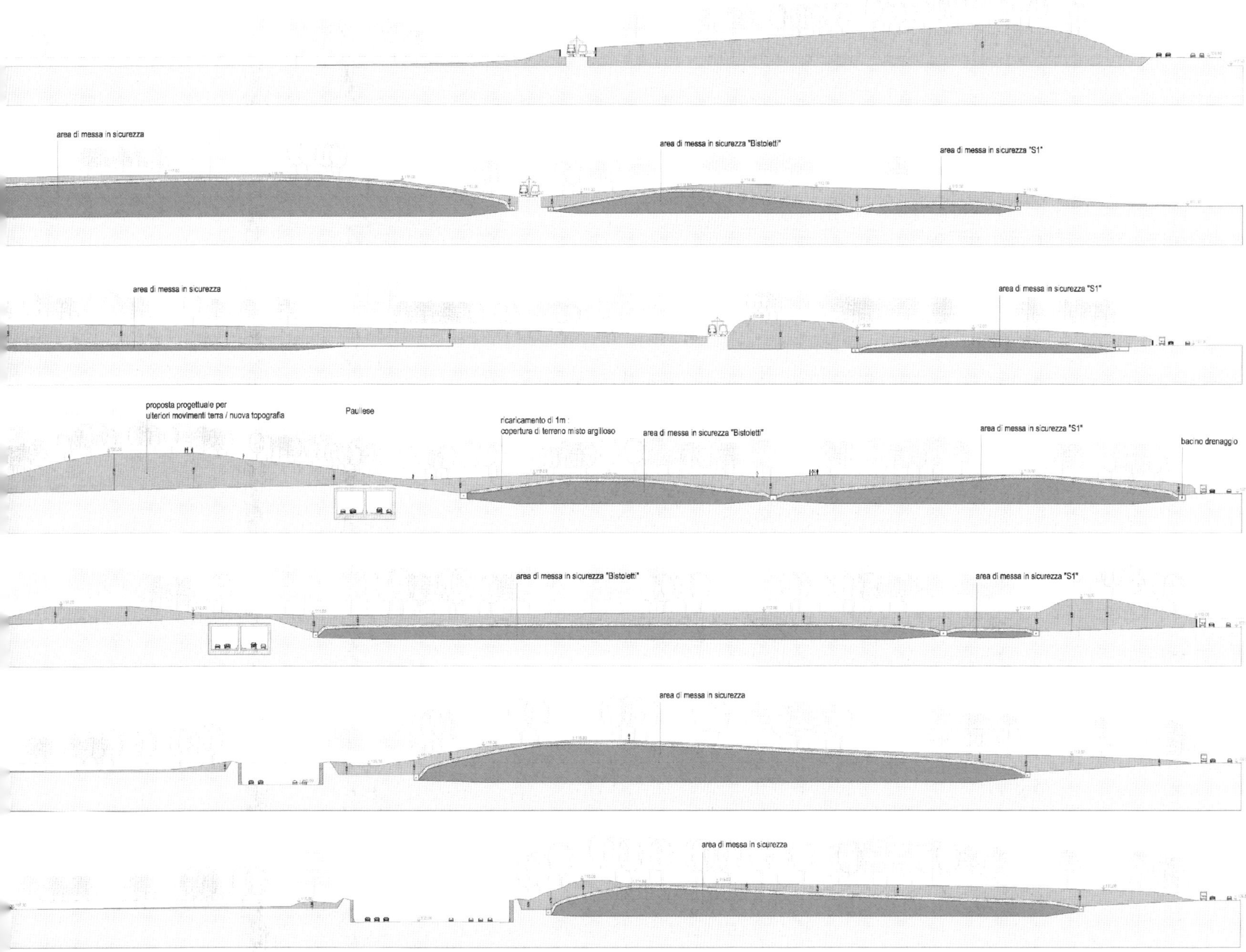

area di messa in sicurezza
area di messa in sicurezza "Bistoletti"
area di messa in sicurezza "S1"
area di messa in sicurezza
area di messa in sicurezza "S1"
proposta progettuale per
ulteriori movimenti terra / nuova topografia
Paullese
ricaricamento di 1m
copertura di terreno misto argilloso
area di messa in sicurezza "Bistoletti"
area di messa in sicurezza "S1"
bacino drenaggio
area di messa in sicurezza "Bistoletti"
area di messa in sicurezza "S1"
area di messa in sicurezza
area di messa in sicurezza

on 8

9

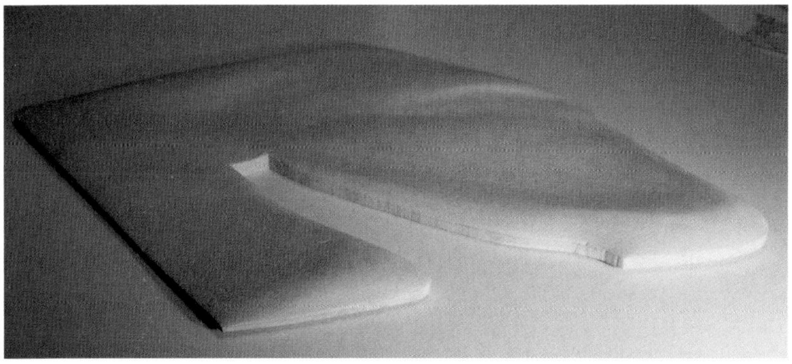

10

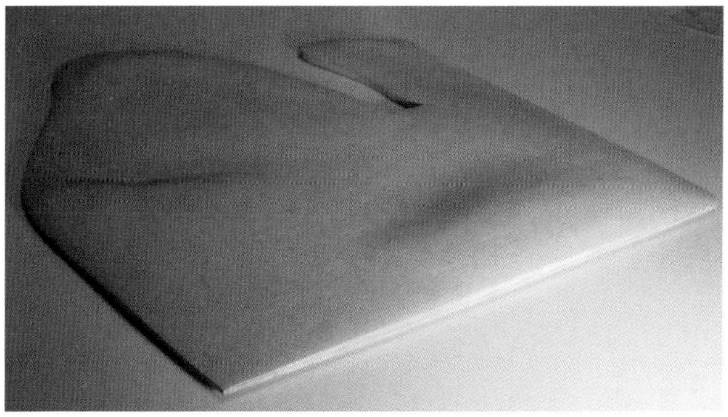

11

12: Hearts and broken hearts
13: Floor of Milan Duomo
14: Model, park
15: Model, detail

12

13

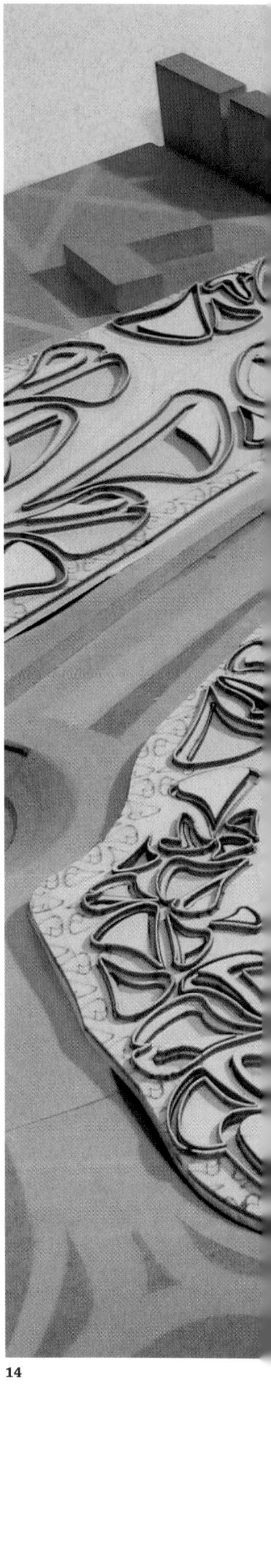
14

15

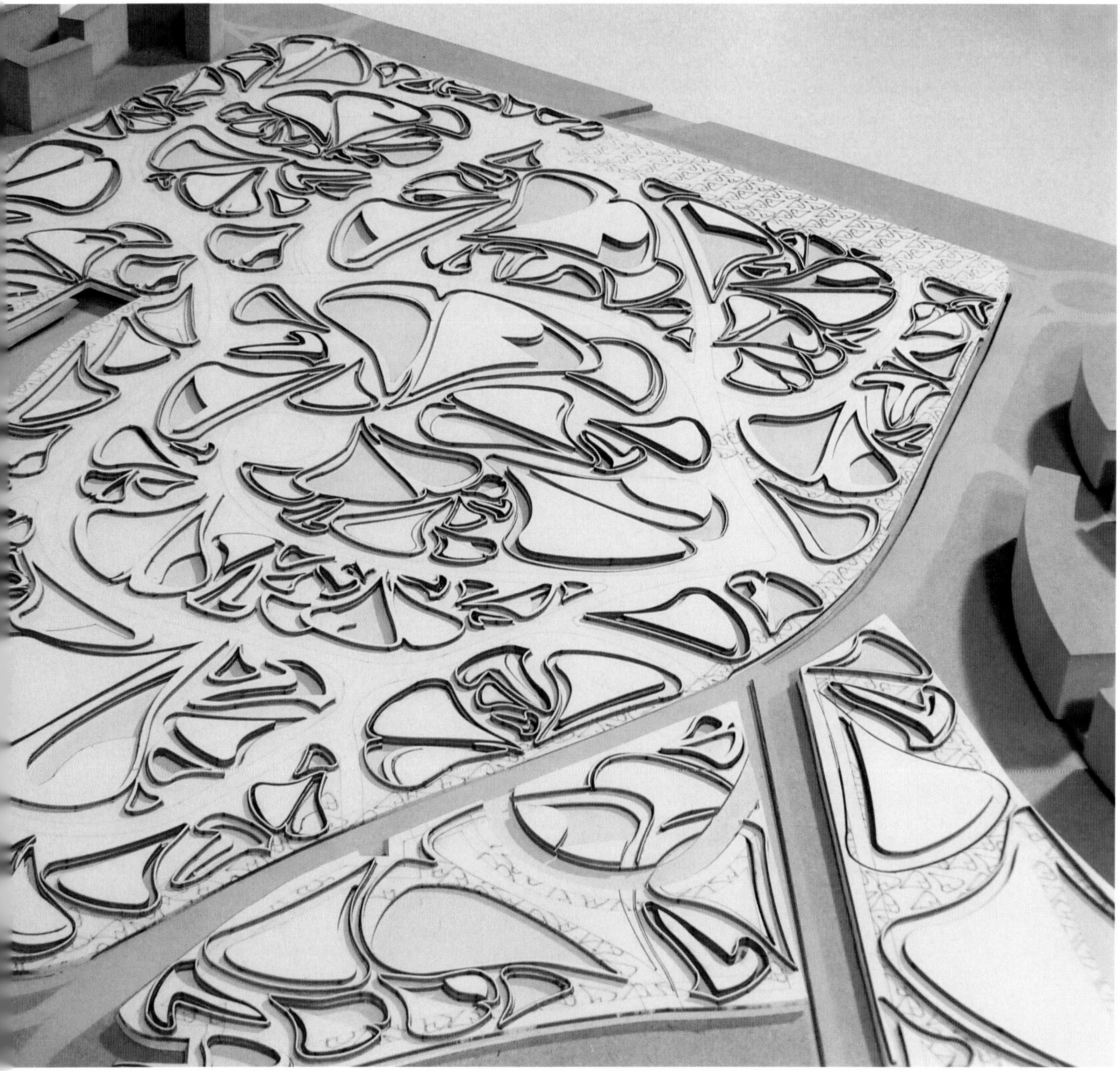

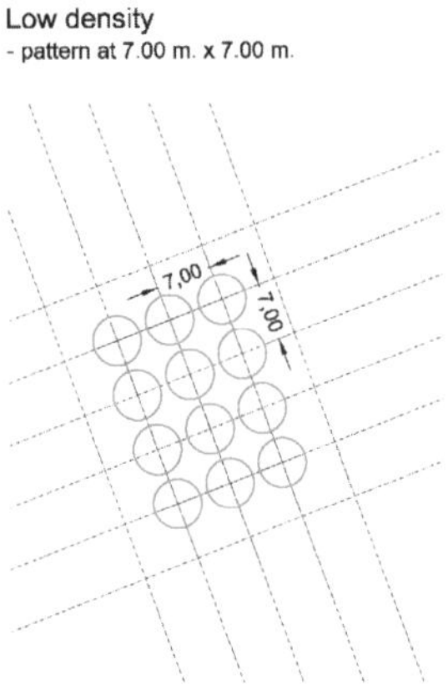

16a

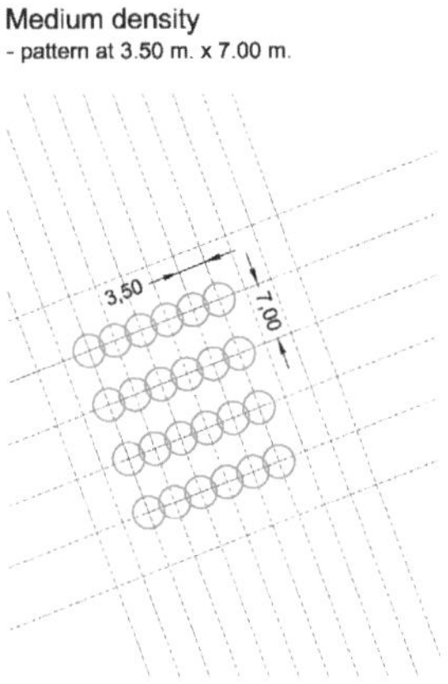

b

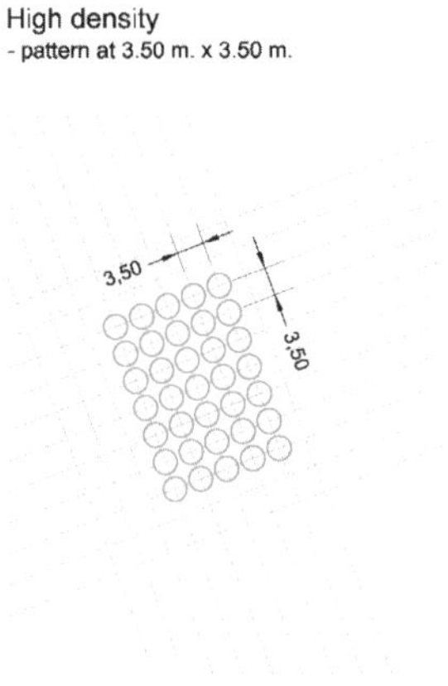

c

PLANTING

16a–c: Planting scheme
17: Lombard trees
18: Tree grid
19–20: Artist's impressions

17

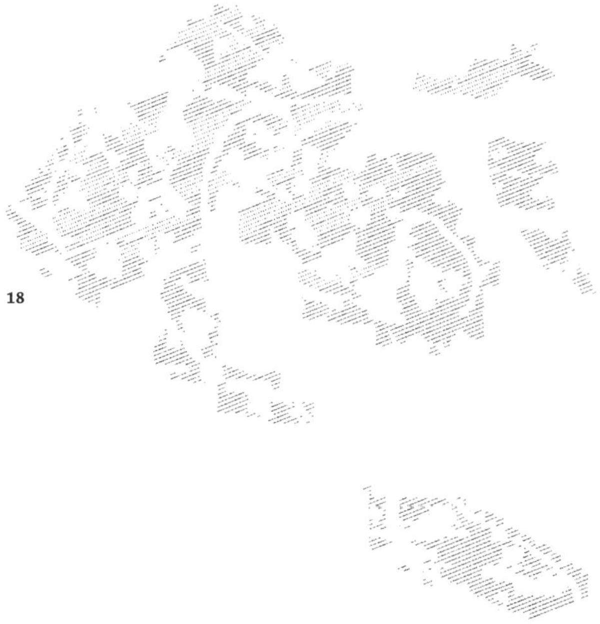

18

19

20

21: Tree plan
22: Gardens and fields

21

22

23

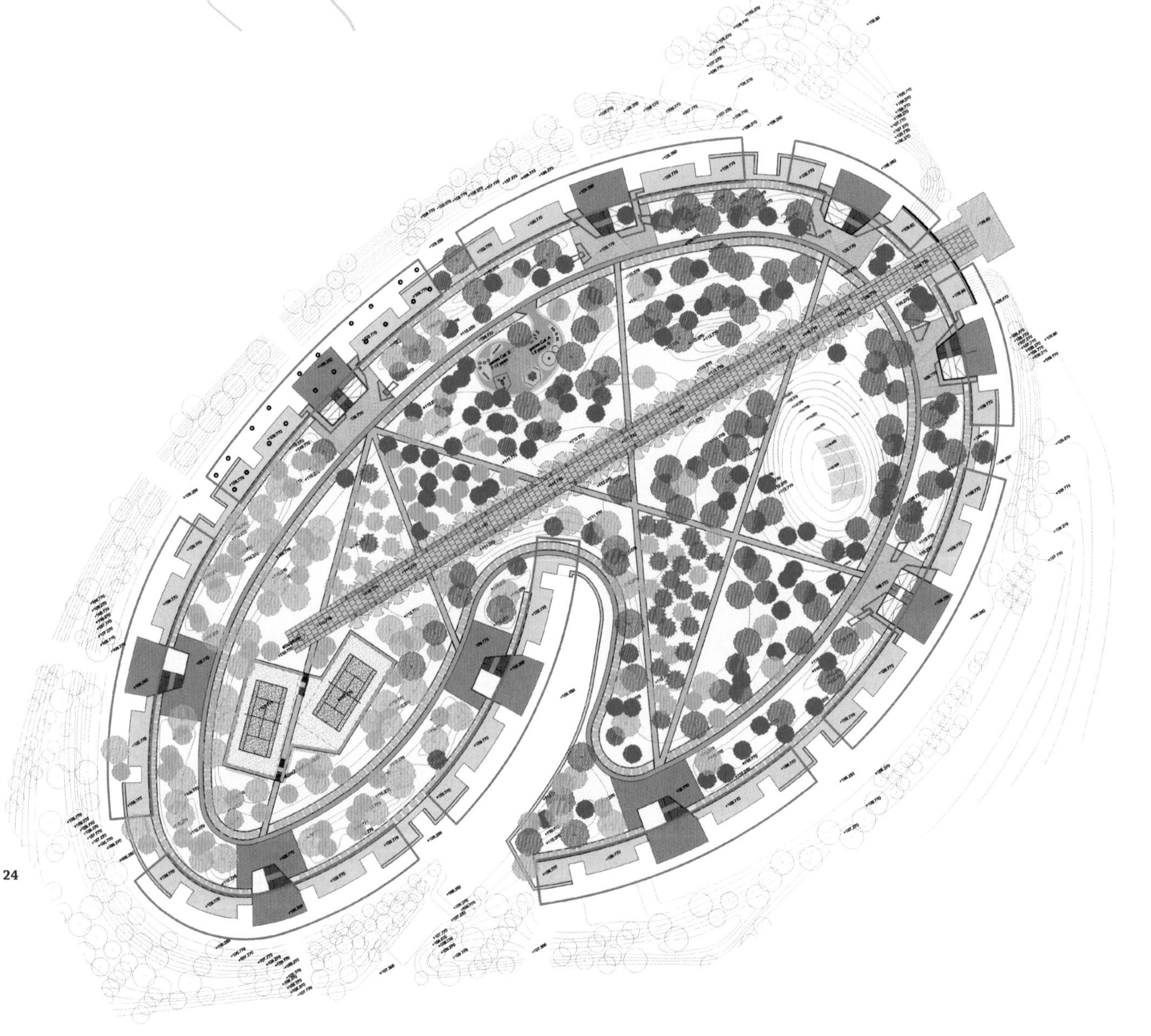

24

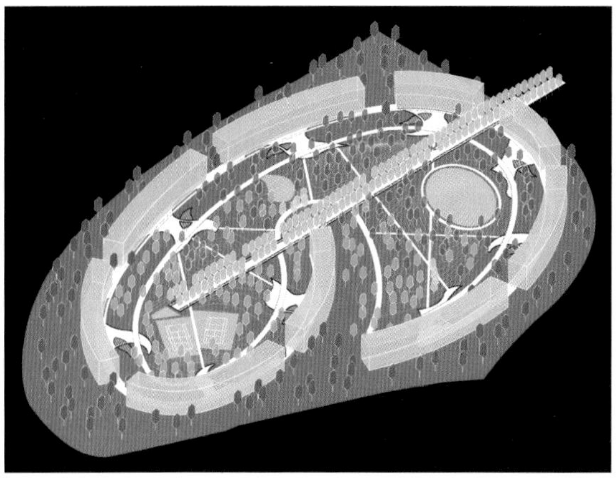
25

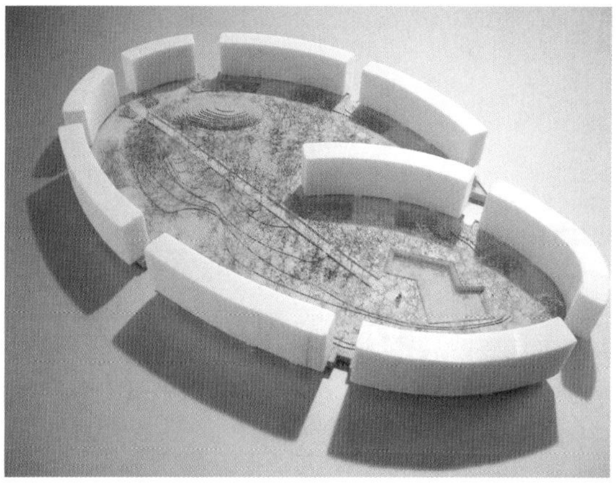
26

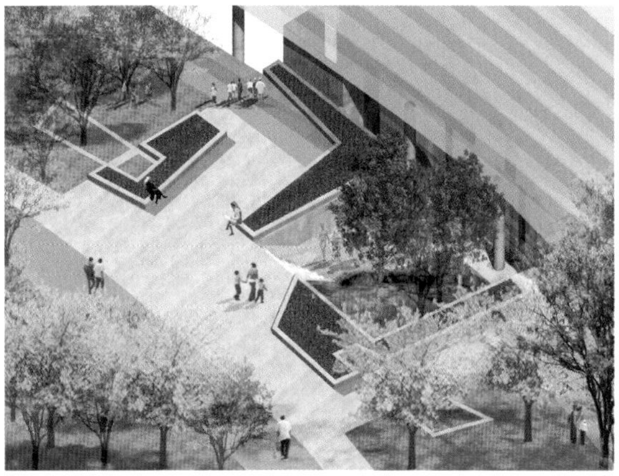
27

28

OVAL GARDEN

23: Routeing, diagram
24: Master plan
25: Conceptual drawing
26: Model
27–28: Artist's impressions

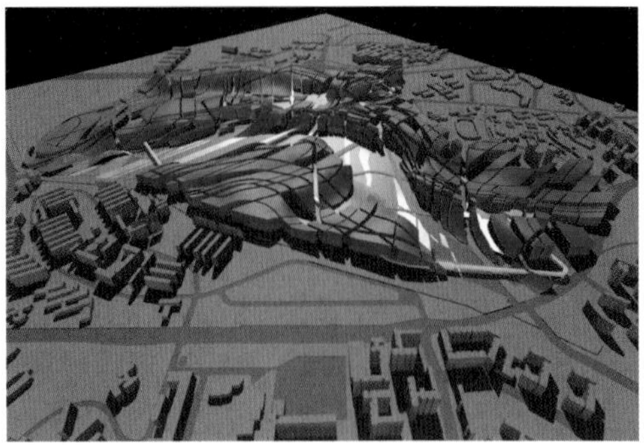

1

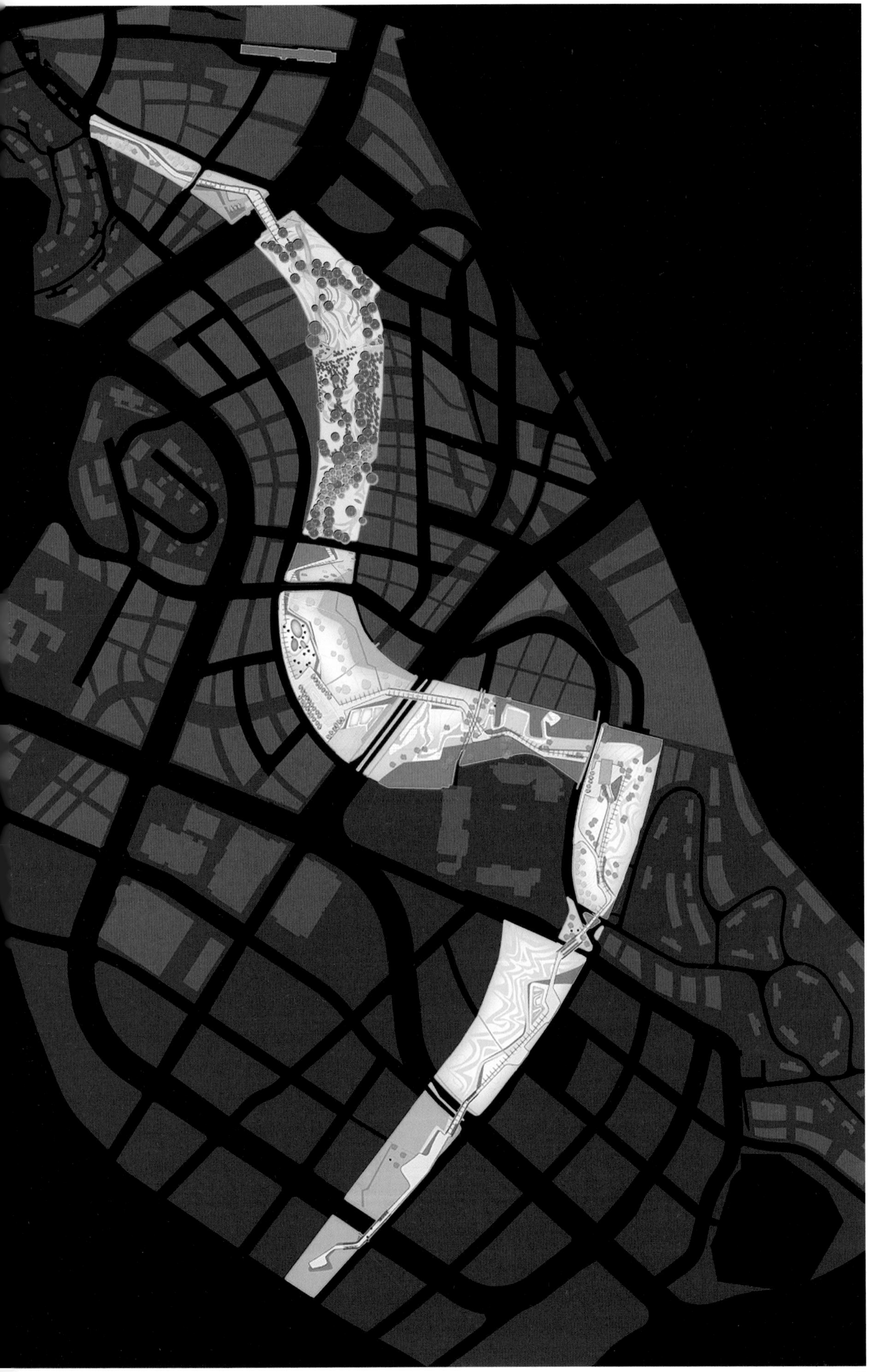

2

1: Urban plan, Zaha Hadid
2: Master plan park
3: Longitudinal section
4: Artist's impression
5: Sansevierias

3

5

ONE NORTH PARK

SINGAPORE

Zaha Hadid's master plan defines a long, meandering open space in the new suburb of Buona Vista. For this area, West 8 created a park design, the first part of which has been completed. The park, with its dramatic topography and exciting sight-lines, provides a shady place for a leisurely stroll. It contains a large collection of tropical plants and trees. The climax is formed by a remarkable water attraction: a stream that flows uphill.

4

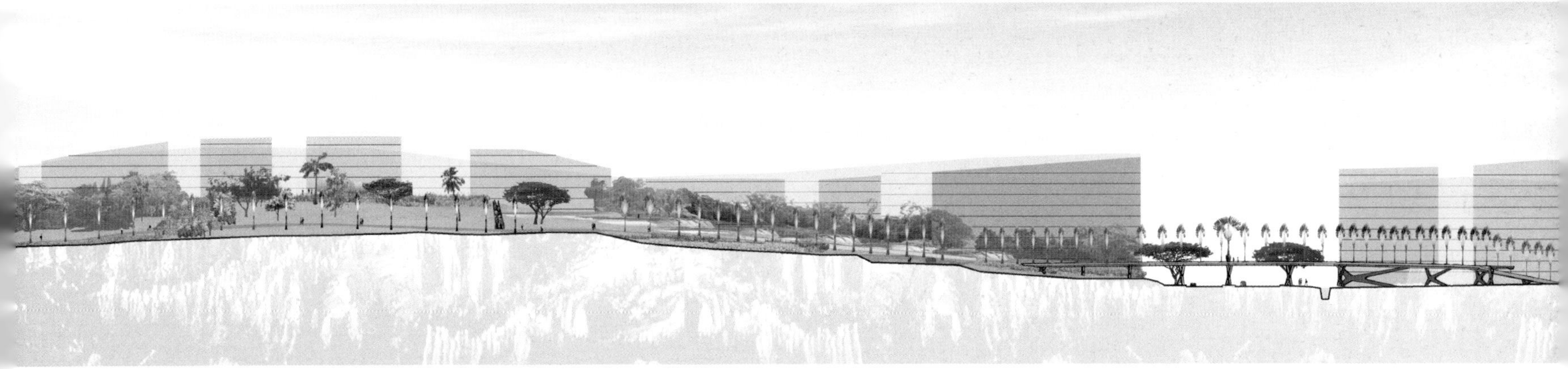

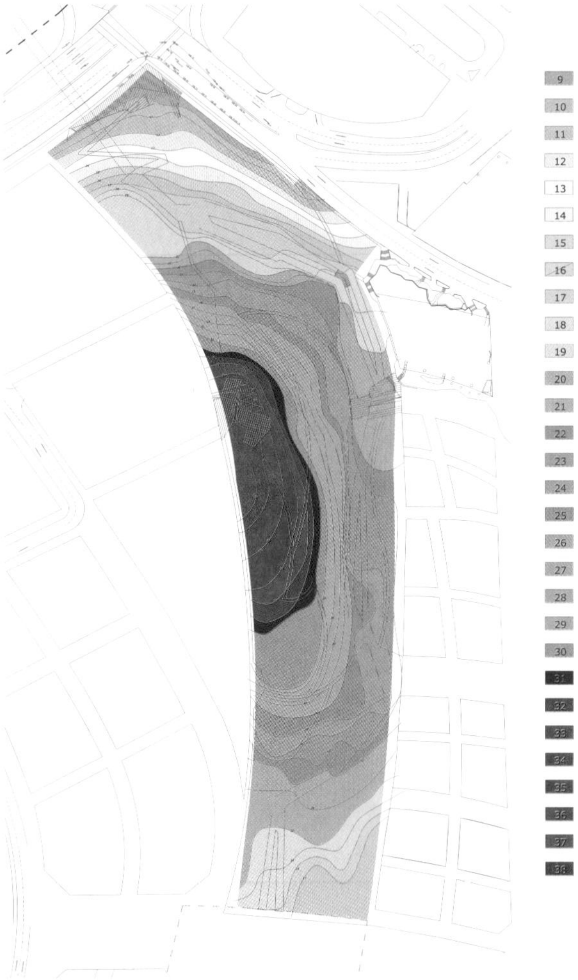

6

7

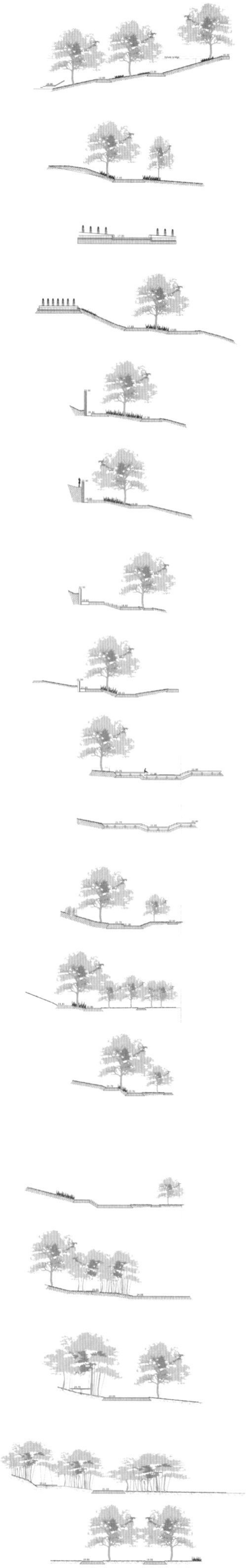

8

9

6: Height lines
7: Study model
8: Cross-sections promenade
9–12: Promenade

10

11

12

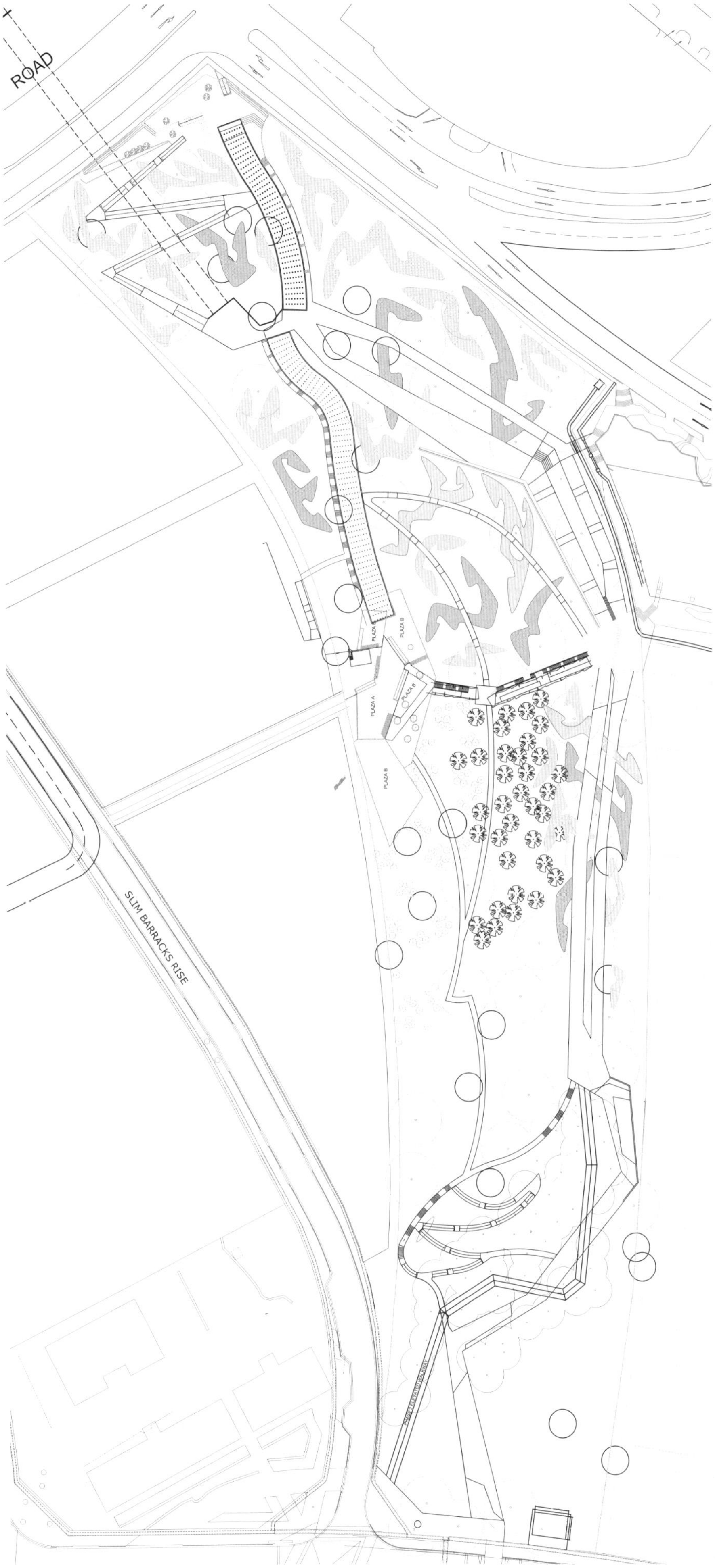

13

14

15

16

17

18

19

BOTANY

13: Vegetation plan
14–18: Types of plants
19: Colour check
20: Sansevierias
21: Planters resting
22: Pattern sketches

20

22

21

23

24

25

26

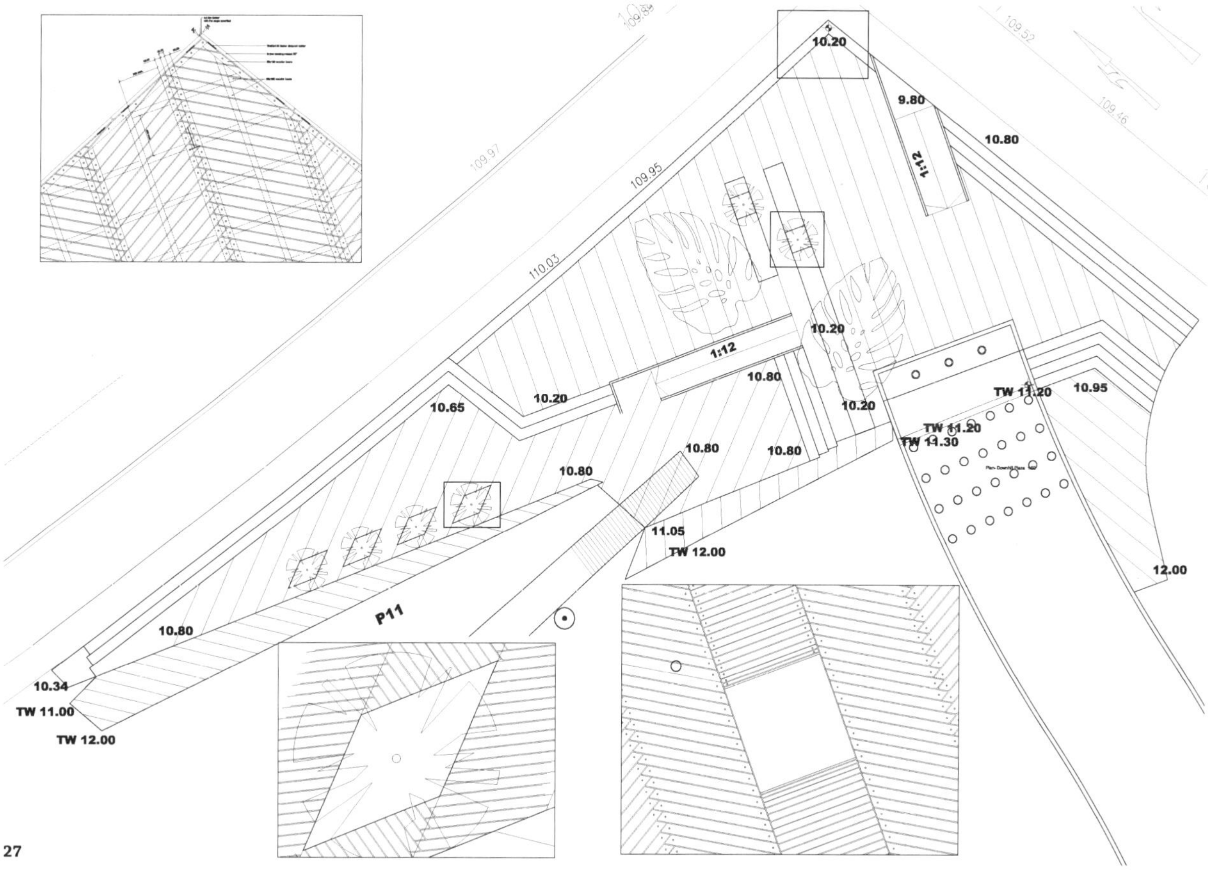

27

28

29

30

ENTRANCES

23–26: Eastern entrance to square

27: Northern entrance, plan

28–30: Northern entrance

31

32

33

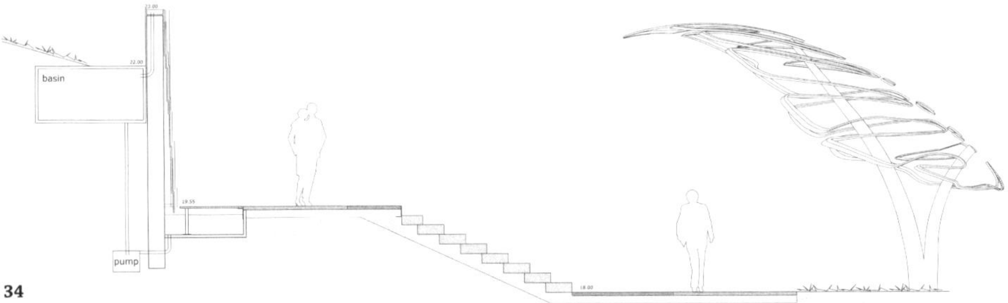

34

WATER WALL

31: Sansevierias with water wall
32–33, 35: By night
34: Technical section
36: Catchment basin
37: Spotlight

36

35

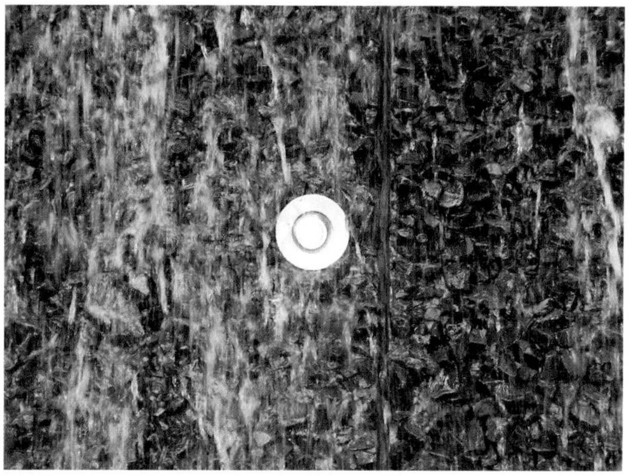

37

38

39

40

41

SHELTERS

38: Artist's impression

39–40: Production prototype

41: Computer sketch

42

43

44

42–44: Park bench
45–48: Installation first prototype shelters

45

46

47

48

JUBILEE GARDENS

LONDON, ENGLAND

Jubilee Gardens lies in the middle of the cultural South Bank district, just under the London Eye. In 1995, West 8 won a competition for the design of the 1.2-hectare city park. West 8 introduced the idea of an undulating landscape with white cliffs. Polyester-concrete panels and strips were fabricated specially for this design. The park's micro-topography offers incomparable panoramas of the London skyline and the Thames.

1

+

2

1: Wimbledon grass
2: White cliffs
3: Elevations
4: London Eye: view over Houses of Parliament
5: London Eye: view of site

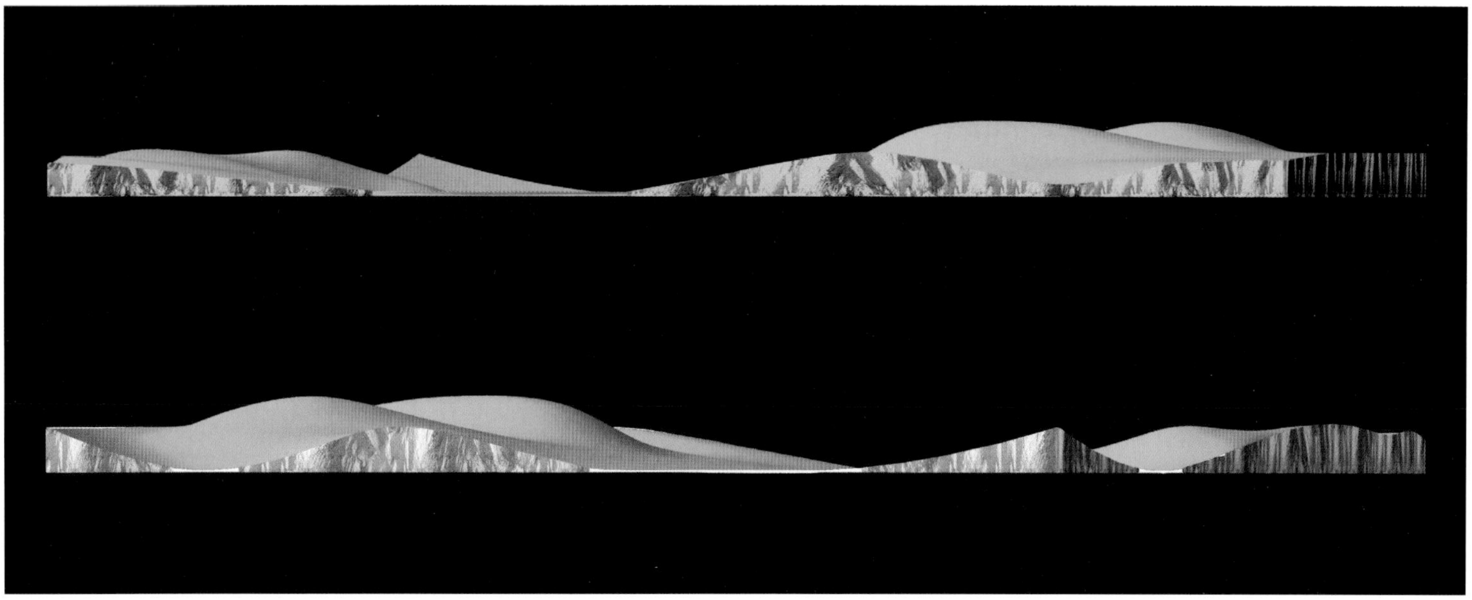
3

4

5

6

7

8

DESIGN SKETCH 1995

6: Artist's impression
7: Queen's Walk
8: View from the Embankment
9: Sequence of parks in Central London
10: Vantage points providing views of the Thames
11: Photo montage: context Queen's Walk

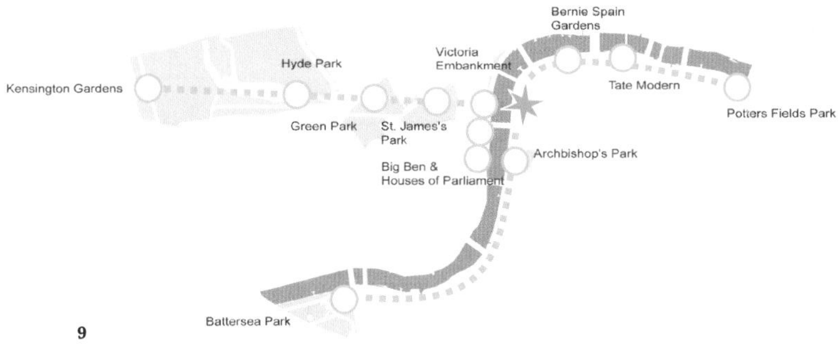
Kensington Gardens
Hyde Park
Green Park
St. James's Park
Victoria Embankment
Bernie Spain Gardens
Tate Modern
Potters Fields Park
Big Ben & Houses of Parliament
Archbishop's Park
Battersea Park

9

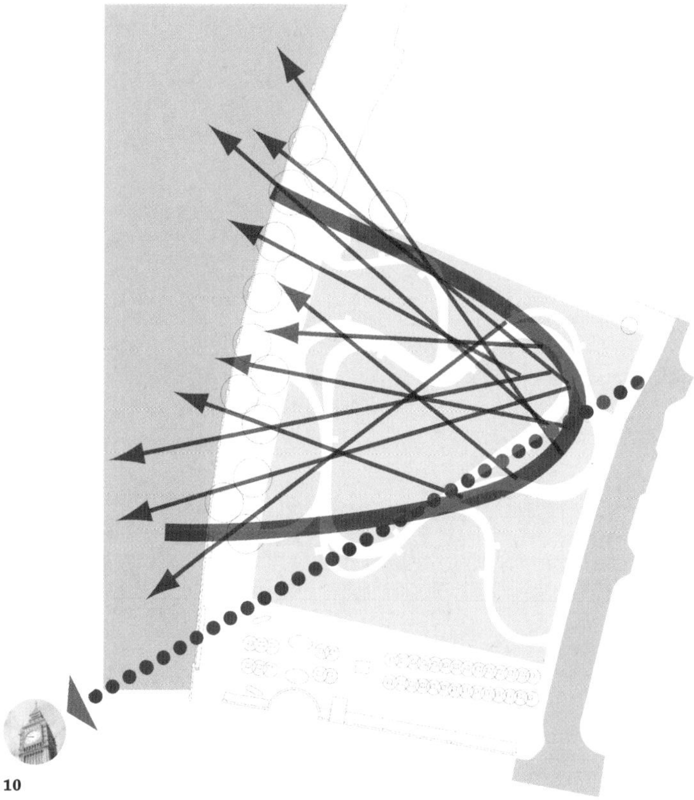

10

11

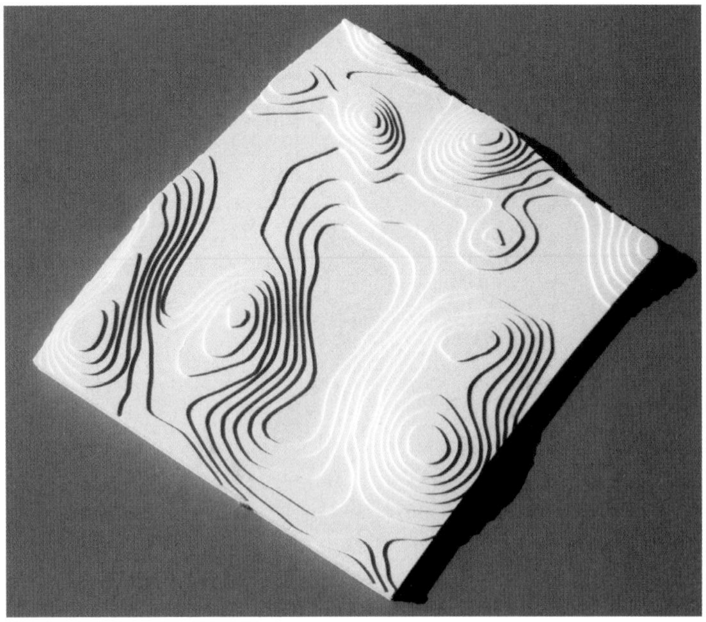

12

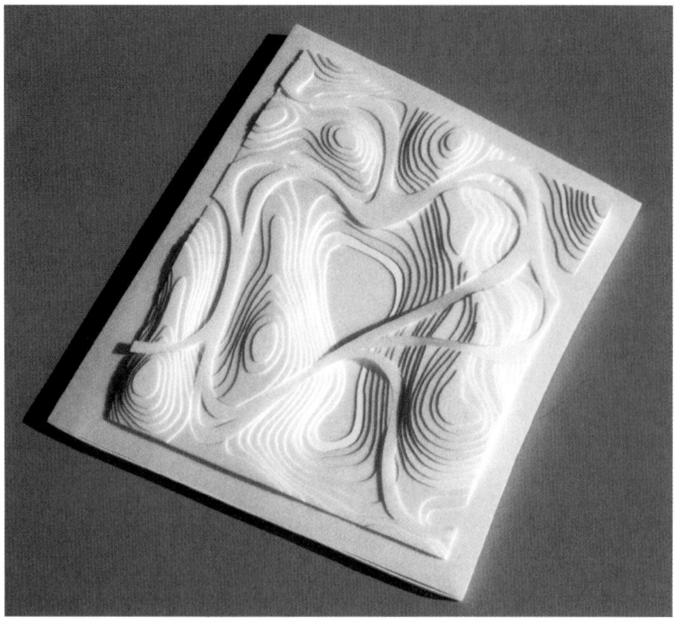

13

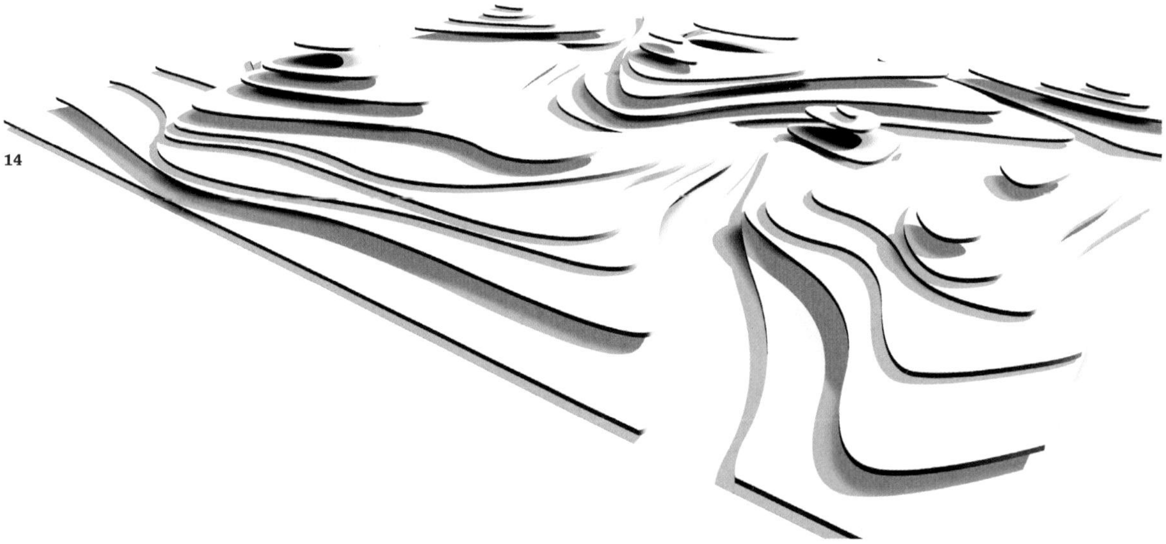

14

TOPOGRAPHY

12–17: Research, models

15

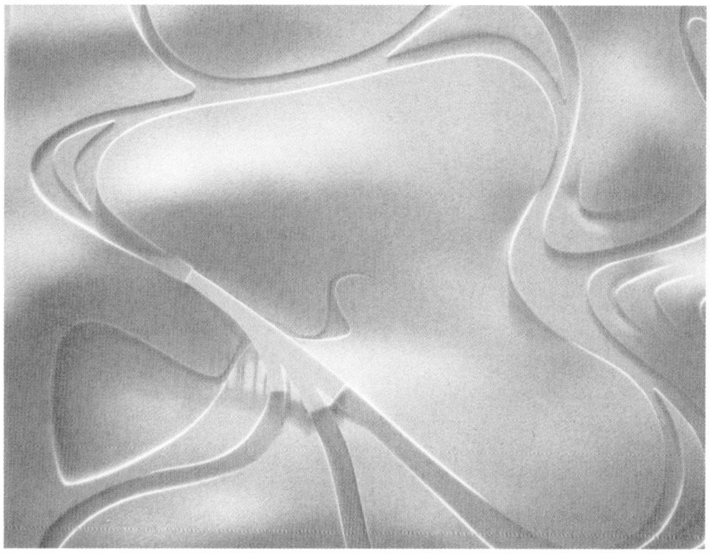

16

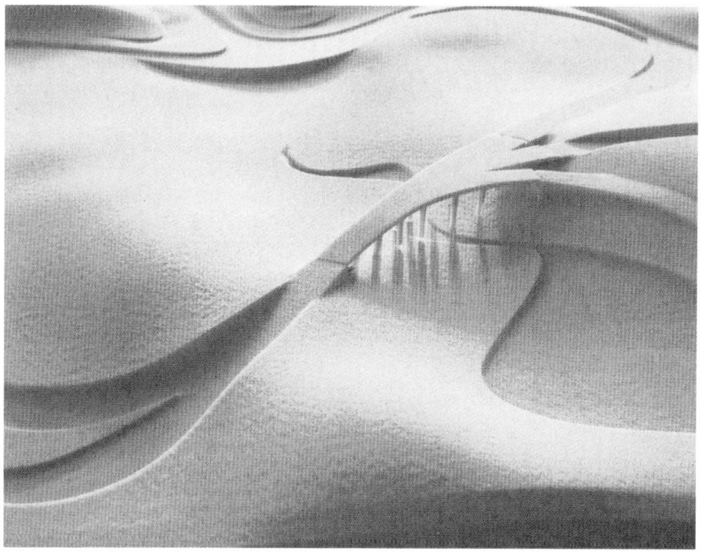

17

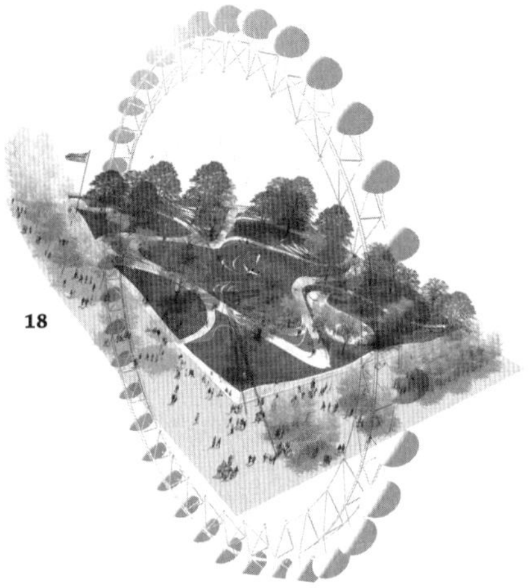

18

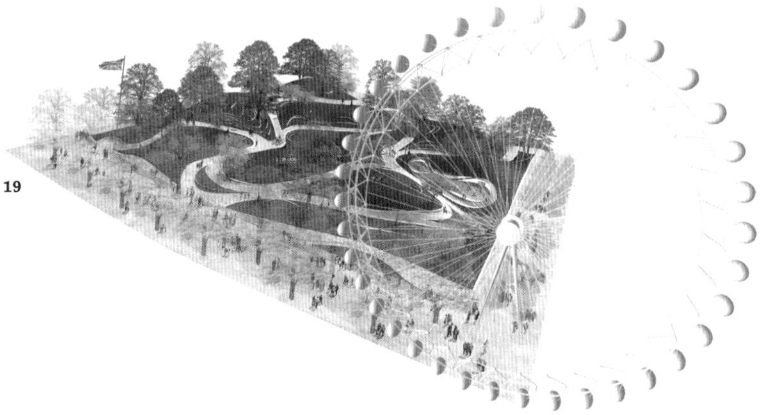

19

18–22: Definitive design, various viewpoints

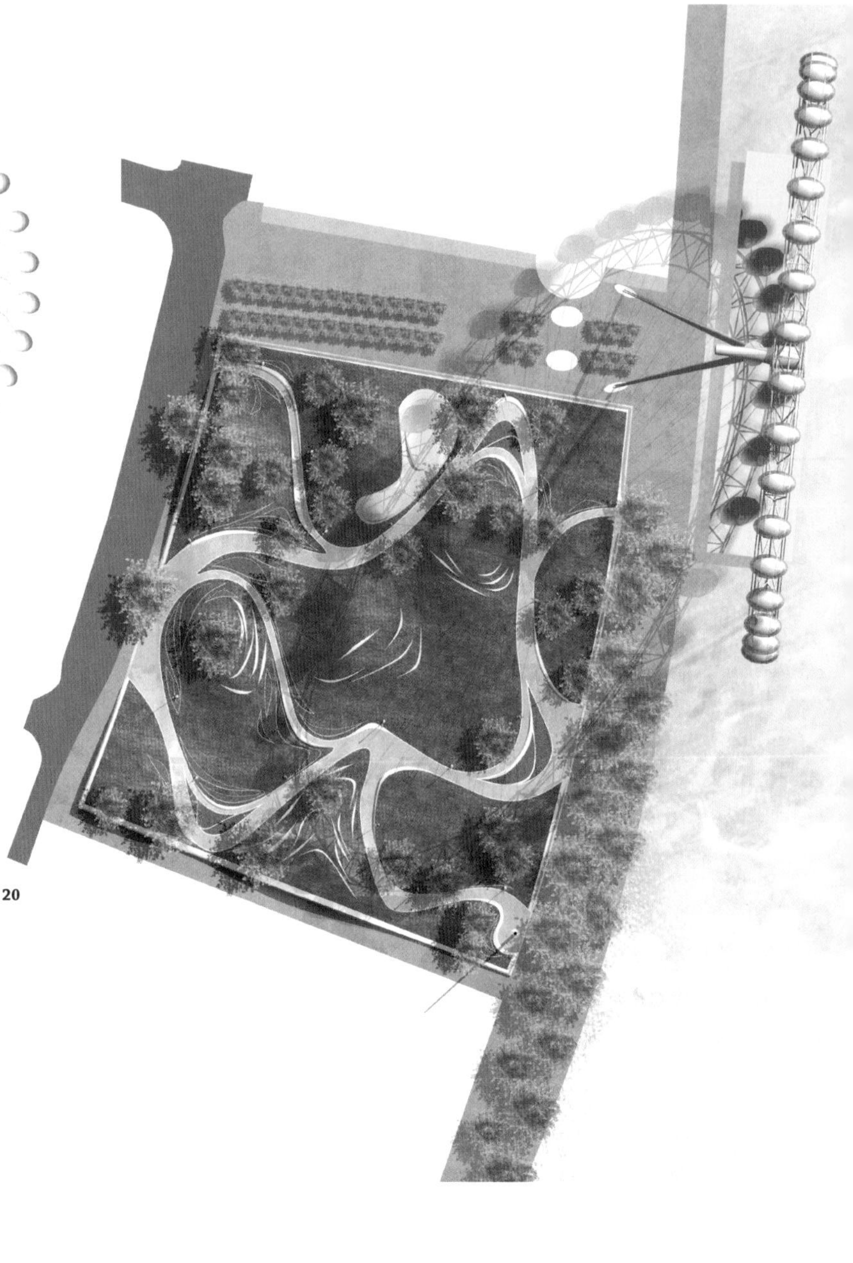

20

22

21

23

24

25

26

23: Elevations
24: Interior
25: Night
26: Queen's Walk in winter

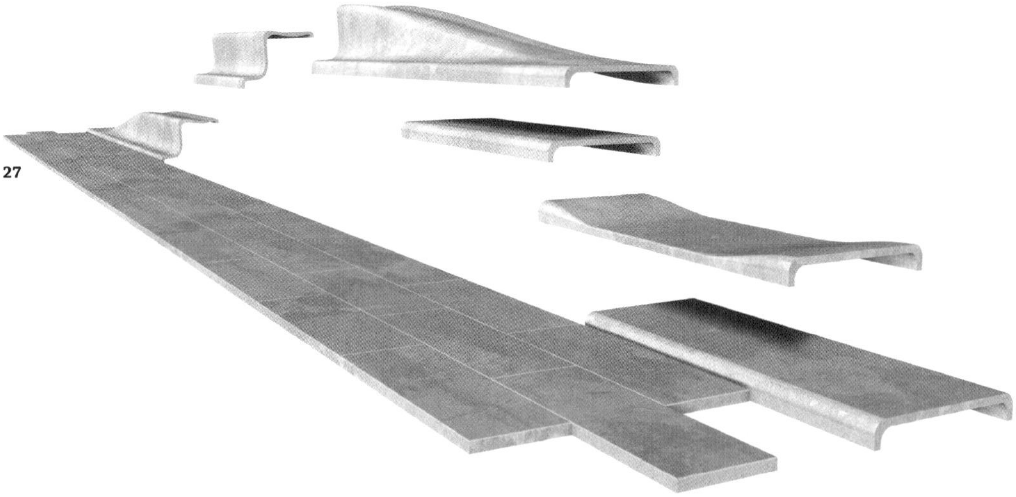

27

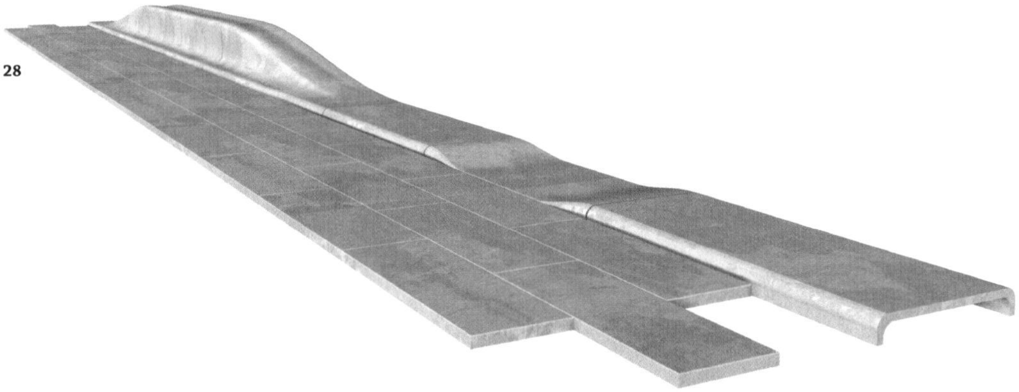

28

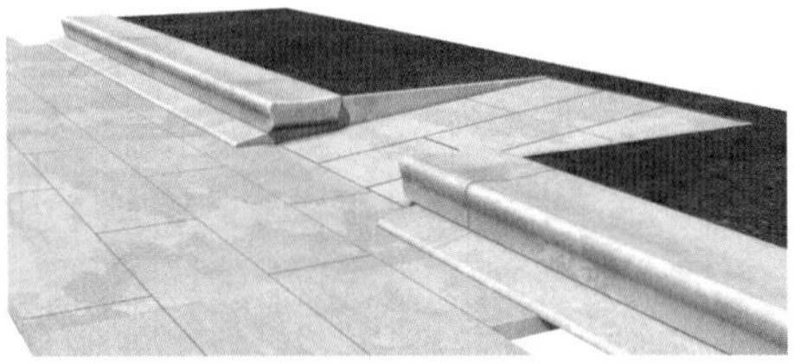

29

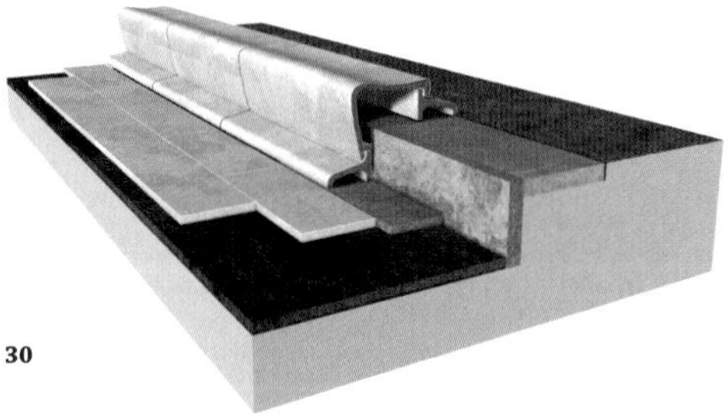

30

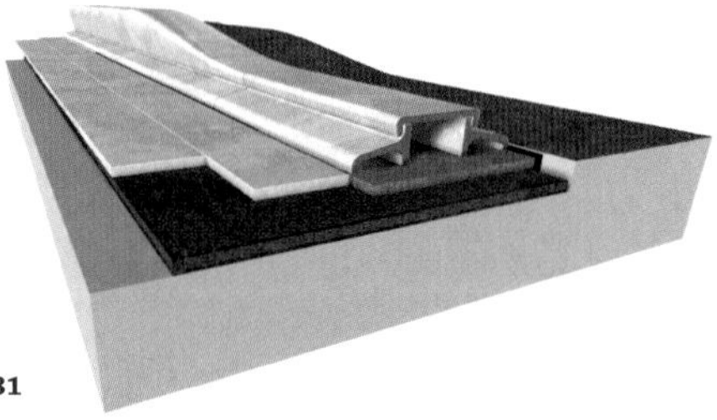

31

27–34: Curbs, made from catalogue of polyester-concrete elements

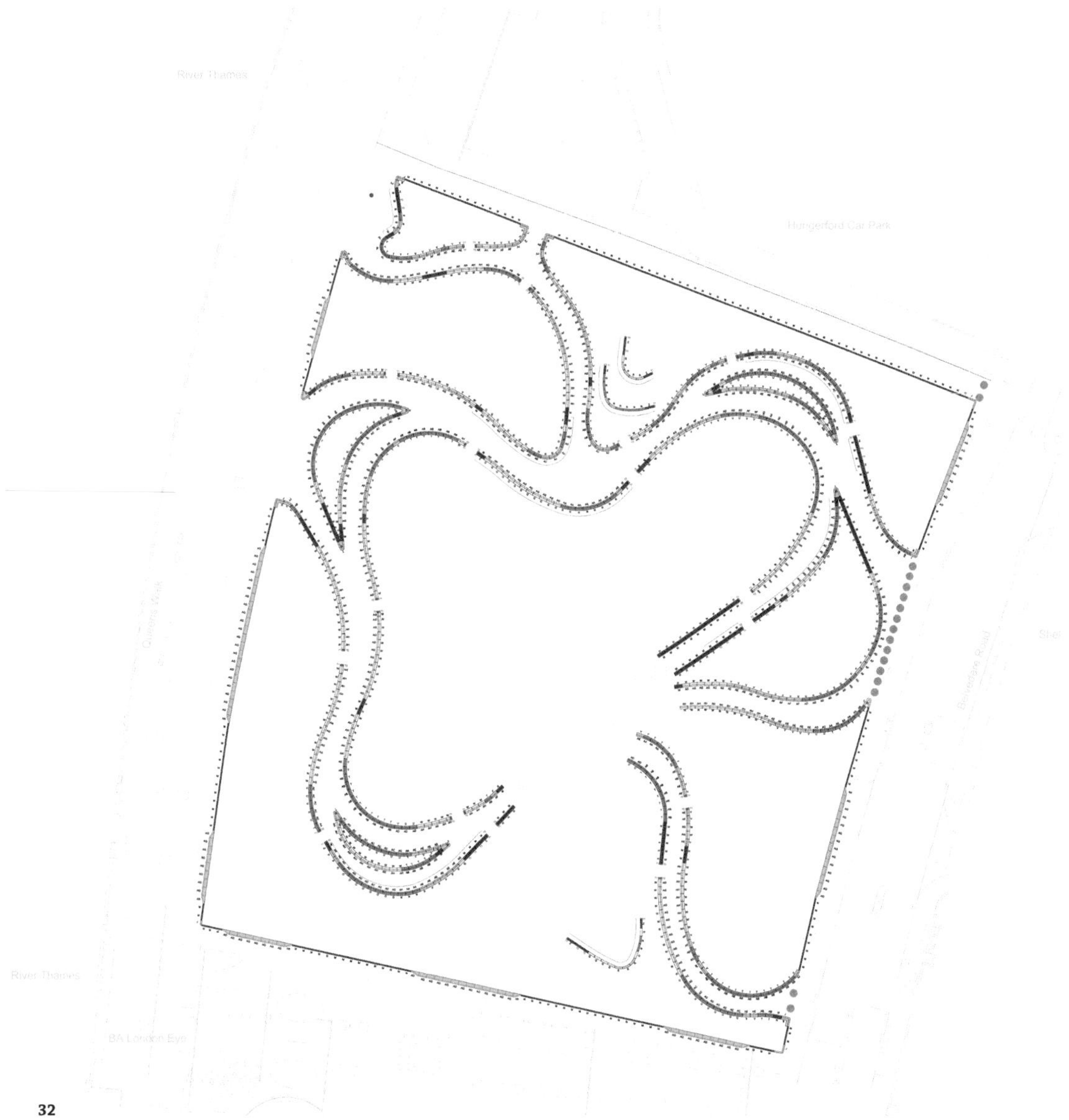
River Thames
Hungerford Car Park
River Thames
BA London Eye

32

33

1. N 2. Ri10,68; Ro11,17 3. 21 pcs.
1. O 2. Ri14,33; Ro14,83 3. 33 pcs.
1. T 2. Ri10,68; Ro11,17 3. 107 pcs.
1. U 2. Ri14,33; Ro14,83 3. 120 pcs.
1. AA 2. Ri10,68; Ro10,68 3. 31 pcs.
1. AC 2. Ri14,13; Ro14,33 3. 82 pcs.
1. AB 2. Ri11,17; Ro11,38 3. 90 pcs.
1. AD 2. Ri14,83; Ro15,04 3. 74 pcs.
1. P 2. Ri25,18; Ro25,72 3. 13 pcs.
1. Q 2. Ri36,51; Ro37,05 3. 36 pcs.
1. V 2. Ri25,18; Ro25,72 3. 105 pcs.
1. W 2. Ri36,51; Ro37,05 3. 195 pcs.
1. AE 2. Ri25,18; Ro24,95 3. 72 pcs.
1. AG 2. Ri36,28; Ro36,51 3. 97 pcs.
1. AF 2. Ri25,72; Ro15,04 3. 45 pcs.
1. AH 2. Ri37,05; Ro37,27 3. 128 pcs.
1. R 2. Ri2,56; Ro3,05 3. 14 pcs.
1. X 2. Ri2,56; Ro3,05 3. 10 pcs.
1. Y 2. Ri1,55; Ro2,03 3. 3 pcs.
1. AI 2. Ri2,36; Ro2,56 3. 3 pcs.
1. AJ 2. Ri3,05; Ro3,25 3. 12 pcs.
1. AL 2. Ri2,03; Ro2,24 3. 3 pcs.
1. H2 2. Ri0,00; Ro0,00 3. 16 pcs.
1. Z 2. Ri0,00; Ro0,00 3. 22 pcs.
1. H 2. Ri0,00; Ro0,00 3. 69 pcs.
1. M 2. Ri0,00; Ro0,00 3. 267 pcs.
1. B 2. - 3. 6 pcs.
1. C 2. - 3. 3 pcs.
1. J 2. - 3. 9 pcs.
1. K 2. - 3. 3 pcs.
1. D 2. - 3. 7 pcs.
1. I 2. Ri0,00; Ro0,00 3. 40 pcs.
1. L 2. - 3. 7 pcs.
1. I2 2. Ri0,00; Ro0,00 3. 34 pcs.
1. AO 2. - 3. 8 pcs.
1. AP 2. - 3. 8 pcs.
1. AQ 2. - 3. 8 pcs.
1. AR 2. - 3. 8 pcs.
1. AS 2. - 3. 8 pcs.

34

35

35–38: Studies for 'cliff face'
39–40: 'Cliff', made from catalogue of polyester-concrete elements
41–42: Samples of chalk texture

36

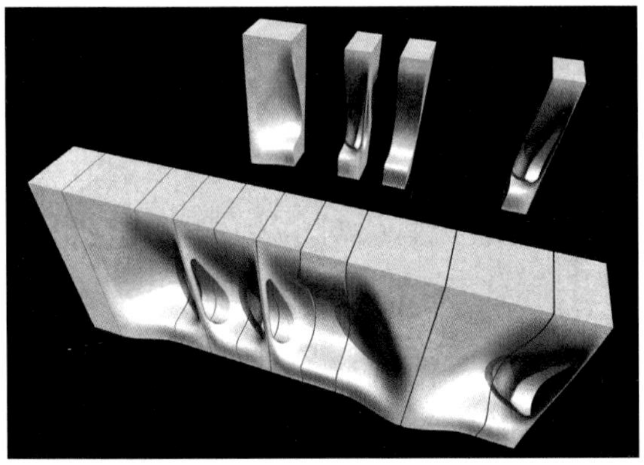

37

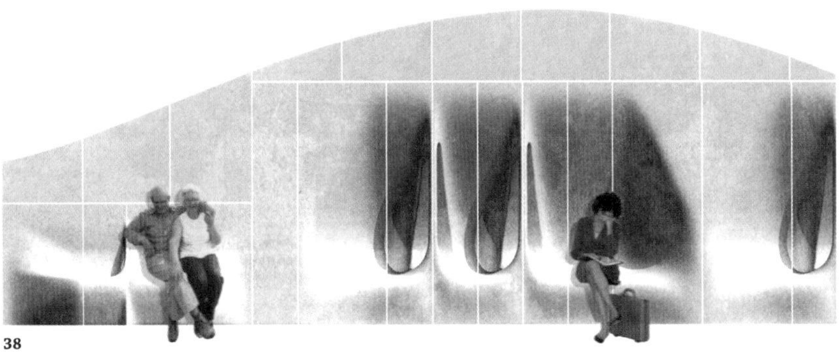

38

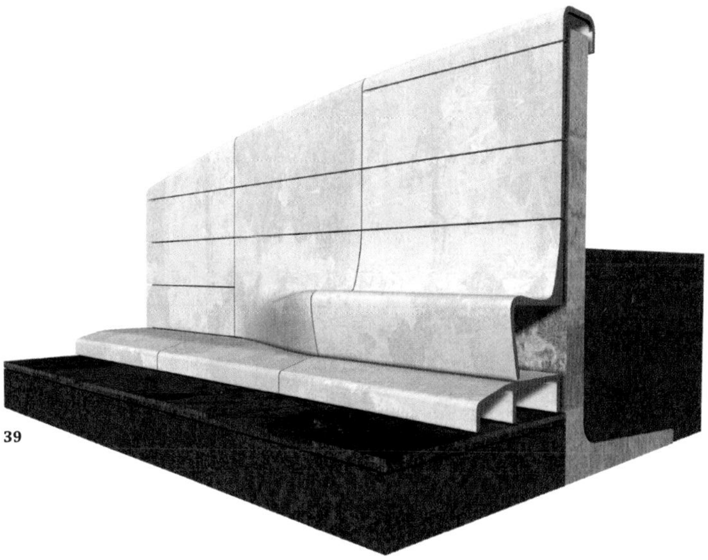
39

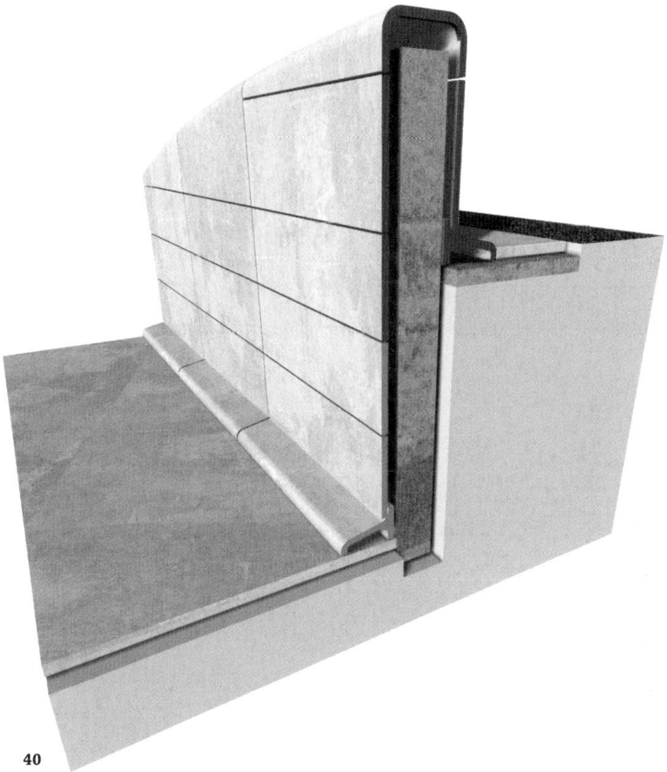
40

41

42

43

CLIFF BENCHES

43: Foam dummy
44–45: Production of prototype
46–47: Models

44

46

45

47

48

49

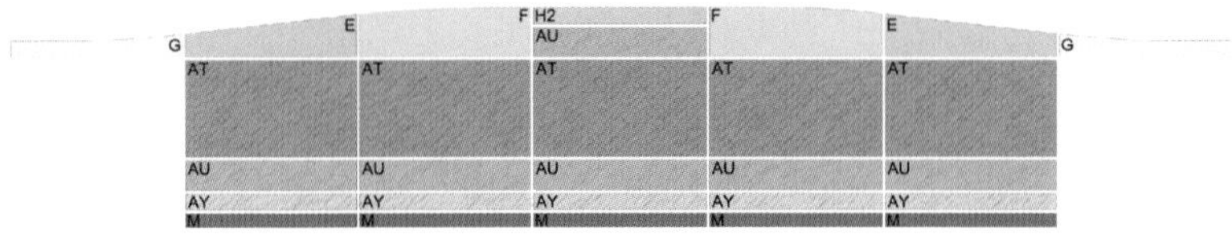

50

51

48–49, 51: First mock-up
50: Different panels

52

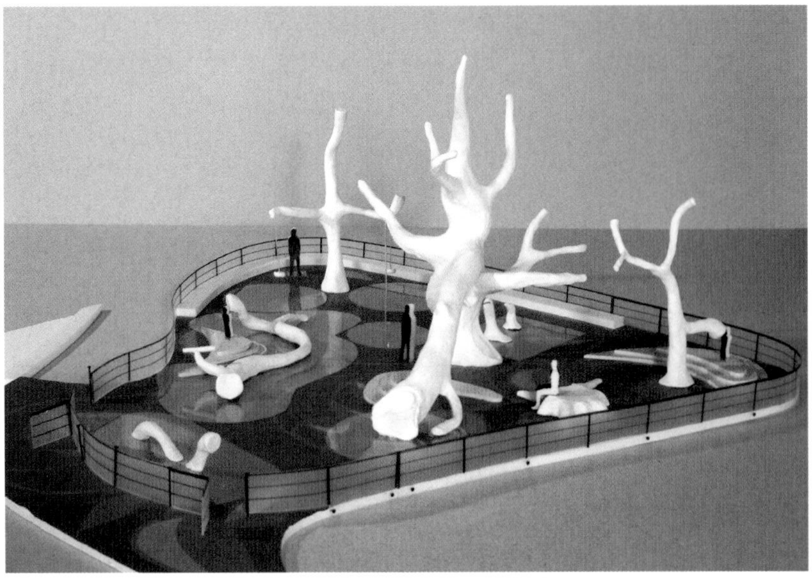
53

54

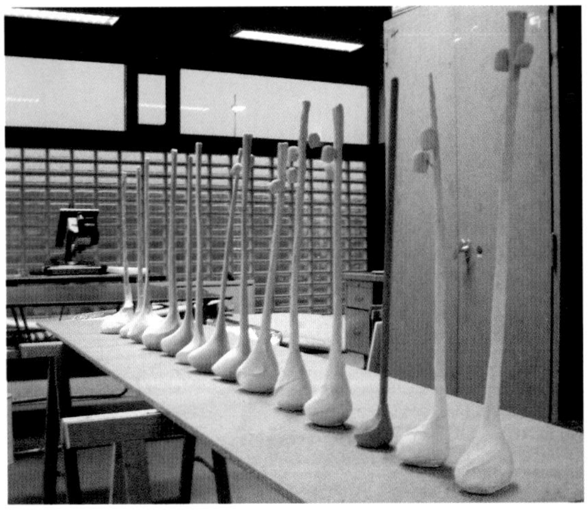
55

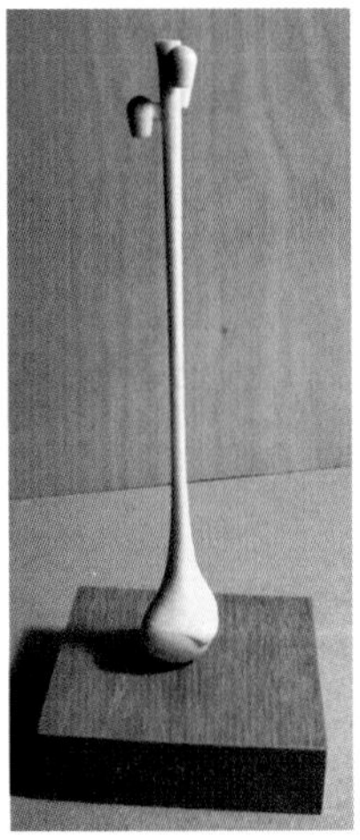
56

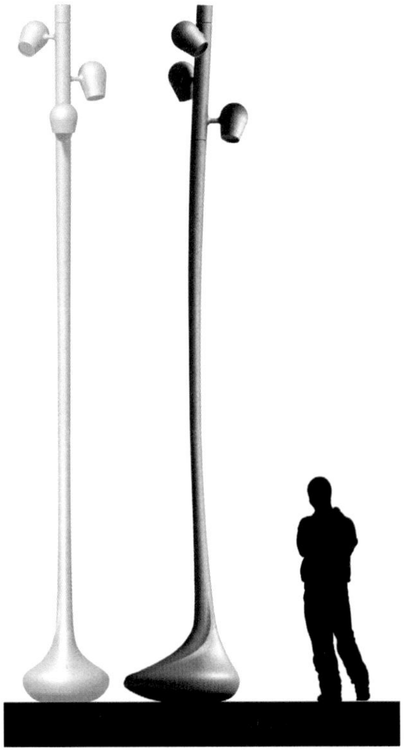
57

52: Last tree from Birnam Forest (Macbeth)
53–54: Magical forest playground

LIGHTING

55–56: Models
57: Design

58: Botanic scheme
59: Technical section

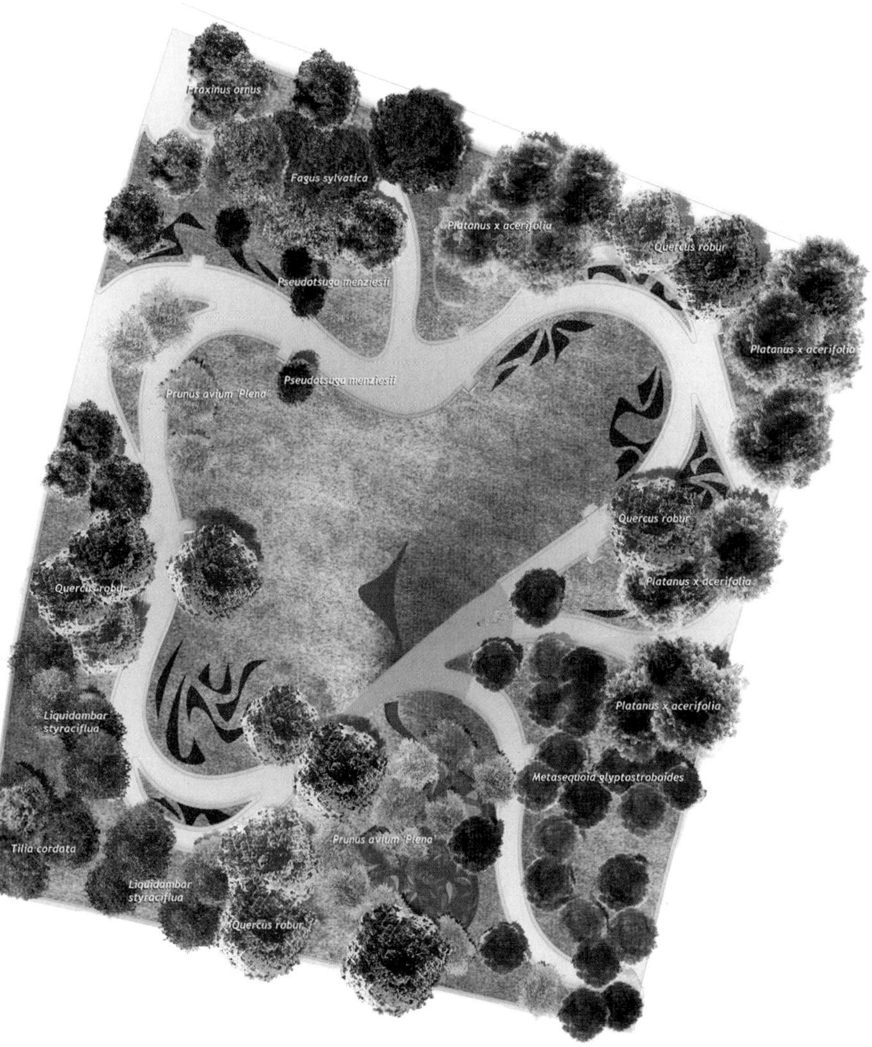

58

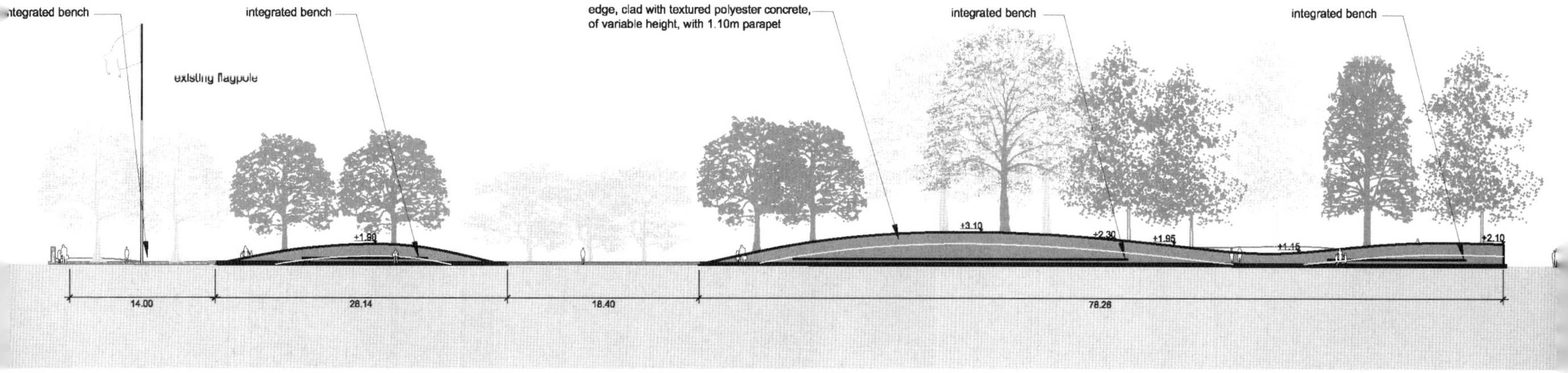

59

1

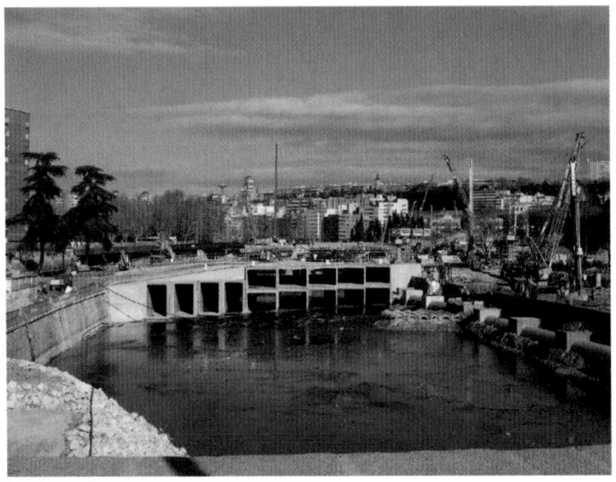

2

1–2: Construction site along river Manzanares

MADRID RIO

SPAIN

Madrid mayor Ruiz-Gallardón's ambition to bury the whole of the M30 highway, which cuts through the centre of the city, in tunnels was fulfilled in less than six years. The city dug 43 kilometres of tunnels into which the exit routes and highway of the six-kilometre section along the River Manzanares disappeared. West 8, working together with MRIO, designed the master plan for the reclaimed riverbanks and the new urban area. Development plans were then prepared for the individual components: Salón de Pinos, Avenida de Portugal, Huerta de la Partida, Jardines de Puente de Segovia, Jardines de Puente de Toledo, Jardines de la Virgen del Puerto and Parque de la Arganzuela. The first parts were completed in spring 2007.

3a

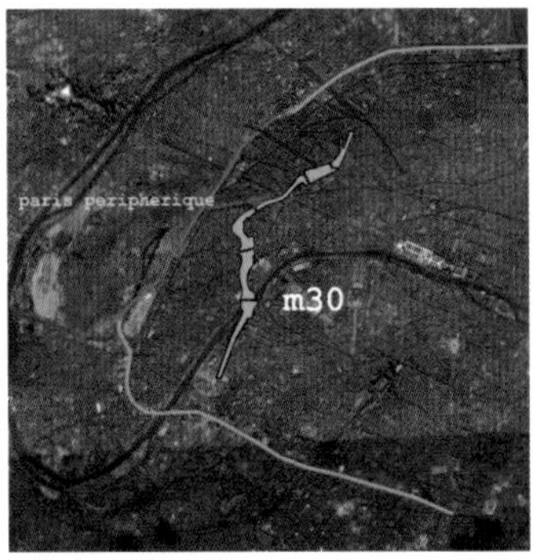

b

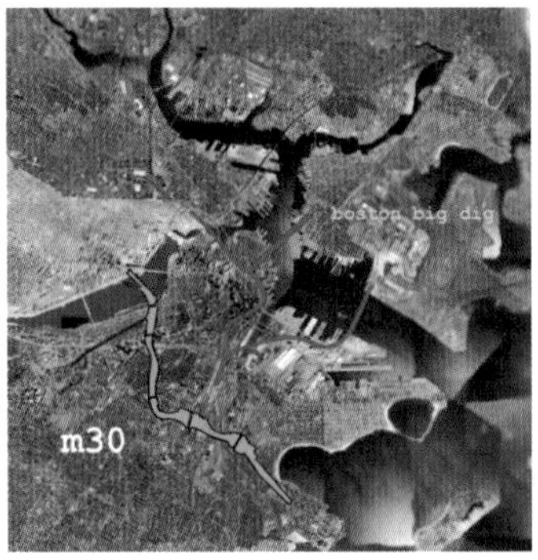

c

3: Size comparison M30 project
a: New York City, FDR Drive, Manhattan
b: Paris, Périphérique
c: Boston, Big Dig

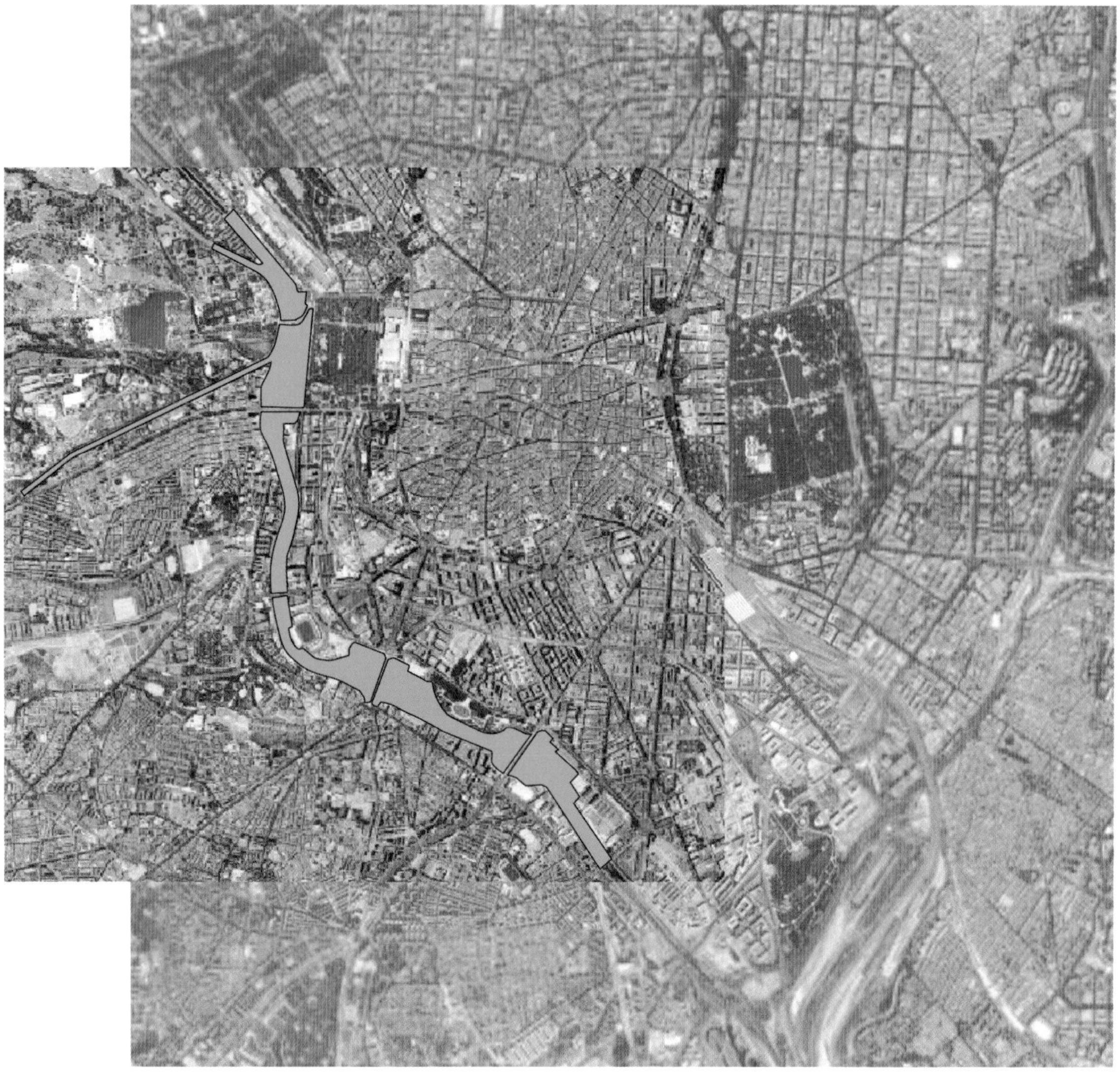

4

5

4: Site within context of Madrid

5: Salón de Pinos, river Manzanares

6

Master plan

7

8

9

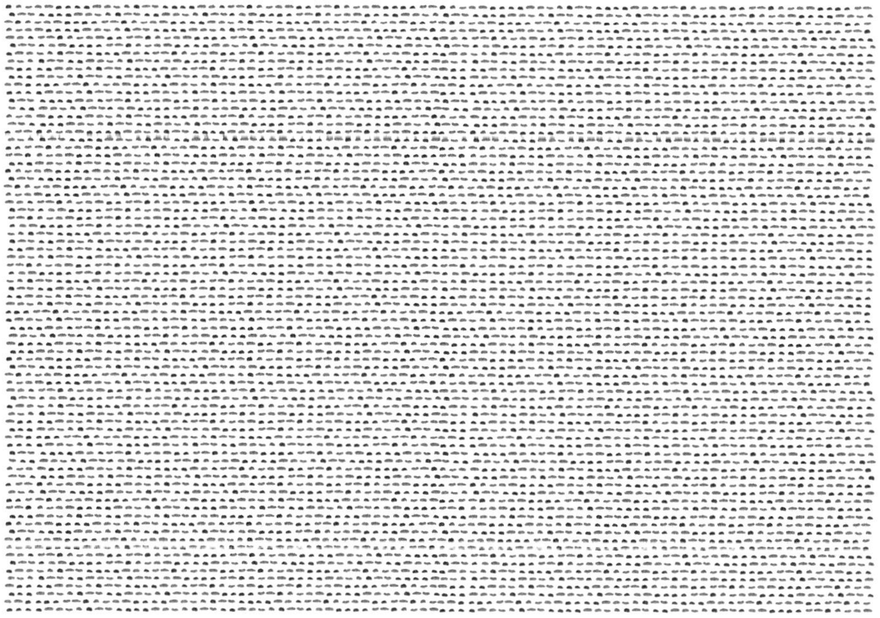

10

SALON DE PINOS

7: Artist's impression

8: Model

9: Section

10: Concept 2.000 pines

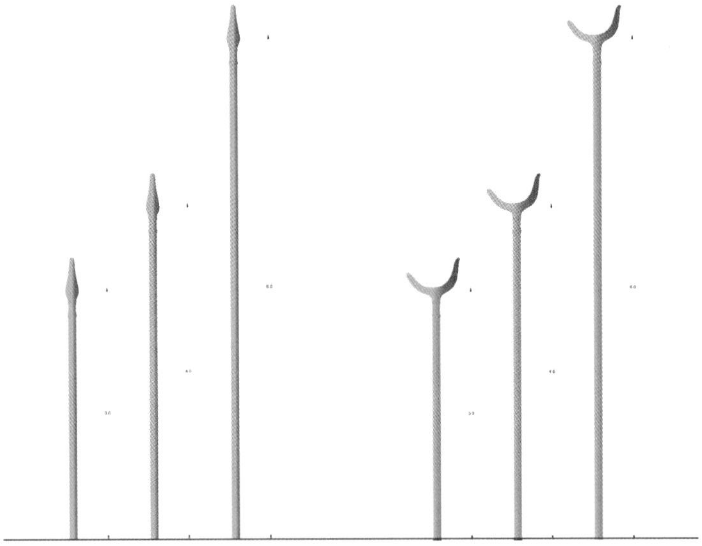

11

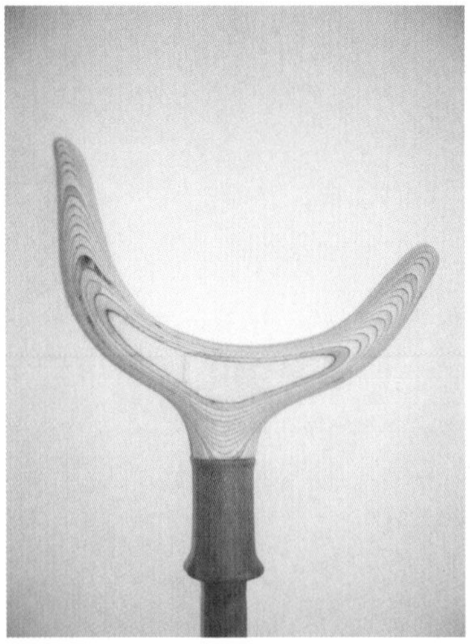

12

13

SALON DE PINOS

11: Tree supports
12: Prototype
13: First mock-up, cast iron
14–15: Model
16: Mountain pine

16

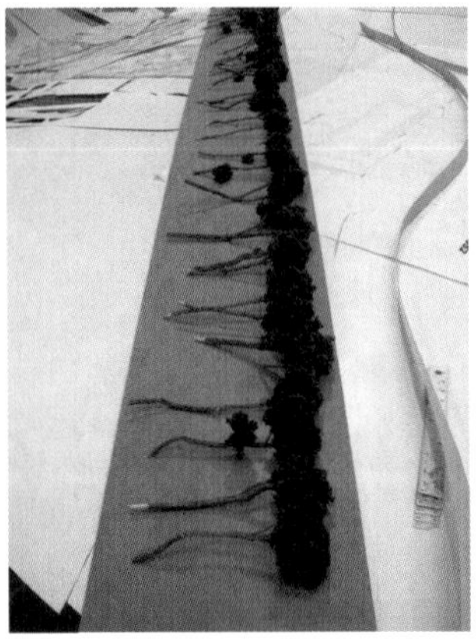

14

15

17

17: Testing site
18-19: Planting

18

19

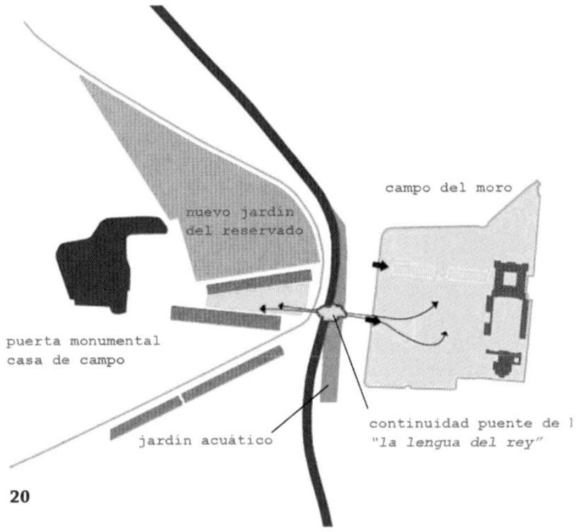

20

21

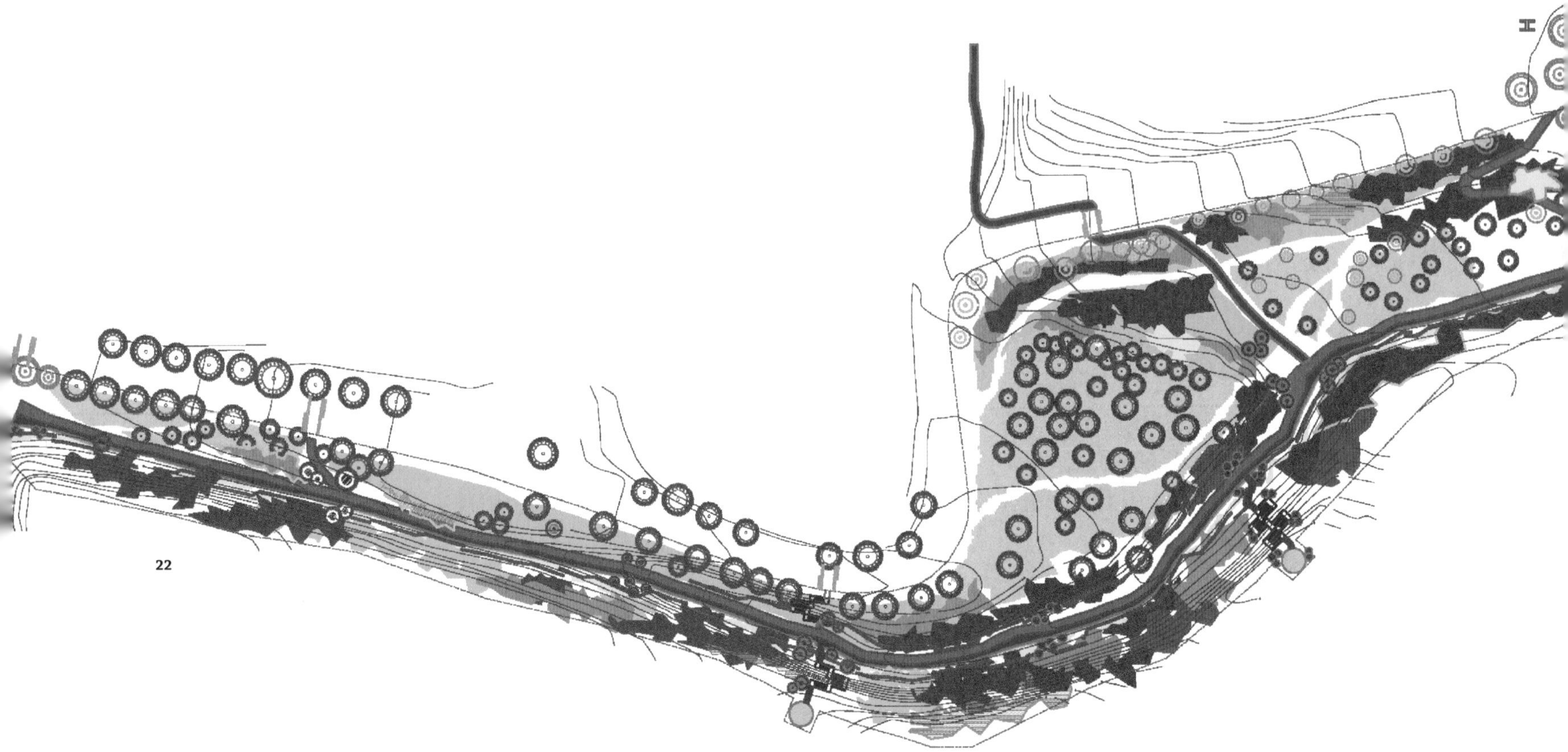

22

HUERTA DE LA PARTIDA

20: Grass bridge to the Royal Palace

21: Historic photo

22: Master plan

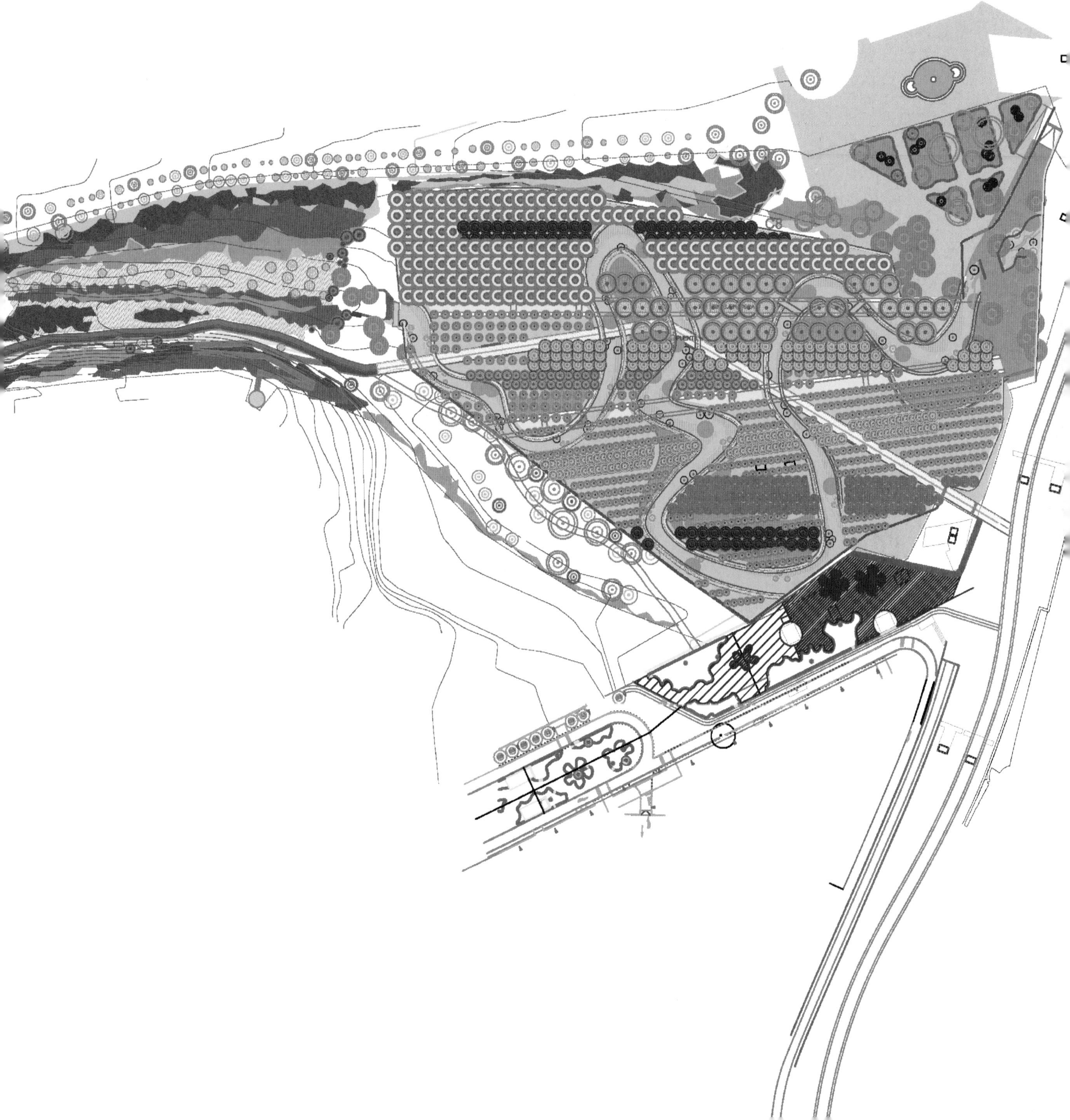
C8

23

24

25

26

23: First year vegetation
24–26: Tree tie
27: Opening ceremony, Mayor Gallardón

28

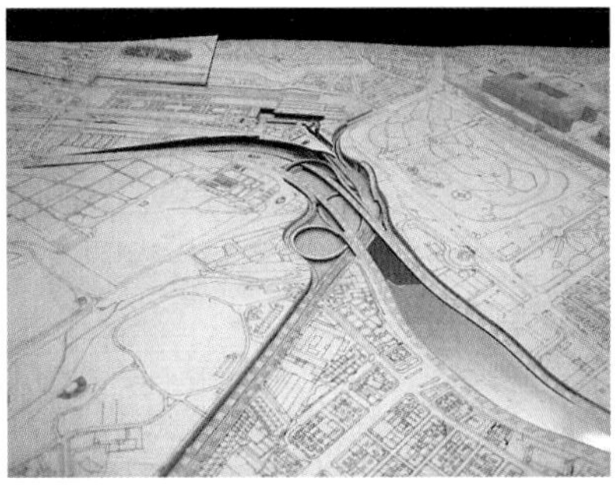
29

33

30

34

31

AVENIDA DE PORTUGAL

28: Highway before construction work
29: Model of the tunnels
30: Avenida during construction
31: New tunnel
32–35: Artist's impressions
36–37: Details of paving concept

35

32

38

39

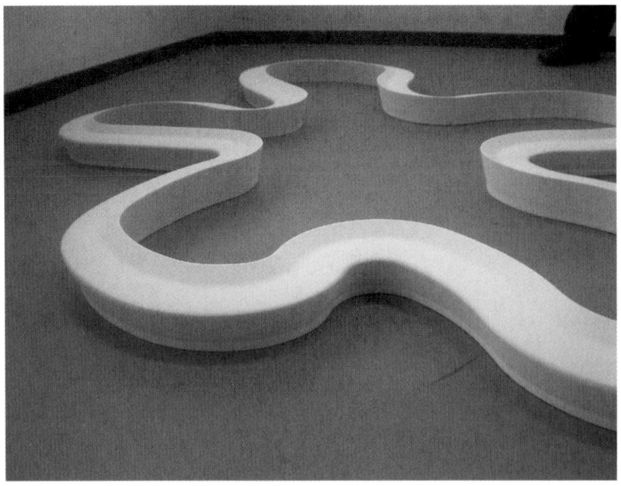

40

41

BENCH / CURB

38: Elements of the bench
39–40: Models
41–45: Photos

42

43

44

46

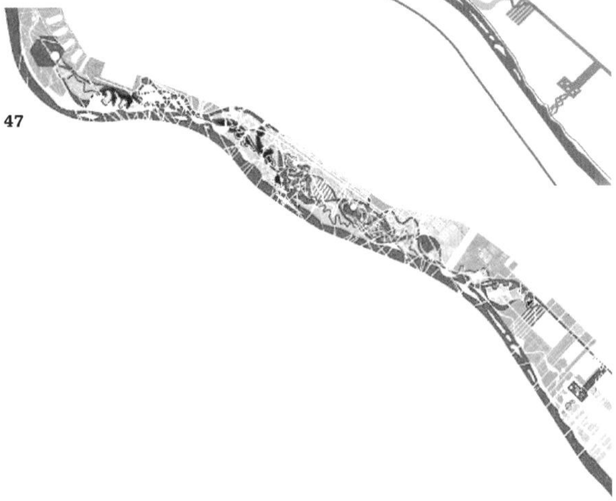

47

48

PARQUE DE LA ARGANZUELA

46: Concept of streams
47: Biotopes
48: Lower park
49: Master plan
50: Fountains
51: Creek section
52: Path section
53: Dry river section

49

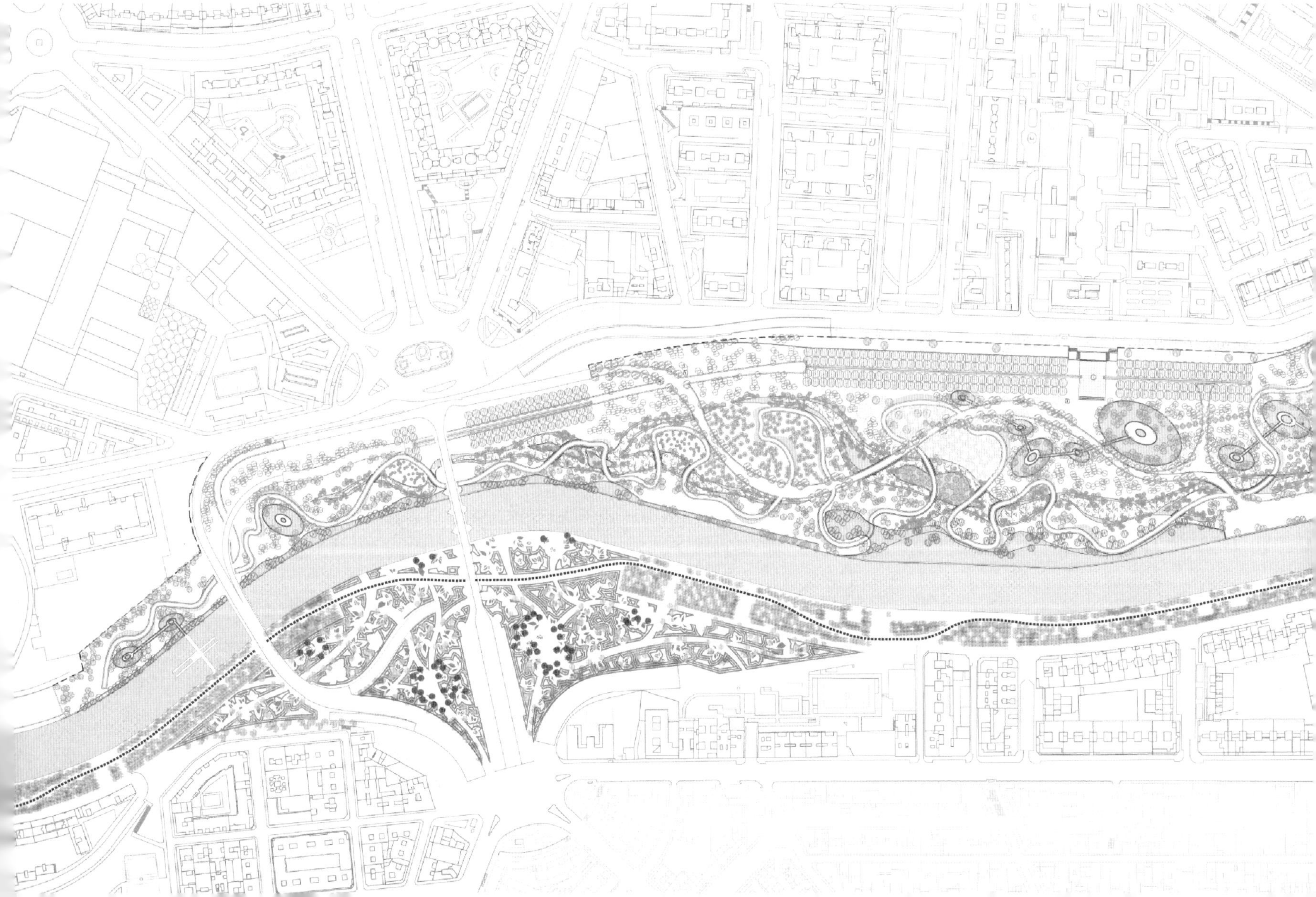

50

51

52

53

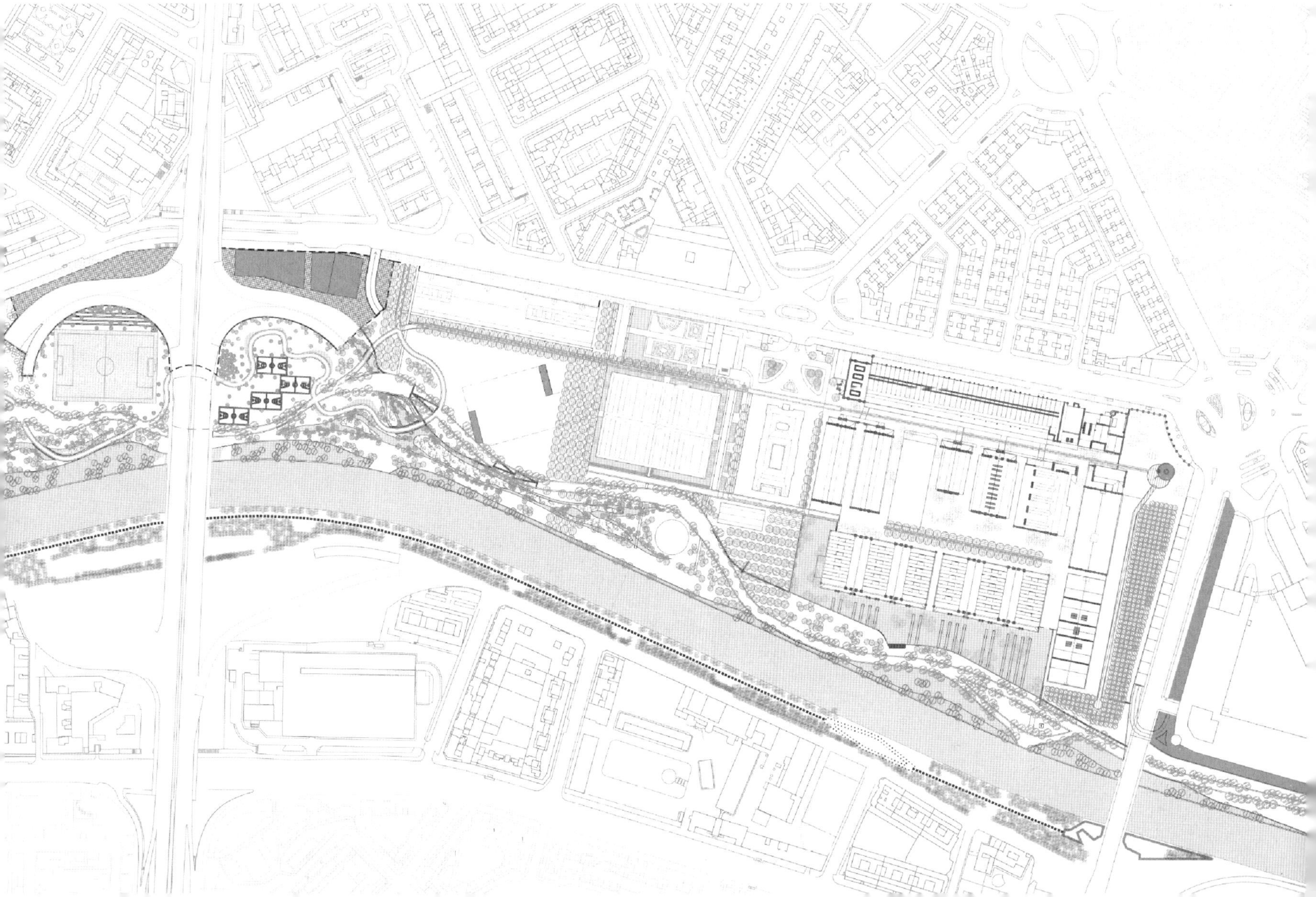

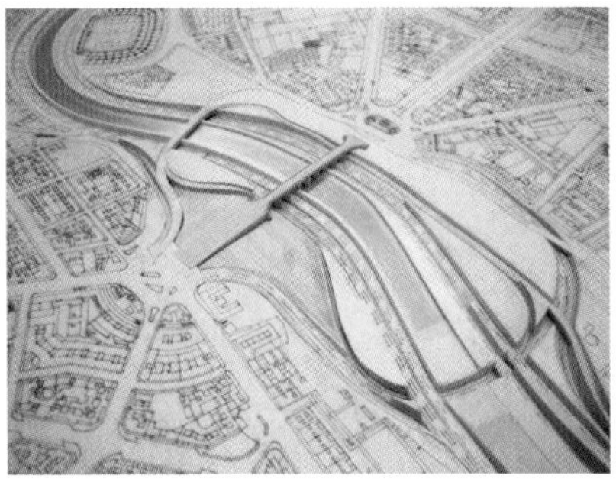

54

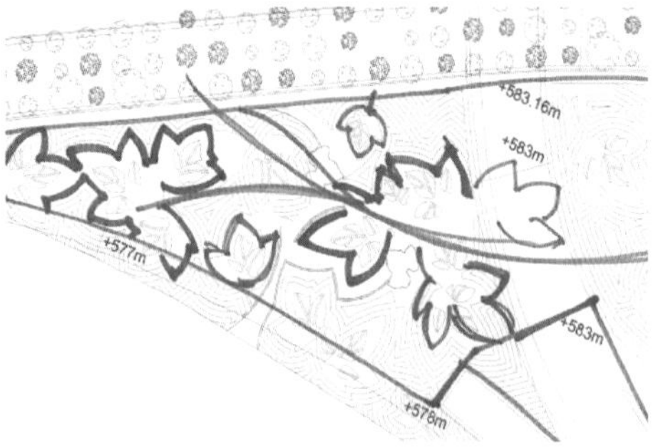

55

RIVER GARDENS AT TOLEDO BRIDGE

54: Model of the tunnels
55–56: Sketches
57: Master plan
58: Artist's impression
59: View from the bridge during construction of the tunnels
60: Quay side rendering

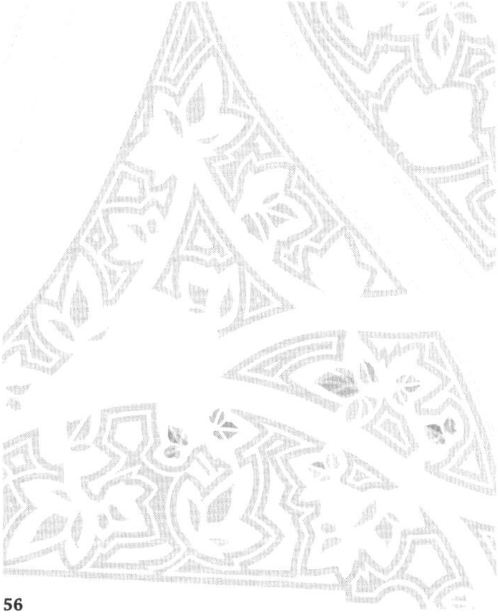

56

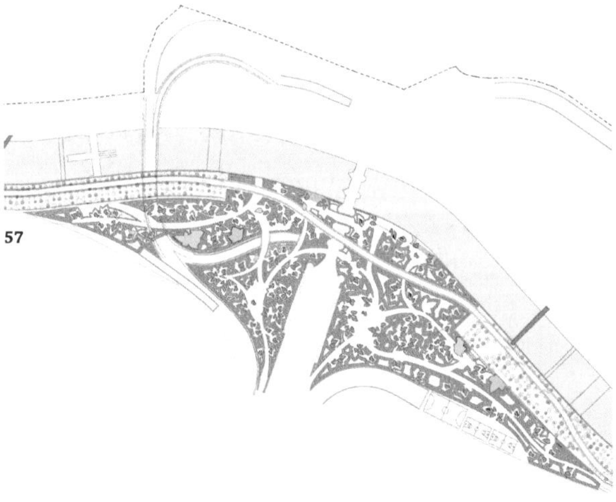

57

58

59

60

WEST8, HISTORY & CREDITS (SHORTLIST)

CREDIT LIST

Kröller-Müller Museum Sculpture Garden, Otterlo (NL)
Client: Kröller-Müller Museum
Design: 1995–1997; 2000; 2005
Realisation: 1996–2007
Credits: Adriaan Geuze, Edzo Bindels, Theo Reesink, Riëtte Bosch, Edwin van der Hoeven, Guido Marsille, Jacco Stuy

Gwandju, Botanical Bridge (TW)
Client: Gwangju Biennale
Design: 2001–2002
Credits: Adriaan Geuze, Jerry van Eyck, Sabine Müller, Pieter Rabijns, Yoon-Jin Park
Botanical adviser: Prof. Oh Koo-Kyoon

Möbius House, 't Gooi (NL)
Client: Wim and Hetty Laverman
Design: 1997–1998
Realisation: 1998–1999
Credits: Adriaan Geuze, Marnix Vink, Inge Breugem, Floor Moormann, Jan Paul de Ridder
Architect: Ben van Berkel

Chaumont-sur-Loire (FR)
Client: Conservatoire International des Parcs et Jardins et du Paysage
Design: 1999
Realisation: 2000
Credits: Adriaan Geuze, Guido Marsille

CBK Sculpture Garden, Dordrecht (NL)
Client: Centrum Beeldende Kunsten (Centre for the Arts)
Design: 1992
Realisation: 1995
Credits: Adriaan Geuze, Cyrus Clark, Dirry de Bruyn, Peter Cue, Casper Lefavre

Jubilee Gardens, London (UK)
Client: South Bank Employers Group
Design: 2005–
Realisation: 2007–2008
Credits: Adriaan Geuze, Edzo Bindels, Jerry van Eyck, Alyssa Schwann, Karsten Buchholz, Freek Boerwinkel, Perry Maas, Riikka Tuomisto, Maarten van de Voorde
In association with AKT Engineers, BDSP Partnership, Soil and Land Consultants, Buro Happold

Expo '02 – Yverdon-les-Bains (CH)
Client: Expo '02
Design: 1998–2000
Realisation: 2001–2002
Credits: Adriaan Geuze, Edzo Bindels, Jerry van Eyck, Daniel Jauslin, Eliana Pereira de Sousa Santos, Freek Boerwinkel, Rudolph Eilander, Marc Lampe, Joost Koningen, Marco van der Pluym, Maarten van de Voorde
In association with Diller + Scofidio, Morphing Systems, Véhovar & Jauslin Architektur, Zürich

Luxury Village, Moscow (RU)
Client: Mercury
Design: 2004–2006
Realisation: 2006
Credits: Adriaan Geuze, Edzo Bindels, Jerry van Eyck, Freek Boerwinkel, Alexander Sverdlov, Javier Muñoz, Karsten Buchholz, Arman Akdogan, Alyssa Schwann, Sander Lap

AEGON Plein, The Hague (NL)
Client: AEGON NV
Design: 1996
Realisation: 2000–2001
Credits: Adriaan Geuze, Edzo Bindels, Freek Boerwinkel, Rudolph Eilander, Inge Breugem, Sabine Müller, Paul Deibel, Guido Marsille, Robert Schütte,Edwin van der Hoeven, Marc McCarthy

Santa Giulia, Milan (IT)
Client: Milano Santa Giulia SpA
Design: 2005–2007
Realisation: 2008–
Credits: Adriaan Geuze, Adriana Mueller, Jacco Stuy, Carlo Missio, Christian Dobrick, Alexander Sverdlov, Juan Figeroa Calero, Enrique González, Silvia Lupini, Robert Schütte, Shachar Zur

Ryckaertsplein, Berchem (BE)
Client: City of Antwerp
Design: 1999–2000
Realisation: 2006
Credits: Adriaan Geuze, Edzo Bindels, Maarten van de Voorde, Justus Slaakweg, Tyler Myer, Eve Robidoux, Pieter Rabijns, Anna Little

Grand Egyptian Museum, Cairo (EG)
Client: Ministry of Culture of Egypt
Design: 2004
Realisation: 2009
Credits: Adriaan Geuze, Edzo Bindels, Jerry van Eyck, Christian Gausepohl, Christine Wahba, Jacco Stuy, Daphne Schuit, Glen Scott, Matthew Halsall, Silvia Lupini, Arman Akdogan, Shoko Yuzawa, Alyssa Schwann
In association with Heneghan Peng Architects, Ove Arup & Partners, Buro Happold, Davis Langdon Schumann Smith, Sites International, Bartenbach Lichtlabor

Pinecone Garden, Padua (IT)
Client: Ortis Artis
Design: 2003
Realisation: 2003
Credits: Adriaan Geuze, Jerry van Eyck, Theo Reesink, Jacco Stuy

Lensvelt Garden, Breda (NL)
Client: Lensvelt B.V.
Design: 1997–1998
Realisation: 1998–1999
Credits: Adriaan Geuze, Edzo Bindels, Edwin van der Hoeven, Guido Marsille, Jan Paul de Ridder, Bert Roete, Olivier Scheffer

Madrid Rio, Madrid (ES)
Client: Municipality of Madrid
Design: 2006
Realisation: 200
Credits: Edzo Bindels, Adriaan Geuze, Martin Biewenga, Christian Dobrick, Sander Lap, Alexander Sverdlov, Marta Roy, Enrique González, Riccardo Minghini, Silvia Lupini, Karsten Buchholz, Perry Maas, Lennart van Dijk, Shachar Zur, Kees Schoot, Claudia Wolsfeld
In association with MRIO arquitectos

Leidsche Rijn Park, Utrecht (NL)
Client: Project Development Leidsche Rijn
Design: 1997–1999
Realisation: 2003–2010
Credits: Adriaan Geuze, Edzo Bindels, Martin Biewenga, Jeroen de Willigen, Esther Kruit, Nigel Sampey, Fritz Coutzee, Jacco Stuy, Rob Grotewal, Bert Karel Deuten, Suzanna van Remmen, Edwin van der Hoeven, Joirs Hekkenberg, Jack van Dijk, Norbert Trolf, Freek Boerwinkel, Maarten Buys, Cyrus Clark, Ard Middeldorp, Robert Schutte, Kees Schoot, Perry Maas, Bas van der Vinne, Sabine Müller/The Wall

One North Park, Singapore (SG)
Client: JTC, Singapore National Parks Board
Design: 2004–2006
Realisation: 2006 first parcel was completed
Credits: Jerry van Eyck, Adriaan Geuze, Freek Boerwinkel, Riëtte Bosch, Glen Scott, Marco van der Pluym, Jung Yoon Kim, Felipe van Klaveren, Sander Lap

Chiswick Park, London (UK)
Client: Stanhope plc
Design: 1999
Realisation: 2000–
Credits: Adriaan Geuze, Edzo Bindels, Jerry van Eyck, Nigel Sampey, Tyler Myer, Jacco Stuy, Sabine Müller, Adriana Mueller, Freek Boerwinkel
Architect: Richard Rogers Partnership

Project Horizon, Various polders (NL)
Client: International Architecture Biennale Rotterdam
Design: 2005
Realisation: 2005
Credits: Adriaan Geuze, Jerry van Eyck, Edzo Bindels, Martin Biewenga, Fanny Smelik, Sander Lap, Marco van der Pluym, Andrew Tang, Jonas Vanneste, Anna Holder, Joost Koningen, Karsten Bucholz, Maarten van de Voorde, Fabian Greiff, Annette van 't Hof, Carlos Peña, José Suraña Fernandez, Rolf Eilander

Aelbrechtskade, Rotterdam (NL)
Redevelopment of quayside
Client: Municipality of Rotterdam
Design: 1990
Realisation: 1992
Size: 2.3 km

Visserijplein, Rotterdam (NL)
Market square
Client: Municipality of Rotterdam
Design: 1990
Realisation: 1995
Size: 0.9 ha

Mercatorplein, Amsterdam (NL)
Competition design urban square
Client: Stadsdeel De Baarsjes
Design: 1992

IJ-oevers, Amsterdam (NL)
Master plan for redevelopment IJ banks
Client: AWF Amsterdam
Design: 1993
In association with OMA, UN Studio, KCAP, Neutelings Riedijk, Light

Binnenrotte, Rotterdam (NL)
Market square
Client: Municipality of Rotterdam
Design: 1993–1994
Realisation: 1994–1995
Size: 3.6 ha

Schouwburgplein, Rotterdam (NL)
Civic, ceremonial and events square Rotterdam
Client: Municipality of Rotterdam
Design: 1991
Realisation: 1996
Size: 1.2 ha

Oostelijk Havengebied (Borneo Sporenburg), Amsterdam (NL)
Transformation of former harbour area into low-rise, high-density neighbourhood, 2 400 dwellings
Client: New Deal
Design: 1993
Realisation: 1996–1997
Size: 24 ha

Barentszplein, Amsterdam (NL)
Square on the IJ river-banks
Client: Dienst Ruimtelijke Ordening Amsterdam
Design: 1994

Wilhelminahof, Rotterdam (NL)
Courtyard design
Client: Bouwfonds Vastgoedontwikkeling bv, Rijksgebouwendienst, Burgerinvest Properties, ING
Design: 1994
Realisation: 1996–1997
Size: 0.7 ha

Woonwijk Kernhem, Ede (NL)
Suburban development, 4 600 dwellings
Client: Municipality of Ede
Design: 1995
Size: 100 ha

IJ-burg, Amsterdam (NL)
Design study for reclaimed land area IJburg
Client: Municipality of Amsterdam
Design: 1994

Chasséterrein, Breda (NL)
Public space strategy for residential campus
Client: Chassé cv (Proper-Stok Woningbouw bv, AM Wonen nv)
Design: 1994
Realisation: 2000–2005
Size: 18 ha

De Uithof, Utrecht (NL)
Public space strategy for university campus, various projects
Client: University of Utrecht
Design: 1995–1996
Realisation: 1999–

GWL terrein, Amsterdam (NL)
Public space design sustainable neighbourhood
Client: Stichting ECO-plan, Stadsdeel Westerpark
Design: 1997
Realisation: 1998–1999
Size: 3.2 ha

Leidschenhage, Leidschendam (NL)
Redevelopment of public space shopping centre
Client: Municipality of Leidschendam
Design: 1996
Realisation: 1998–2000

Carrascoplein, Amsterdam (NL)
Design for urban landscape under railway viaducts
Client: Gemeentelijk Grondbedrijf Amsterdam
Design: 1997
Realisation: 1998
Size: 2.8 ha

De Neude, Utrecht (NL)
City square in historical context
Client: Municipality of Utrecht
Design: 1996
Realisation: 1998
Size: 1.2 ha

UCP (Utrecht City Project), Utrecht (NL)
Master plan and public space strategy for transport node
Client: BVR
Design: 1996–1997

2010, Almere (NL)
Design study for urban development Almere
Client: Municipality of Almere, BVR
Design: 1996

18 september-plein, Eindhoven (NL)
Square
Client: Municipality of Eindhoven
Design: 1996

Plein West / Jaarbeurs / Heycop, Utrecht (NL)
Reception square of convention centre
Client: Royal Dutch Jaarbeurs Utrecht
Design: 1997–1998
Realisation: 1999
Size: 1.5 ha

Nolensplein, Venlo (NL)
Market square
Client: Municipality of Venlo
Design: 1996–1998
Realisation: 1999
Size: 2.1 ha

AEGON Plein, The Hague (NL)
Station square and reception square of insurance company headquarters
Client: AEGON nv
Design: 1996
Realisation: 2000–2001
Size: 1.5 ha

Vathorst, Amersfoort (NL)
Master plan for urban development of 10,000 dwellings and 45 ha business park
Client: Municipality of Amersfoort, consortium Vathorst Beheer bv
Design: 1996
Realisation: 1998–2010
Size: 300 ha
In association with Kuiper Compagnons

De Laak, Vathorst, Amersfoort (NL)
Urban design and supervision of watercity
Client: Ontwikkelingsbedrijf Vathorst bv
Design: 1999–2008
Realisation: 2000–2010
Size: 100 ha

H.J. van Heekplein, Enschede (NL)
Master plan and supervision for town centre extension, mixed use
Client: Municipality of Enschede
Design: 1999
Realisation: 2001–2003
Size: 11 ha

Zeeburg, Amsterdam (NL)
Design study for 6 000 houses in wetland area
Client: Municipality of Amsterdam
Design: 1997–1998
Size: 200 ha
In association with Neutelings Riedijk

Borneo Sporenburg Bridges, Amsterdam (NL)
Designs for a cycle bridge and two pedestrian bridges
Client: Municipality of Amsterdam
Design: 1998–1999
Realisation: 2000
Size: span 93 m / 25 m, width 3.5 m / 4 m

Singels, Ypenburg, Amsterdam (NL)
Urban design residential neighbourhood, 652 dwellings
Client: Bouwcollectief d'Artagnan
Design: 1998–1999
Realisation: 2000–2002
Size: 17.5 ha

Master plan Stadshart, Lelystad (NL)
Master plan for redevelopment of town centre, mixed use
Client: OMS Beheer bv, Municipality of Lelystad, William Properties bv
Design: 1999
Realisation: 2000–2010
Size: 44 ha

Stalberg-Oost, Venlo (NL)
Villa park, 200 villas
Client: Heijmans Vastgoed Rosmalen
Design: 1998–2000
Realisation: 2001–
Size: 14 ha

Drinkwaterleidingterrein Sliedrecht, Sliedrecht (NL)
High-density residential development on the river-bank, 200 dwellings
Client: Watertoren nv
Design: 2001
Size: 2 ha

Park Hoogveld, Heerlen (NL)
Villa park, 450 villas
Client: Hoogveld bv
Design: 1999–2001
Realisation: 2002–2007

Zernikecomplex, Groningen (NL)
Master plan for redevelopment of university campus
Client: Rijksuniversiteit Groningen, Hanze Hogeschool
Design: 1999
Realisation: 2002–2010

Deelplan 4, Ypenburg, Amsterdam (NL)
Public space new urban centre
Client: RABO Vastgoed bv, Forum Invest bv, Rapp + Rapp
Design: 1999
Realisation: 2006

Frihavn, Copenhagen (DK)
Urban development of former harbour area
Client: Port of Copenhagen, TK Development
Design: 2000
Realisation: 2001–2007

Cronenburgh, Loenen aan de Vecht (NL)
Extension of historical village, 200 dwellings
Client: Municipality of Loenen aan de Vecht
Design: 2001–2002
Realisation: 2006–2012

Kanaaleiland, Bruges (BE)
Design public space, bridge and roof for visitors of the historical town centre
Client: City of Bruges, Department Waterwegen, Zeewegen en Kust
Design: 2000
Realisation: 2001–2002

Glastuinbouw, Nieuwdorp (NL)
Design study for glasshouses area in the province of Zeeland
Client: ZLTO
Design: 2001
Realisation: study not to be realised
Size: 71 ha

Maastricht Airport Businesspark, Maastricht (NL)
Spatial development scenarios
Client: LIOF, Maastricht Airport Authority

Kings Crescent Regeneration, London (UK)
Redevelopment of residential area
Client: Peabody Trust, United House Limited
Design: 2000–2005
Realisation: 2004 (process stopped)
Size: 4.2 ha

Watersite, Vilvoorde (BE)
Redevelopment of Het Broek residential area
Client: City of Vilvoorde
Design: 2003
Realisation: 2006
Size: 13.5 ha

Waterrijk, Woerden (NL)
Design and supervising development of residential neighbourhood, 1 200 dwellings
Client: Municipality of Woerden
Design: 1998
Realisation: 2000–2015
Size: 46 ha

Historic Centre, Leidschendam (NL)
Design and supervising of redevelopment historic centre around a lock
Client: Municipality of Leidschendam-Voorburg, Schouten de Jong, Bouwfonds MAB Ontwikkeling
Design: 2000–2001
Realisation: 2005–2015

Station, Hasselt (BE)
Master plan for the development of new quarter around main public transport terminal
Client: City of Hasselt, Euro Immostar, NMBS, LRM
Design: 2001
Realisation: 2005–
Size: 2.25 ha

Schuytgraaf veld 16 / 17, Arnhem (NL)
Design and supervising development of residential neighbourhood
Client: GEM Schuytgraaf
Design: 2005
Realisation: 2007–2010
Size: 20 ha

Kiosken, Enschede (NL)
Design for three kiosks for the daily market
Client: Municipality of Enschede
Design: 2002
Realisation: 2004

Scarborough (UK)
Urban regeneration, public space strategy
Client: Yorkshire Foreword
Design: 2002

Bridlington (UK)
Urban regeneration, public space strategy
Client: Yorkshire Foreword
Design: 2004

HST Terminal, Brussels (BE)
Urban regeneration of railroad yard HST Terminal
Client: Euro Immostar
Design: 2002
Size: 75 ha

South Dagenham, London (UK)
Master plan for the redevelopment of former industrial area into urban neighbourhood
Clients: LDA (London Development Agency), LBBD (London Borough of Barking & Dagenham), LBH (London Borough of Havering)
Design: 2000
Realisation: not defined
Size: 32 ha

Westrandweg, Amsterdam (NL)
Study, spatial integration of new highway in urban landscape
Client: Municipality of Amsterdam
Design: 2003
Size: 20 km

Town square, Middlesbrough (UK)
Design for public square
Client: Municipality of Middlesbrough
Design: 2003
Realisation: 2004–2006
Size: 1.8 ha
In association with Erick van Egeraat associated architects

Nieuw-Rhijngeest, Oegstgeest (NL)
Framework plan / urban design / supervision for contemporary water city
Client: Municipality of Oegstgeest
Design: 2000–2007
Realisation: 2007–2015
Size: 48 ha

Parkhaven, Rotterdam (NL)
Development study of leisure and living programme around the Euromast
Client: dS+V Municipality of Rotterdam
Design: 2003

Kop van Feijenoord, Rotterdam (NL)
Master plan for the restoration of urban tissue
Client: dS+V Municipality of Rotterdam
Design: 2005

Park Strijp S, Eindhoven (NL)
Design and supervising redevelopment of former Phillips factory grounds
Client: Park Strijp Beheer
Design: 2001
Realisation: 2002–2010
Size: 29 ha

Parc Jean-Baptist Lebas, Lille (FR)
Design urban park
Client: Ville de Lille, LMCV
Design: 2002–2003
Realisation: 2004–2005
Size: 4.9 ha
In association with Lalou + Libel

Stratford City, London (UK)
Master planning new urban heart
Client: Chelsfield plc, Stanhope plc, London & Continental Railways Ltd, Westfield, Firstbase
Design: 2003
Realisation: planned 2015
Size: 75.4 ha
In association with Fletcher Priest Architects, Ove Arup

Stratford City, London (UK)
Master planning public space, design for Olympic Village
Client: First Base Ltd London
Design: 2002
Realisation: 2010
Size: 22 ha

Seeufer, Zurich (CH)
Urban design vision for reorganisation of the public Zurich lake shore
Client: City of Zürich
Design: 2003
Realisation: study
Size: approx. 5 km

Waterfront Bodensee, Rorschach (CH)
Redesign of the Bodensee waterfront
Client: Stadt Rorschach
Design: 2003
Realisation: start 2007
Size: 1.8 ha

Nieuw Crooswijk, Rotterdam (NL)
Urban regeneration plan, public space design, supervising architectural designs
Client: Ontwikkelingscombinatie Nieuw Crooswijk (joint venture of Era Bouw, Proper-Stok, Woning Bedrijf Rotterdam)
Design: 2003
Realisation: 2007–2016
Size: 2 025 dwellings

Structuurplan, Emmen (NL)
Master plan for the development of the town of Emmen till 2020
Client: Municipality of Emmen
Design: 2005
In association with Pau

Avenida Roosevelt, San Juan (PR)
Traffic boulevard / urban landmark
Client: Arte Publico with Ministry of Transportation
Design: 2004
Realisation: construction documents
Size: 400 m (pilot)

Ferry Terminal Area, Tromsø (NO)
Ferry terminal and commercial programme master plan and public space design
Client: City of Tromsø, Port Authority
Design: 2003
Realisation: construction documents
In association with Space Group Architects

Overstad, Alkmaar (NL)
Transformation of former industrial area into multifunctional town centre
Client: Municipality of Alkmaar, Ontwerpatelier Overstad
Design: 2005
Realisation: 2007–2015
Size: 28 ha

Luxury Village, Moscow (RU)
Public space design for luxury goods shopping mall
Client: Mercury
Design: 2004–2006
Realisation: 2006
Size: 2.5 ha
In association with Projekt Meganom

Rotterdam Central Station, Rotterdam (NL)
Design for Central Station and adjacent urban development
Client: Prorail, Ontwikkelings Bedrijf Rotterdam, dS+V
Design: 2004–2006
Realisation: 2010
Team CS: Benthem Crouwel Architekten, Meyer en Van Schooten Architecten, West 8

Strijp S, Eindhoven (NL)
Urban design for former Philips plant
Client: Park Strijp Beheer
Design: 2001
Realisation: 2007–
Size: 62 ha

Supervisie West-Corridor Eindhoven, Eindhoven (NL)
Supervision of urban design and regeneration plans in the West-Corridor zone
Client: Municipality of Eindhoven
Design: 2003
Realisation: 2007–

Dolderse Hille, Den Dolder (NL)
Transformation of former mental hospital site into a mixed-use development
Client: De Seystere Veste, Stichting Altrecht
Design: 2004
Realisation: 2008–2012

Foyer / Lippensplein, Knokke (BE)
Boulevard and entrance square
Client: Municipality of Knokke
Design: 2004
Realisation: 2005–2006
Size: 3.75 ha

Leerpark, Dordrecht (NL)
Design of mixed-use development of schools, sports, culture, dwellings and commerce
Client: Heijmans nv, Proper-Stok Woningbouw bv
Design: 2004
Realisation: 2005–2013
Size: 35 ha

De Vijverberg Zuid, Doetinchem (NL)
Villa park, 170 villas
Client: Municipality of Doetinchem, Goldewijk projectontwikkeling, Bemog projectontwikkeling, Rijnbouw bv
Design: 2005
Realisation: 2009

Pedagogenbuurt, Utrecht (NL)
Public space design in urban regeneration project
Client: Municipality of Utrecht
Design: 2005
Realisation: 2006–2009
Size: 2.4 ha

Island Brygge, Copenhagen (DK)
Master plan for the redevelopment of former industrial area into urban neighbourhood
Client: Port of Copenhagen, Nordkranen AS, NCC property development
Design: 2004
Size: 15.6 ha
In association with PLOT Architects

Master plan Havengebied, Goes (NL)
Transformation of former industrial harbour into residential watertown
Client: Municipality of Goes, Proper-Stok Woningbouw bv
Design: 2004
Realisation: 2008–
Size: 60 ha

Krugerbrug, Antwerp (BE)
Cycle bridge over railroad tracks
Client: City of Antwerp
Design: 2004
Size: span 95 m, width 12 m

Minoco Wharf, London (UK)
Public space design in high-density development along the River Thames
Client: Clearstorm Ltd
Design: 2006

Voetgangersbrug (footbridge), Wenduine (BE)
Design of wooden pedestrian bridge
Client: AWZ Oostende
Design: 2005
Realisation: 2007
Size: span 90 m, width 3 m

Vlaardingse Vaart Bridge, Vlaardingen (NL)
Steel pedestrian bridge
Client: Municipality of Vlaardingen
Design: 2005
Realisation: 2007–2008
Size: span 65 m, width 5.5 m

Parque Lineal de Manzanares, Madrid (ES)
Public space on top of the tunnel of the M30 urban motorway
Client: Municipality of Madrid
Design: 2005–2007
Realisation: 2006–2010
Size: 120 ha
In association with Burgos & Garrido Arquitectos, Porras & La Casta Arquitectos, Rubio & Álvarez-Sala Arquitectos

Stadshart Den Helder Haalbaarheidsstudie, Den Helder (NL)
Master plan for the transformation of city centre and marine port
Client: Zeestad bv, Woningstichting Den Helder, Proper-Stok Ontwikkelaars, Johan Matser Projectontwikkeling
Design: 2006–2007
Realisation: 2008–
Size: 24 ha

Spoorhavengebied, Roosendaal (NL)
Master plan for the transformation of industrial area into new urban core
Client: Municipality of Roosendaal, Proper-Stok Woningbouw bv, Robo Vastgoed bv
Design: 2006–2007
Realisation: 2009–
Size: 20 ha

Museum Plaza, Louisville, Kentucky (US)
Public park and reception square
Client: Wilson-Brown, Greenberg, Poe Companies
Design: 2006
Realisation: 2008–
Size: 3 ha
In association with REX
Local partner: MESA, Dallas TX

Knokke-Heist, Knokke-Heist (BE)
Master plan for redevelopment of coastal boulevard and squares
Client: Municipality of Knokke-Heist
Design: 2006
Realisation: 2007
Size: 16.3 ha

North Lotts, Dublin (IR)
Master plan for redevelopment of former docklands
Client: Dublin Dockland Development Authority
Design: 2006
Realisation: 2008–
Size: 34 ha

Pegaso, Madrid (ES)
Landscape design for business park
Client: Inmobiliaria Urbanitas, S.L.
Design: 2006–2007
Realisation: 2007–2008
Size: 40 ha

Island in Maashaven, Rotterdam (NL)
Design study for landfill in harbour basin and new urban neighbourhood
Client: Proper-Stok Woningbouw bv, Dura Vermeer bv, Amvest, Ballast Nedam bv
Design: 2006–2007
Size: 22 ha

Ruimtelijke Visie Zuiderzeeland, Zuiderzeeland (NL)
Design vision for water management and spatial development
Client: Waterschap Zuiderzeeland
Design: 2007

Toronto Waterfront, Toronto (CA)
Master plan for revitalisation of Toronto waterfront
Client: TWRC (Toronto Waterfront Revitalisation Corporation)
Design: 2006
Realisation: approx. 2009
Size: 3.5 km
In association with DuToit Allsopp Hillier, Schollen & Company, Diamond + Schmitt Architects, Arup, Halsall Associates, David Dennis Design

Parkhouse 50, Phoenix, Arizona (US)
Public space and park design, private garden, commercial zone
Client: Parkhouse 50
Design: 2006–2007
Realisation: 2008
Size: 4 ha
Local partner: MESA, Dallas TX

Markeroog, IJmeer (NL)
Winning competition proposal for the spatial development of lake area east of Amsterdam
Design: 2006
In association with Royal Boskalis Westminster nv, AT Osborne, Witteveen + Bos

Klein Koninkrijk, 's-Gravendeel (NL)
Design study, transformation of former industrial area into mixed-use neighbourhood
Client: Bureau Drechtsteden
Design: 2007
Size: 36 ha

Mirandastrook ZuiderAmstel, Amsterdam (NL)
Master plan urban for green spaces and mixed-use development
Client: Municipality of ZuiderAmstel
Design: 2006
Size: 21 ha

Garden, Bunnik (NL)
Private garden
Client: Otten family
Design: 1995
Realisation: 1996

Garden, Breukelen (NL)
Private garden
Client: Kahn family
Design: 1992
Realisation: 1995

VSB Headquarters Garden, Utrecht (NL)
Office garden with bridge
Client: VSB (now Fortis)
Design: 1994
Realisation: 1994–1995

ABN Amro Bank, Amsterdam (NL)
Competition design for gardens, vertical patios
Client: ABN Amro Bank
Design: 1992
Architect: Neutelings Riedijk

Garden for Arts Centre CBK, Dordrecht (NL)
Design sculpture garden
Client: Centrum voor Beeldende Kunst Dordrecht
Design: 1992
Realisation: 1995

Sculptural Garden Kröller-Müller Museum, Otterlo (NL)
Extension and renewal of sculpture garden
Client: Kröller-Müller Museum
Design: 1995–2000
Realisation: 1996–2001
Size: 28 ha

Interpolis Garden, Tilburg (NL)
Public park
Client: Interpolis Tivoli nv
Design: 1997
Realisation: 1998

EEA Garden, Rotterdam (NL)
Office garden
Client: Erick van Egeraat associated architects
Design: 1993
Realisation: 1994
Size: 200 sqm

Wilhelmina Kinderziekenhuis, Utrecht (NL)
Open-space design for children's hospital
Design: 1996
Realisation: 1998–1999

Sphinx Garden, Borneo Sporenburg, Amsterdam (NL)
Patio garden
Client: New Deal
Design: 1997
Realisation: 2001
Size: 1 500 sqm

Univé, Zwolle (NL)
Open-space design including roof-garden and patio garden for insurance company
Client: Univé
Design: 1997
Realisation: 1997–1998
Architect: De Zwarte Hond

Noorder Dierenpark, Emmen (NL)
Master plan for the extension of the Noorder Dierenpark zoological park
Client: Noorder Dierenpark
Design: 1997–2001
Realisation: 2001–2002
Size: 37 ha

Lensvelt Garden, Breda (NL)
Open-space design for Lensvelt headquarters
Design: 1997–1998
Realisation: 1998–1999

Makeblijde, St. Maartensdijk (NL)
Vertical garden expo Makeblijde
Client: Makeblijde
Design: 1999

Montecity, Milan (IT)
Design private garden for apartment ensemble, public park and public spaces
Client: Milano Santa Giulia S.p.A.
Private Park
Design: 2005–2007
Realisation: 2008
Size: 4.3 ha
Public Park
Design: 2006–2008
Realisation: 2009
Size: 28.7 ha
Adjacent public areas
Design: 2006–2008
Realisation: 2009
Size: 12.1 ha

Chaumont Garden, Chaumont-sur-Loire (FR)
Temporary garden
Client: Conservatoire International des Parcs et Jardins et du Paysage
Design: 1999
Realisation: 2000

Erasmian Garden, Arboretum Trompenburg, Rotterdam (NL)
Enclosed garden in arboretum
Client: Breeze of Air
Design: 2001
Realisation: 2002–

Binnentuin Carré, Woerden (NL)
Green courtyard for apartment block
Client: Proper-Stok Woningbouw bv
Design: 2005
Realisation: 2007
Size: 0.5 ha

Buitenruimte Afrika Museum, Berg en Dal (NL)
Open-space design for outdoor museum
Client: Afrika Museum
Design: 2005–2006
Realisation: 2006–2007
Size: 9.2 ha

Cour de Loges, Lyon (FR)
Open-space design of housing block courtyard
Client: ING Real Estate
Design: 2005
Realisation: 2007–2008
Size: 2 800 sqm

Jubilee Gardens, London (UK)
Public park along the South Bank of the River Thames in Central London
Client: South Bank Employers' Group
Design: 2005–2006
Realisation: 2007–2008
Size: 1.5 ha
In association with AKT engineers, BDSP Partnership (mechanical / electrical), Soil and Land Consultants, Buro Happold (security)

Lohmann Garden, Münster (DE)
Private garden
Client: Lohmann family
Design: 2006
Size: 2 100 sqm

Olive Loop, Dallas, Texas (US)
Residential garden
Client: Developers combination
Design: 2006–2007
Local partner: MESA, Dallas TX
Realisation: 2008
Size: 1 ha

PARK DESIGNS

Stadspark Overbos, Beverwijk (NL)
Competition design for public park
Client: Stichting Groene Long
Design: 1989

Parc Urbain Eura-Lille, Lille (FR)
Competition design for urban park
Client: Eura Lille
Design: 1992
Size: 8.5 ha

Park Monbijou, Berlin (DE)
Competition design for urban park
Client: Municipality of Berlin
Design: 1993

Vertical Landscape, Petrosino Park, New York, New York (US)
Manifest for new landscape architectural vernacular
Client: Storefront gallery
Design: 1996

Park Leidsche Rijn, Vleuten-De Meern (NL)
Competition design public park
Client: Projectbureau Leidsche Rijn
Design: 1997–1999
Realisation: 2003–2010
Size: 300 ha

Expo.02, Swiss National Expo, Yverdon-les-Bains (CH)
Master plan and design of expo terrain
Client: Expo.02
Design: 1998–2000
Realisation: 2001–2002
Size: 4 ha
In association with Diller and Scofilio, Morphing Systems, Véhovar & Jauslin Architektur

Buona Vista Park, One North Park, Singapore (SG)
Public park
Client: JTC, National Parks Board
Design: 2004
Realisation: Parcel One completed in 2006
Size: 3.7 ha Parcel One (13 ha total)
In association with Studio Steed, Singapore

Centraal Park Amsterdam Noord, Amsterdam (NL)
Competition design public park
Client: Municipality of Amsterdam, Stadsdeel Amsterdam-Noord
Design: 2005–2007
Realisation: 2007–2010
Size: 30 ha

Grand Museum of Egypt Park, Cairo (EG)
Museum park and urban esplanade
Client: Ministry of Culture, Egypt
Design: 2004–2005
Realisation: 2009
Size: 40 ha
In association with Heneghan Peng Architects, Ove Arup & Partners, Buro Happold, Raafat Miller Consulting, Arab Consulting Engineers, Shaker Consultancy, Davis Langdon Schumann Smith, Sites International, Bartenbach Lichtlabor

De periferie als centrum, Utrecht (NL)
Case study for regional forest and landscape development in the province of Utrecht
Client: Direktie bos- en landschapsbouw SBB
Design: 1989

Eastern Scheldt storm surge barrier, Zeeland (NL)
Landscape design for the delta works
Client: Rijkswaterstaat Directie Zeeland
Design: 1990
Realisation: 1991–1992

Landscaping Schiphol Airport, Amsterdam (NL)
Landscape design for national airport
Client: Schiphol Airport
Design: 1992
Realisation: 1994–1998
Size: half a million birch trees

Hoogovens; 101 hoofdkantoor laboratoria, IJmuiden (NL)
Landscape design for steel works
Client: Corus
Design: 1991
Size: 800 ha

RPD, Randstad Internationaal, Den Haag (NL)
Study for models for spatial development of the Randstad
Client: RPD
Design: 1990

Terneuzen Kanaalzone, Terneuzen (NL)
Landscape design borders Canal Gent-Terneuzen
Client: Rijkswaterstaat
Design: 1992
In association with Bureau Waardenburg

Rotterdam: AIR-Alexander, Rotterdam (NL)
Manifests for the urbanisation of the Randstad
Client: Rotterdamse Kunststichting (now RRKC)
Design: 1993

Noise Barrier A16, Dordrecht (NL)
Design research for noise barrier along Highway A16
Client: Municipality of Dordrecht
Design: 1993

Buckthorncity (Rotterdam 2045 Manifestation), Coast of Holland, Rotterdam (NL)
Concept design for landfill, landscape development and urbanisation in the North Sea
Client: Municipality of Rotterdam, foundation Rotterdam 2045
Design: 1995
Size: 4 473 ha

Gasmeer Groningen, Groningen (NL)
Landscape design for water retainment, recreation, ecological zones and urbanisation east of Groningen
Client: Oostaan bv
Design: 1996–1997
Size: 1 500 ha
In association with De Zwarte Hond

Landscaping Papendorp, Utrecht (NL)
Landscape design for office park
Client: Projectbureau Leidsche Rijn
Design: 2001
Realisation: 2002–2004
Size: 12.8 ha

Park Schuytgraaf, Arnhem (NL)
Design for the linear park / green structure of Schuytgraaf
Client: GEM Schuytgraaf
Design: 2001
Realisation: 2006–2007

Chiswick Park, London (UK)
Master plan and landscape design of business park
Client: Stanhope plc
Design: 1999
Realisation: 2002–2006
Size: 33 ha
Architect: Richard Rogers Partnership

Battersea Power Station, London (UK)
Public space design
Client: Parkview International Plc
Design: 2004–2006
Realisation: initial concept stage
In association with Arup AGU

Fort bij Vechten, Vechten (NL)
Design study for one of the forts of Nieuwe Hollandse Waterlinie
Client: Province of Utrecht
Design: 2006–2007
Realisation: 2008
Size: 2.5 ha
In cooperation with Rapp + Rapp

New Coastal Vision, North Sea (NL)
Future perspective for next 100 years of the Dutch coast
Client: Royal Boskalis Westminster nv
Design: 2006–2007
Realisation: not yet known
Size: 18,500 ha

COMPETITION DESIGNS

Prix de Rome
1st prize for the Prix de Rome in landscape architecture and urban design
Design: 1990

PPP, Bergen op Zoom (NL)
1st prize in competition for the design of the environment of the station area in Bergen op Zoom
Client: Stichting PPP
Design: 1993

Diemerzeedijk, Amsterdam (NL)
Landscape competition design for the coverage of a polluted soil depot
Client: Municipality of Amsterdam
Design: 1994

Landschaftspark Riem, Munich (DE)
Competition design for landscape park
Client: MRG Maßnahmeträger München-Riem GmbH
Design: 1995
Size: 215 ha

Waterfront Thessaloniki, Thessaloniki (GR)
Competition design for the development of the Thessaloniki waterfront
Client: Municipality of Thessaloniki
Design: 1996

Westergasfabriek Westerpark, Amsterdam (NL)
Competition design for transformation of former gas factory into an urban park
Client: Municipality of Westerpark
Design: 1997

Papendorp Bridges, Papendorp (NL)
Competition design for two bridges
Project Office Leidsche Rijn
Design: 1998

San Michele Cemetery, Venice (IT)
Competition design for the extension of the cemetery
Client: City of Venice
Design: 1998

Siemens Silver City, Munich (DE)
Competition design for science village for Siemens
Client: Siemens Real Estate GmbH & Co OHG
Design: 2001
Size: 41 ha

San Sebastián, San Sebastián (ES)
Competition design for urban park
Client: Municipality of San Sebastián
Design: 2001

Parco Forlalini, Milan (IT)
Competition design for urban park
Client: Municipality of Milan
Design: 2002
Size: 550 ha

Arroyo Parkway, Pasadena, California (US)
Competition design for new identity of the Arroyo Parkway
Client: City of Pasadena
Design: 2002

Antwerpen Spoor Noord, Antwerp (BE)
Competition design urban park and office development
Client: City of Antwerp
Design: 2004
Size: 6 ha

Victoria and Albert Museum, London (UK)
Competition design for V&A's patio garden
Client: Victoria and Albert Museum
Design: 2003

Paris, Les Halles (FR)
Competition design for garden
Client: SEM Paris
Design: 2004
Size: 3 ha
In association with MVRDV

Giardini di Porta Nuova, Garibaldi Repubblica, Milan (IT)
Competition design for urban park
Client: Municipality of Milan
Design: 2004
Size: 25 ha
In association with Studio Power & Paolo Pommodoro

Port Autonome, Bordeaux, Bordeaux (FR)
Competition design for commercial centre
Client: ING Real Estate
Design: 2004

Wieringerrandmeer, Wierringerrandmeer (NL)
Competition design, landscape design for lake around former island Wieringen
Client: Heijmans Arcadis
Design: 2003

Grand Moulin, Paris (FR)
Competition design for public space
Client: City of Paris
Design: 2003
Size: 1 ha

Fiets- en Voetgangersbrug, Hoorn (NL)
Competition design for pedestrian bridge
Client: Municipality of Hoorn
Design: 2005
Size: span 140 m, width 5 m

Theaterplein, Antwerpen (BE)
Competition design for public space
Client: City of Antwerp
Design: 2004
Realisation: not realised
Size: 2.8 ha

Hoek van Holland, Rotterdam (NL)
Competition design for new dune landscape and urbanisation for the Municipality of Rotterdam
Client: Bontebal vastgoed bv, ING Real Estate, PWS woningstichting
Design: 2005

Le Lac, Bordeaux (FR)
Competition design for mixed-use development on Lake of Bordeaux
Client: ING Real Estate, Cogedim
Design: 2005

Flageyplein, Brussels (BE)
Competition design for public square
Client: City of Brussels
Design: 2005
Size: 2.9 ha

Neues Wohnen in Jenfeld, Hamburg (DE)
Urban regeneration of a former military base into housing neighbourhood
Client: Freie & Hansestadt Hamburg
Design: 2005–2006
Realisation: 2008
Size: 29 ha

Schelde Kaai, Antwerp (BE)
Competition design, master plan for River Scheldt quaysides
Client: City of Antwerp
Design: 2006
Realisation: not realised
Size: 7 km

Coney Island, New York, New York (US)
Landscape strategy and perimeter design for the New York Aquarium
Client: New York Aquarium, Wild Life Association, NYEDC
Design: 2006
Realisation: not realised
In Association with Weisz & Yoes

Carlsberg Competition, Copenhagen (DK)
Competition design for redevelopment of former brewery in the centre of Copenhagen
Client: Carlsberg Brewery
Design: 2007

EXPO 2010, Shanghai (CN)
Competition design for the Dutch pavilion
Client: Ministry of Economic Development
Design: 2006

Urban Plan, Isle Saint Denis, Paris (FR)
Master plan for Isle Saint Denis
Client: ING Real Estate
Design: 2007
Realisation: not realised
Size: 10 ha

Governors Island, New York, New York (US)
Competition design for park
Client: Governors Island Preservation and Education Corporation
Design: 2007
In association with Rogers Marvel Architects, Diller, Scofidio & Renfro, SMWM, Quennell Rothschild

In Holland Staat Een Huis, Rotterdam (NL)
Exhibition and design study of consequences of further suburbanisation of the Randstad
Client: NAI
Design: 1995
Realisation: 1995

Colonizing The Void, Venice (IT)
Dutch contribution to the VI Mostra Internazionale di Architettura
Client: NAI
Realisation: 1996

90.000 Pakjes Margarine (90,000 packets of butter), Groninger Museum (NL)
Exhibition on the heroic history of the Dutch landscape
Client: Groninger Museum
Realisation: 1997

Spoleto Festival, Charleston, South Carolina (US)
Pavilion of Spanish moss in Cypress Gardens swamp
Client: Spoleto Festival
Design: 1996
Realisation: 1997
Size: 30 sqm

The Flood, Rotterdam (NL)
Adriaan Geuze, curator of the second International Architectural Biennale Rotterdam
Client: International Architecture Biennale Rotterdam
Design: 2004–2005
Realisation: 2005

Project Horizon, various polders (NL)
Billboard project, inflatable cows to draw attention to the beauty of Dutch polders
Client: International Architecture Biennale Rotterdam
Design and realisation: 2005

Wonder Holland, Rome (IT)
Entry to the Dutch design manifestation
Client: Royal Netherlands Embassy
Production: Rob van 't Hof
Design: 2004
Realisation: 2004

West 8, NAi Rotterdam (NL)
Traveling exhibition about West 8 park projects
Design: 2005

WEST 8, 2007

Shany Barath
Rikus Beekman
Simone de Bergh
Martin Biewenga
Edzo Bindels
Freek Boerwinkel
Riëtte Bosch
Simone Breitkopf
Maarten Buijs
Caja Cabbollet
Cyrus Clark
Christian Dobrick
Wilbert Duyvesteyn
Christoph Elsässer
Fiona Endres
Gaspard Estourgie
Jerry van Eyck
Juan Figueroa Calero
Christian Gausepohl
Adriaan Geuze
Enrique González
Fanny Guilmet
Yichun He
Pieter Hoen
Edwin van der Hoeven
Annette van 't Hof
Saskia Imming
Kristin Jensen
Mark Johnson
Reinaldo Jordan
Berthine Knaut
Joost Koningen
Rob Koningen
Leander Kwakernaak
Sander Lap
Felix Lauffer
Silvia Lupini
Perry Maas
Marja Maliepaard
Harrie van Oorschot
Sylvia Pietjouw
Marco van der Pluym
Nicolette Pot
Askar Ramazanov
Petra Rudolf
Marc Ryan
Igor Saitov
Carlos Saldarriaga
Safiyeh Salehi Mobarakeh
Glenn Samson
Kees Schoot
Robert Schütte
Alyssa Schwann
Eva Silberschneider
Jasna Stefanovjka
Jacco Stuy
Andrew Tang
Riikka Tuomisto
Maarten van de Voorde
Peter Vredeveld
Christine Wahba
Joris Weijts
Claudia Wolsfeld
Shachar Zur

CONTACT DETAILS

West 8 urban design & landscape architecture b.v.
Schiehaven 13M (Maaskantgebouw)
3002 AE Rotterdam
The Netherlands
tel: +31 [0] 10 – 485 5801
fax: +31 [0] 10 – 485 6323
www.west8.nl

PHOTO CREDITS

Archives West 8

Ger Dekkers/Het Oversticht, Zwolle: p. 7

Gemeentemuseum Den Haag, The Hague: p. 12

Ellen Kooi: p. 21

Mauritshuis Royal Picture Gallery, The Hague: p. 10

Jeroen Musch: pp. 2; 24: fig. 1-2; 26: fig. 4-5; 27: fig. 6; 49: fig. 4-5; 57: fig. 26; 58: fig. 27-28, 30; 61: fig. 32-35; 62: fig. 36-38; 65: fig. 39-40; 66: fig. 41-42; 67: fig. 43-47; 68: fig. 48-49; 69: fig. 50; 70: fig. 51, 53; 72: fig. 1; 124: fig. 20-21; 125: fig. 22-23; 126: fig. 24; 127: fig. 25-27; 175: fig. 3-4; 176: fig. 5-7; 182: fig. 13-15; 183: fig. 16-17; 184: fig. 18

Museum Boijmans Van Beuningen, Rotterdam: p. 11

National Gallery, London: p. 11

Cas Oorthuys/Nederlands Fotomuseum, Rotterdam: p. 17

Rijksmuseum, Amsterdam: p. 12

SELUX: pp. 92: fig. 2-3; 96: fig. 13; 101: fig. 26; 107: fig. 43-45